Farewell to

Farewell to Flatbush

The 1957 Brooklyn Dodgers

RONNIE JOYNER

McFarland & Company, Inc., Publishers
Jefferson, North Carolina

Library of Congress Cataloguing-in-Publication Data

Names: Joyner, Ronnie, author.
Title: Farewell to Flatbush : the 1957 Brooklyn Dodgers / Ronnie Joyner.
Description: Jefferson, North Carolina : McFarland & Company, Inc.,
Publishers, 2022 | Includes bibliographical references and index.
Identifiers: LCCN 2022001985 | ISBN 9781476686783 (paperback : acid free paper) ∞
ISBN 9781476644462 (eBook)
Subjects: LCSH: Brooklyn Dodgers (Baseball team)—History. | Ebbets Field
(New York, N.Y.)—History. | Flatbush (New York, N.Y.)—History. | Brooklyn
(New York, N.Y.)—History | Baseball—New York (State)—New York—History. |
BISAC: SPORTS & RECREATION / Baseball / History
Classification: LCC GV875.B7 J69 2022 | DDC 796.357/
640974723—dc23/eng/20220224
LC record available at https://lccn.loc.gov/2022001985

British Library cataloguing data are available

ISBN (print) 978-1-4766-8678-3
ISBN (ebook) 978-1-4766-4446-2

Front cover images and design by Ronnie Joyner

Printed in the United States of America

McFarland & Company, Inc., Publishers
Box 611, Jefferson, North Carolina 28640
www.mcfarlandpub.com

To the Flatbush Faithful—the few still on the bases and the many who've already crossed the plate.

Table of Contents

Preface

Why write a book on the 1957 Brooklyn Dodgers, a team that finished third in the National League with an unspectacular record of 84 wins and 70 losses? The answer, really, is pretty simple once you look beyond that year's won-loss record and instead viewing the ballclub in the context of decades of Brooklyn teams that came before them—and the zero Major League Brooklyn teams that came after them.

On February 2, 1957, the Brooklyn Dodgers held their opening workout of spring training. By the time they held their next one, they would be the *Los Angeles* Dodgers. While the 1957 ballclub would not achieve glory like the Dodgers of 1955, or infamy like "Dem Bums" of 1951 (and many other gut-wrenching seasons), the third-place '57 team was special for one key reason—they were the last chapter in the storied book of *Brooklyn's* Dodgers. The Los Angeles Dodgers would mine new riches out in the golden west, but Dodgers' East Coast legacy would forever belong to Brooklyn. Pulitzer Prize–winning *New York Times* sportswriter Arthur Daley said it best when he wrote,

> The richest of all baseball legends is the one that has flowered in Flatbush. It cannot be transplanted to alien soil, such as Los Angeles. It's a tree that grew in Brooklyn—a nut tree, if you will. There it must forever remain, gnarled and withered from lack of nutrition and affectionate care. The Dodgers are indigenous to Brooklyn. They must leave the glorious legend behind. "Everything happens to Brooklyn," is the oldest, and truest, of baseball maxims. Name one zany or out-of-the-ordinary happening and the odds are a million to one that the Dodgers were involved in it.

Daley, a native New Yorker who covered sports from 1926 until his death in 1974, witnessed much of the Brooklyn Dodgers' history firsthand, and, as evidenced above, recorded it with amazing style, wit, and insight. I, on the other hand, wasn't born until six years after the Dodgers played their last game in Brooklyn; I am not a New Yorker; and I definitely do not consider myself a *writer*, so Arthur Daley's lofty place as a great chronicler of Brooklyn Dodgers history is in no danger from my text. But, I've always felt a kinship with the Brooklyn fans who had their Dodgers taken from them, so I've long felt I had something of value to add to the narrative—and here's why.

Born in Washington, DC, and raised in a family that rooted for the hapless Washington Senators for decades (my grandfather loved watching the base-stealing exploits of George Case in the 1940s, and my father thought the world of slick-fielding shortstop Eddie Brinkman in the 1960s), I, like the fans in Brooklyn, felt the sting of watching helplessly as my home team abandoned our city for greater riches elsewhere. As a nine-year-old who idolized the slugging of Frank "The Capitol Punisher" Howard, I was deeply saddened when Howard and the Senators moved to Texas to become the Rangers following the 1971 season. Ironically, Howard was originally scouted by the Brooklyn Dodgers in 1956 and '57, and would ultimately make his big-league debut with the 1958 Los Angeles Dodgers, so maybe there was a bit of baseball foreshadowing going on there.

Similar to promises made to Brooklyn fans of 1957, Washington fans of 1971 were promised a new team to immediately replace the team that left for Texas. We had reason to believe, too, because there had been a precedent for this in the not-too-distant past. Washington fans first experienced the heartbreak of losing a ballclub following the 1960 season when the original Senators left DC to become the Minnesota Twins. Without missing a beat, Washington fielded a new team in 1961—an expansion team. The name on the jersey fronts still read "Senators," but the players wearing the 1961 uniforms were a completely different bunch—a rag-tag mix of aging veterans, journeymen, and unknown prospects. After decades of losing, the Senators of 1960 were a team on the rise, its roster boasting quality players like Harmon Killebrew, Bob Allison, Jim Lemon, Zoilo Versalles, Pedro Ramos and Camilo Pasqual. (Many of these players would help propel the Twins to the 1965 World Series where they would lose to—you guessed it—the Dodgers. More wicked baseball foreshadowing, perhaps.)

Meanwhile, the new Senators of 1961 featured an opening day roster made up of names like Coot Veal, Willie Tasby, and Pete Daley. The expansion Senators struggled to win for their entire 11-year existence, only once topping the .500 mark, but they had a strong core of dedicated fans who, because of the replacement club of 1961, believed baseball officials when they said Washington would get another new team following the 1971 season. But year after year, it never materialized. Finally, when many folks had given up hope, baseball returned to DC in

2005 when the Montreal Expos moved their franchise to Washington. It took 35 years, but Washington once again had big league baseball. On the other hand, 64 years after the Dodgers left for Los Angeles, Brooklyn still does not have a Major League baseball team.

Maybe it was the experience of having watched my home team pull up stakes and leave town, but later in life I found myself and my good friend Bill Bozman (who helpfully proofread this book) becoming associated with a few organizations whose sole purpose was to keep alive the memories of defunct franchises. The St. Louis Browns Historical Society, the Philadelphia Athletics Historical Society, the Washington Senators Historical Society and the Boston Braves Historical Society. My work for these organizations usually revolved around my skills as a baseball artist. As a natural progression, I always wanted to do a project involving the mother-of-all defunct franchises—the Brooklyn Dodgers.

So in 2005 I decided to illustrate/write/design a baseball card set commemorating the 1957 Brooklyn Dodgers. My hopes were that I'd have the set finished in 2007, just in time for the 50th anniversary of the franchise's last season in Flatbush. As it turned out, I didn't complete the set until 2012, but I couldn't have been happier with the final product. For the card fronts, I painted portraits of every player who took the field for the '57 Dodgers (36 total), plus manager Walt Alston and coaches Billy Herman, Jake Pitler, Joe Becker, and Greg Mulleavy. For the card backs I wrote player biographies relevant to the '57 season, as well as drawing Topps-style cartoons for each player. The response to the set was extremely positive, like none other I'd received to date, so it left me wanting to do a fuller tribute to the team.

And that brings me full circle to this book, *Farewell to Flatbush: The 1957 Brooklyn Dodgers.* This book is essentially an exercise in reverse engineering my 1957 Brooklyn Dodgers baseball card set, one that takes the condensed saga told in that set and expounds upon it. Reproductions of the cards from the set are included here to enhance the text with life and color. A general overview of the history of the Brooklyn Dodgers is also included to provide a frame of reference to what's most important here—the 1957 Brooklyn Dodgers season and the end of an era in Flatbush.

Introduction

On February 23, 1960, two-and-a-half years after the Brooklyn Dodgers played their final game in Flatbush, some 200 somber-faced fans gathered at a once majestic, but now dilapidated and abandoned ballpark. They were there to bid farewell to the old place, for on this day the unthinkable would begin—the demolition of Ebbets Field, the beloved home of the Dodgers for nearly half a century. Surrounded by streets whose names the ballpark had lifted to national renown—Bedford Avenue, Sullivan Place, McKeever Place and Montgomery Street—Ebbets Field would soon cease to exist. Its razing would toss a final symbolic shovelful of dirt on the grave of the Brooklyn Dodgers who had already died in the hearts of many fans when the club fled the borough for the promise of greater treasure to be mined out west in golden California. A 22-million-dollar apartment complex would be built where Ebbets Field stood, so there would finally be tangible closure for many fans—no more ghostly Ebbets Field standing on the corner as a daily reminder of their departed Dodgers.

* * *

The Brooklyn Dodgers–Ebbets Field; Ebbets Field–the Brooklyn Dodgers. Theirs was a symbiotic relationship in the creation of the now larger-than-life legend and myth of the *Brooklyn* Dodgers. And the glue that bonded the Brooklyn Dodgers and Ebbets Field was, of course, the fans and the community. For 44 years—1913–57, the lifespan of Ebbets Field—the team, the fans, and the ballpark came together from April till September, slow-curing a concrete-strong legacy that would stand the test of time. How can it be said that the Brooklyn Dodgers stood the test of time if the franchise and its ballpark no longer exist? Because the Brooklyn Dodgers continue to live in the hearts and minds of their aging fans, and will continue to live on long after the last person to have seen the Dodgers play at Ebbets Field has passed. What Brooklyn put together, no man could put asunder—be he a profit-chasing owner or a wrecking-ball crane operator.

* * *

Introduction

Crash! A two-ton iron wrecking ball, painted white with red stitches to resemble a baseball, struck the first blow in the demolition of Ebbets Field by slamming into the roof of the visitors dugout. Beneath that roof had once sat decades' worth of great Brooklyn Dodgers opponents—Kid Gleason, Joe Tinker, Edd Roush, Pie Traynor, Stan Musial, and Willie Mays to name a few. Men whose spirited play against the Dodgers had helped forge the tough-luck legacy that came to define "Dem Bums" until they finally broke through with a World Series victory in 1955. The onlookers watched this disturbing scene much in the way one might gawk at a train wreck, unable to look away in spite of the dark nature of what they were seeing.

Harry Avirom Affiliates Incorporated, a local demolition company, was in charge of the razing. Harry Avirom was president of the company and a longtime Brooklyn resident and Dodgers fan. He had made it clear that he would use great sensitivity in destroying the park. In fact, Avirom wanted Dodgers fans to have as many artifacts from the stadium as they wanted. He listed dugout telephones, benches, lockers, steel from the roof and fittings, flagpoles, and railings as examples of items which could be had by fans who merely showed up to collect them. "Some people might like to get two or three items to place in their game room or patio," Avirom said. "They just have to come out to the ballpark to get them. Even Giants fans are welcome!" A mere four years later, Avirom would be up in Harlem to oversee the destruction of the Polo Grounds, the longtime home park of the "other" team he'd referenced prior to razing Ebbets Field—the New York Giants.

A team of Avirom workers stood back while the wrecking ball pounded the dugout, waiting for their signal to join in the destruction. They were a formidable-looking bunch, wearing boots, khaki work pants, and hardhats. Each worker also wore a blue "Dodger" warm-up jacket emblazoned with Harry Avirom Inc on the back and a "uniform" number on the front left chest. It was a special touch the Kratter P.R. men had thoughtfully whipped up for the occasion. The Avirom men gripped massive sledgehammers. Just a few years earlier, prior to the start of the 1955 World Series and not far from where these workers now waited, another formidable-looking bunch posed for photographers. They wore ballcaps instead of hardhats, however, and held baseball bats instead of mauls—but they were just as destructive ... Dodgers sluggers Duke Snider, Gil Hodges, Roy Campanella and Carl Furillo.

* * *

In baseball, the elements required for creating a legacy of epic scope are simple: (1) colorful players and memorable on-field events; (2) vibrant and interesting community and fans; (3) a unique ballpark. Some franchises have one of these elements. Others may have two. But very few have all three. Those franchises that possess all three of these elements have gone beyond the niche of simple baseball history, instead achieving greater permanence by weaving themselves into the broader fabric of mass Americana. The New York Yankees, Boston Red Sox, and Chicago Cubs have achieved this. The St. Louis Cardinals are in the discussion, even though the ballparks in which they played (and currently play) do not have the aura which surrounds Yankee Stadium, Fenway Park or Wrigley Field. All of the franchises mentioned here still exist, and that's a distinct advantage when it comes to adding to a legacy or keeping a past legacy in the public consciousness. That is why it is so amazing that the Brooklyn Dodgers, a franchise that has not played a game in over 50 years, is as well known today as it was the day it pulled out of Flatbush. In fact, it's quite possible that the Brooklyn Dodgers are even better known today than they were in 1957, their last year in the borough.

The Brooklyn Dodgers, like most big league franchises of their time, was an eclectic mix of players, managers, coaches, front office executives, and employees—colorful enough that they would likely have had an enduring legacy with or without an iconic ballpark. But that legacy would certainly have been smaller in scale, possibly confined to local fans who followed the club and hardcore baseball historians. Look no further than other defunct teams for examples of this. The Washington Senators, who played at Griffith Stadium, left DC for Minnesota following the 1960 season. In their history the Senators won as many World Series titles as the Brooklyn Dodgers—exactly one—yet the Nats were largely forgotten outside of Washington in the decades that followed the team's departure. The Philadelphia Athletics, who played at Shibe Park/Connie Mack Stadium, left for Kansas City following the 1954 season. Having won five World Series titles, their on-field achievement was greater than that of the Washington Senators and Brooklyn Dodgers combined, yet the mention of the *Philadelphia* Athletics to the average person born after the baby boom generation is likely to get no more than a look of confusion. These clubs, along with other defunct teams like the New York Giants, Boston Braves and St. Louis Browns, also had colorful histories, but their legacies have faded while the legend of the Brooklyn Dodgers has only grown with the passage of time.

* * *

The final wheel in the demolition of Ebbets Field was set in motion on December 31, 1959, for it was that day that the Dodgers' lease expired.

Introduction

Matt Burns was the lone Dodgers employee left behind at Ebbets Field after the rest of the operation moved west two years earlier. It was his job to take care of all duties related to Ebbets Field, and the last of his duties was the formality of handing the keys to the ballpark over to Seymour Goldsmith, vice president of the Kratter Corporation—the company that would build the massive housing project on the 5½-acre site that the Brooklyn Dodgers had called home from 1913 to 1957.

Goldsmith passed by somber reminders of Dodgers/Ebbets–past as he made his way through the ballpark to meet Burns and a small gathering of officials and press. Still hanging from the right field upper tier, outside at the corner of Sullivan and Bedford, was the familiar sign that read "NEXT GAME—Dodgers vs _____." The Pirates were the last team to have its name filled into that blank for the game of September 24, 1957, but the blank had remained empty ever since. The iconic, rounded, brick entrance to the park still looked the same as it had in its glory days, with "Ebbets Field" still spelled out in large letters at the top, but the large arched windows now featured many sad, broken panes of glass. The lack of turnstiles as Goldsmith passed through the entrance was a clear sign that Ebbets Field's days hosting ballgames—or any paying event—were over. There had been a few events held at Ebbets Field after the Dodgers left—a demolition derby, a stunt-driver auto thrill show, a circus, soccer matches, college baseball games—but those activities had now ceased in preparation for the scheduled razing of the park. And, in the minds of many Brooklyn fans, those events were viewed as sacrilege—an insult to the hallowed ground of Ebbets Field.

The now-imminent demolition of Ebbets Field also put to an end the desperate hopes of many that Brooklyn would receive a new big-league franchise to replace the departed Dodgers, a hope to which they'd grasped for two years. Their best opportunity to see that hope realized had come as discussions of a third professional league, the Continental League (joining the American and National Leagues), were taking place. Dodgers icon Branch Rickey was part of the group planning the new league. His inclusion added legitimacy to the plan, but formation of the league never got off the ground and was officially killed when Major League Baseball began its expansion in 1961.

As Goldsmith continued his journey through the stadium to meet Burns, he was surrounded by more reminders of Ebbets Field's rich history and its bleak future. Unlike the missing turnstiles, the concession stands, program kiosks, and souvenir stands remained in their accustomed places, but they appeared stark in the cavernous darkness, empty of the goods they used to sell. The visitors' clubhouse and the umpires' dressing room were padlocked, but the home clubhouse was open. The lockers were still there—lockers that had once been home to Dodgers greats like Zack Wheat, Rube Marquard, Dazzy Vance, Billy Herman, Don Newcombe, and Gil Hodges. Those names were no longer visible on the lockers, as

Introduction

they'd been taped over and rewritten with the unfamiliar names of members of the last soccer team to rent the park. There was, however, one locker that still bore a name that would one day be added to the esteemed roster in Cooperstown—"Campanella"—and in that locker hung Campy's number 39 gray road jersey. At Campanella's request, the locker and jersey would be given to him at the ceremony planned for the impending demolition of Ebbets Field.

The once-bustling commissary under the stands was empty except for a solitary gentleman who told Goldsmith that the group he was looking for was gathered under the leftfield stands. It was a dreary scene as Goldsmith made his way from the Dodgers bullpen in right field, across the outfield grass, and to a door in the left-centerfield wall where the group—and Angel, a stray mutt that had made Ebbets Field its home—awaited him. The once-lush green grass was patchy and weed-infested, and the stands that had so often been filled with zealous fans were eerily empty. Handshakes were exchanged and Burns handed the keys over to Goldsmith, who accepted them on behalf of Marvin Kratter, president of the Kratter firm. With that, the stage was set for the final act in the story of the Brooklyn Dodgers—the demolition of Ebbets Field.

* * *

Colorful players and memorable on-field events came to define the Brooklyn Dodgers. Through the late 1800s and early 1900s, a number of Brooklyn ballclubs laid the foundation upon which the Brooklyn Dodgers would build their legacy. The Eckfords, the Atlantics, the Excelsiors, the Mutuals, the Hartfords, the Wonders, the Grays—and many others—would play seminal baseball in Brooklyn, building interest and passion in the burgeoning game among those who lived in the borough. When the dust settled and the first modern World Series was played in 1903, it was the Superbas who represented Brooklyn in the National League (they finished fifth in 1903), and they would continue to represent the borough through 1957.

The Superbas were formed in 1899 when the Grays merged with the minor league Baltimore Orioles, and it was at this time that Charles Ebbets, a loyal employee of the ballclub since its founding in 1883, became a part owner of the team. Ebbets would soon become the principal owner of the club, and while Brooklyn would always struggle financially during Ebbets' ownership of the team, he saw to it that the team was always respectable. Ebbets died in 1925, but he had done a fine job of stabilizing the franchise and firmly rooting it into the National League and the borough of Brooklyn.

While Ebbets' team was technically named the "Superbas," the nickname "Trolley Dodgers" was often used by sportswriters covering the club. It caught on with fans over time, and a shortened version, "Dodgers," finally became official in 1932 when it first appeared on players' jerseys. The great Roger Kahn explained it best when he wrote,

> As far as anyone knows, the nickname proceeded from benign to absurdity. Brooklyn, being flat, extensive and populous, was a stronghold of the trolley car. Enter absurdity. To survive in Brooklyn one had to be a survivor of trolleys. After several unfortunate experiments in nomenclature, the Brooklyn National League Baseball Team became the Dodgers during the 1920s, and the nickname endured after polluting buses had come and the last Brooklyn trolley had been shipped from Vanderbilt Avenue to Karachi.

Brooklyn was a perennial also-ran from 1903 through 1915, but they finally rewarded fans with pennants in 1916 and 1920—although they lost the World Series both times. Brooklyn outfielder Casey Stengel had a fine season while helping his club to the 1916 N.L. flag, but even his .364 Series average couldn't stop Babe Ruth and the Boston Red Sox from defeating Brooklyn, four games to one. Stengel, already known for his quirky sense of humor, was also known by Brooklyn management as an annual contract holdout headache, so they traded him to Pittsburgh following the 1917 season. During a game in 1919, Stengel was being unmercifully taunted by the Ebbets Field fans as his Pirates played his former club in Brooklyn. Later in the game, Stengel strutted to home plate to take his at-bat, boos and jeers raining down. Then, with perfectly choreographed flair, Stengel stepped back, turned to the crowd and tipped his hat—and out of his cap flew a sparrow. The catcalls and taunts turned to cheers and applause—and Casey Stengel became an instant crowd favorite at Ebbets Field.

The 1920 Series saw the Cleveland Indians defeat Brooklyn, five games to two. Brooklyn made dubious World Series history in Game Five when right-handed spitballer Burleigh Grimes gave up the first-ever Series grand slam. Then, later in the same game, Clarence Mitchell hit into the Series' first-ever (and still only) unassisted triple play. Grimes had a way of blaming everyone but himself for his failures. He blamed Detroit Tigers scout Jack Coombs for the grand slam, saying Coombs had given him bad advice on the Indians—an American League team Brooklyn had not scouted. Grimes later took another loss, this time in the Series finale, and subsequently blamed his teammates. He claimed a few of Brooklyn's key players had stayed out beyond curfew and didn't show up in shape to play. Grimes also blamed Brooklyn second baseman Pete Kilduff, stating that Kilduff was tipping the spitter to the Indians by picking up dirt and rubbing it in his glove every time Grimes threw the pitch. By doing this, Kilduff was ensuring that he could dry the ball a bit with the dirt in his glove before throwing it if it was hit to him. Clarence Mitchell was also a spitballer—a rare left-handed one. Still, it was not a pitch that earned him infamy—it was a batted ball. With two on and none out, Mitchell hit a line drive to Indians second baseman Bill Wambsganss who was shaded up the middle. Wamby made a leaping catch, stepped on second base to double up Kilduff (who was on his way to third), then tagged out Otto Miller (who was on his way to second from first base). In a split second, Mitchell had become the answer to a World Series trivia question that is still being asked to this day.

* * *

With the New Year's Eve formalities of the Kratter Corporation taking possession of the keys to Ebbets Field now over, the countdown to D-Day—Demolition Day: February 23, 1960—began in earnest. Prior to the wrecking ball descending upon the visitors' dugout on that cold February day, ceremonies were held. The event began promptly at 11:00 a.m. as recorded by the familiar Bulova clock, still keeping perfect time atop the scoreboard in right-centerfield. In addition to the 200 spectators there to pay their last respects, there was an assemblage of various officials, a brass band, and a handful of former Brooklyn Dodgers players. Events opened with a final raising of the United States flag up the centerfield flagpole. It was quickly realized that the flag had been hung upside down, the international sign of distress, but officials assured everyone that it was simply a mistake—not an intended message.

Next, renowned singer Lucy "Star Spangled Soprano" Monroe belted out the National Anthem with musical accompaniment by the 69th Regiment National Guard Band. Monroe, the official soloist for the American Legion and the Veterans of Foreign Wars, spent much of her career singing the National Anthem (over 5,000 times by her estimation), and had done so at Ebbets Field prior to countless games over the years. The difference this time, however, was that neither Monroe nor the musicians in the band seemed to take any pleasure in their performance, and even their spirited rendition of the Anthem could not lift the feeling of gloom that hung over the proceedings.

* * *

Twenty-one years elapsed between Brooklyn's pennant of 1920 and their next one in 1941, and those were tough years on the field and in the stands. Wilbert Robinson managed the club from 1914 to 1931, and the team was referred to as the "Robins" under his leadership. While he

Introduction

had delivered the pennants of 1916 and 1920, Brooklyn was mediocre or worse for the remainder of his tenure, save for a run at the 1924 flag that saw them finish second to the New York Giants. Robinson, a former catcher, was affectionately called "Uncle Robbie" because of his rotund shape and jovial, congenial nature. These characteristics often resulted in his being somewhat unfairly portrayed as buffoonish, but the fact of the matter was that he was a solid baseball man who specialized in developing pitchers. That said, Robinson was a colorful, happy-go-lucky guy, and was certainly partly responsible for the silly way he was portrayed in the press. One particular incident from Brooklyn's 1915 training camp in Daytona Beach, Florida, stands out.

Aviator Ruth Law was flying in the area, serving as a tourist attraction. As the Brooklyn players discussed the novelty of Law's flights, their conversation eventually turned to the possibility of catching a baseball dropped from her plane. None of the players stepped up to take the challenge, so the 52-year-old Robinson decided to try. Law, however, forgot the baseball on the day of the challenge—but a resourceful member of the ground crew gave her a grapefruit to drop instead. No one told Robinson of the switch. The grapefruit knocked Robinson to the ground as it crashed into his mitt, exploded, and soaked him in warm juice. Thinking the juice was his own blood, Robinson panicked and called out for help. Players rushed to his aid only to break out in uproarious laughter as they saw that Uncle Robbie was fine—just drenched in grapefruit juice.

Brooklyn's play on the ballfield during the last few years of Robinson's career with the franchise did more to cement his clownish reputation than the grapefruit caper. Following Ebbets' death in 1925, Robinson took on the role of club president in addition to his duties as manager. Having perhaps bitten off more than he could effectively chew, the team's play slipped over the next few years. Not only did they play poorly, their on-field blunders were epic and became the stuff of legend. It was during this time that they became known as the "Daffy Dodgers" or the "Daffiness Boys," a label coined by famed and controversial journalist Westbrook Pegler that stuck with them well into the 1930s.

* * *

Following Lucy Monroe's singing of the "Star Spangled Banner," the band played a few more tunes, ending with a melancholy rendition of "Auld Lang Syne." Marvin Kratter offered an olive branch to Brooklyn fans by announcing that his colossal new apartment complex would feature a baseball diamond for Little Leaguers. The fans seemed to take no con-solation in Kratter's statement that the Little League team that would play there would be known as the Brooklyn Dodgers, the only team left in America to be so named. Al Helfer, pre-war broadcast partner of Dodg-ers announcer Red Barber, emceed the program. Longtime Dodgers pub-lic address announcer Tex Rickards was there, and he took one last turn at the Ebbets Field microphone. Had there been any fans out in the leftfield seats, fans who used to drape their coats over the railing, Tex may have made his usual request of them—"Will the people in the leftfield boxes please remove their clothing?" But the leftfield boxes were empty on this day. Lee Allen, a Hall of Fame historian, was there, and he was presented the keys with which Charles Ebbets had opened the park in 1913.

* * *

Despite the dismissal of Wilbert Robinson following the 1931 sea-son, the Dodgers continued their daffy brand of baseball through much of the decade. There were many guilty parties in the development of their clownish reputation—characters like: Dazzy Vance, Jumbo Elliott, Van Lingo Mungo, Pea Ridge Day, Boots Poffenberger, Boom-Boom Beck, Hot Potato Hamlin, Babe Phelps, and Frenchy Bordagary to name a bunch—but it was Babe Herman who became the unfortunate poster child of the Daffiness Boys. A lifetime .324 hitter who hit an eye-popping .381 in 1929 followed by .393 in 1930, Herman is unfairly best remem-bered for his poor fielding, comedic base-running, and humorous man-gling of the English language. Whether fair or not, Herman's zany legacy was forever sealed one August day when he doubled into a double-play at Ebbets Field—a play in which all three Dodgers base runners simulta-neously arrived at third base.

Lousy attendance was an unfortunate side effect of the poor prod-uct the Brooklyn Dodgers put on the field, and the Great Depression only exacerbated the attendance problems. The Dodgers were in real trouble by 1938, deeply in debt and in danger of going out of business. A bankrupt Brooklyn franchise was bad for the entire National League, so the owners consulted National League president Ford Frick for sugges-tions as to how to improve the situation with the Dodgers. For answers, Frick turned to the most successful general manager in the league—Branch Rickey of the Cardinals. Rickey would later directly impact the good fortunes of the Dodgers, but at this time he suggested his old friend Larry MacPhail be given the job of resurrecting the Dodgers.

While MacPhail could be loud and boorish, was a heavy drinker, and had a volatile temper, he was a savvy businessman with a genius ability to run a baseball franchise. He'd proved it when Rickey had assigned him to turn around the Cardinals' failing minor league Columbus team. He'd succeeded again with the Cincinnati Reds, but was now available being that he'd recently quit them after punching out team owner Powell Crosley.

MacPhail believed in the philosophy that one had to spend money to make money. That was not necessarily what the Dodgers' creditors wanted to hear, but they went along with MacPhail's plan—and the turnaround was swift. He upgraded the experience of attending a Dodgers game by refurbishing Ebbets Field, dressing the ushers in slick uniforms, dressing the ballplayers in new redesigned uniforms, and installing lights for night baseball. He made listening to the games a joy for fans by bringing Red Barber on board as radio announcer. Most importantly, however, he immediately improved the product on the field by acquiring good, established players like Dolph Camilli, Billy Herman, Leo Durocher, Mickey Owen, Dixie Walker, Joe Medwick, and Kirby Higbe, to name a few, as well as signing top prospects like Hugh Casey, Whitlow Wyatt, Pee Wee Reese, and Pete Reiser. To ensure that there would be a constant flow of new prospects, MacPhail signed 15 scouts, bought six minor league teams, and inked working agreements with six other clubs. The Dodgers had finished sixth in 1937, the year prior to MacPhail joining the team. They finished seventh in his first season at the helm, but his changes began to get traction in 1939 as the Dodgers rose to a third-place finish. The year of 1940 saw them climb to second place, and in 1941 the Brooklyn Dodgers became pennant winners.

* * *

There was a small group of former Brooklyn Dodgers players in attendance at the Ebbets Field demolition-day ceremony. Right-handed pitcher Carl Erskine—"Oisk," as the Brooklyn fans affectionately called him—was there. Erskine, who had treated the Flatbush faithful to years of gutsy pitching—including two Ebbets Field no-hitters—looked dignified in shirt-and-tie and winter overcoat. As he was always willing to do, he pleasantly obliged the photographers' request for a good photo opportunity. He stood next to the baseball-painted wrecking ball, perfectly positioned so as to look as if he was in mid-pitching delivery with the wrecking ball in his pitching hand. It was a clever bit of dark humor. But below the friendly smile, Erskine was introspective about the demolition of the park, telling reporters, "You know, when I look at the field now I see the past. I think of things that happened in this nook and that cranny. I'm

remembering bad pitches I made out there, and great days we had. That
dugout's empty," he said as he pointed to the soon-to-be-destroyed visitors
dugout, "but when I look at it, I can see all the men that used to be there.
It's like losing an old friend."

* * *

With the Deadball Era and the Daffiness Boys a thing of the past, it was the 1941 ballclub that began building the modern legacy of the Brooklyn Dodgers; a legacy of excellent execution on the field, performed by a colorful array of players—but ending in gut-wrenching heartbreak. It was a dynamic that spawned the motto "Wait till next year," and elevated the expression "Dem Bums" to nationwide recognition. As for excellent play on the field, Dolph Camilli validated the high price Larry MacPhail had paid for his services, slugging 34 long balls while driving in 120 runs and winning the league's Most Valuable Player award. The outfield was highly productive, with Pete Reiser batting a league-leading .343 with 14 homers, Joe Medwick hitting .318 with 18 homers, and Dixie Walker checking in with a .311 average. Pee Wee Reese established himself as the Dodgers' shortstop of the future in his first big league season. Second baseman Billy Herman provided more defensive strength up the middle while batting .291 with 41 RBIs. And catcher Mickey Owen solidified the middle strength by earning a spot on the National League All-Star team. Right-handers Kirby Higbe and Whitlow Wyatt were 20-game winners on the mound, while Hugh Casey, Curt Davis, and Freddie Fitzsimmons were solid in their roles starting and relieving.

So, yes, manager Leo Durocher's team had completed MacPhail's rebuilding program, but they were just getting started at building the Brooklyn Dodgers' star-crossed legacy of the 1940s and 1950s. Matched against a powerful New York Yankee team in what became known as the Subway Series, the Dodgers dropped the first two games of the 1941 Series but battled back to win game three and were one strike away from winning game four when disaster struck at Ebbets Field. Yankee batter Tommy Henrich swung and missed Hugh Casey's next pitch for the final out, but the ball got past Mickey Owen and Henrich reached safely. The Yanks jumped on the opening, rallied, and won the game, 7–4. The Yankees closed out the Series by winning game five, 3–1. The four-games-to-one Yankee victory belied how closely fought the Series was, with three games won or lost by a slim one-run margin. But what everyone would remember was the ill-fated way the Dodgers lost—by

Introduction

Mickey Owen's "dropped third strike." While it was not altogether fair to blame Owen (was he crossed up on the pitch by a Casey spitter?), the heartbreaking way the Dodgers would continue to lose became a common theme over the next decade and a half, steadily building their unique legacy.

* * *

Seventy-year-old Otto Miller, the first man to catch a ballgame at Ebbets Field (April 5, 1913), was on hand for the demolition-day cere-mony. Yes—the same Otto Miller who was tagged out for the third out of Bill Wambsganss' unassisted triple-play in the 1920 World Series. Miller spent his entire 13-year big league career with the Dodgers. When asked about the first game at Ebbets Field, the old catcher accurately recalled that the Dodgers had lost, 1–0, to the Phillies. Miller picked up two hits in the game, although he made no mention of that to reporters on hand. Miller sat quiet and expressionless as he watched the wrecking ball crush the dugout roof, but he, like Erskine, was most likely contemplating all the history he witnessed and participated in at Ebbets Field. Miller had scouted for the Dodgers following his playing days, and he still lived in Brooklyn. He died tragically at 72 in a fall from a fourth-floor window at the Brooklyn Eye and Ear Hospital just days after surgery for cataracts. It was never determined if it was an accident or suicide.

* * *

Two months after the Yankees beat the Dodgers in the 1941 World Series, the United States was pulled into World War II following the Jap-anese attack on Pearl Harbor. After all the work Larry MacPhail had done to resuscitate the Brooklyn Dodgers, military enlistments and the draft would ravage their lineup and derail their progress as it did most other major and minor league teams. But lineups stayed mostly intact for a good part of 1942, and that allowed the Dodgers to make a run at another pennant. They had nudged the Cardinals out of the 1941 pen-nant by a mere 2½ games, but this time the Cardinals would return the favor by edging the Dodgers out of the N.L. flag by just two games.

Brooklyn held an eight-game lead in mid–July when Pete Reiser, hitting a hefty .356, ran into Sportsman's Park's concrete centerfield wall while chasing a long drive by Cardinal outfielder Enos Slaughter. Reiser suffered a separated shoulder and a fractured skull, and was told by doctors to sit out the rest of the season, but the Dodgers, desper-ate for another shot at the World Series, allowed Pete to return. Hind-sight proves that Reiser should not have returned so soon—if at all that season. He struggled to hit .200 through the rest of the campaign, and the Dodgers, while playing excellent ball in September, could not catch the Cardinals, who had overtaken them in the weeks following Reiser's injury. Reiser was never again the same player he'd been prior to the injury.

To add insult to injury, there was trouble at the top in the Dodgers front office. Despite the turnaround of their team on the field and increased attendance in the stands, stockholders had grown tired of Larry MacPhail's extravagant spending—and he'd grown tired of his battles with them. MacPhail decided to accept a military commission (he'd already served in World War I), so he resigned from the Dodgers, making way for the man who would lead them to their greatest period of success—MacPhail's old pal, Branch Rickey.

* * *

As a bookend to the appearance of Otto Miller, Ebbets Field's first Dodger catcher, the great Roy Campanella, Ebbets Field's last Dodger catcher, was an honored guest at the demolition-day ceremony. Technically, it was Joe Pignatano who was the last Dodger to work behind the plate at Ebbets Field, but it was Campanella who had started that game (September 24, 1957), and nobody at the demolition ceremony seemed to care about the details. They loved Campy and were happy to see him in attendance. Campanella, handsomely dressed in a wool winter coat, leather gloves, and a fedora, sat in his wheelchair, dignified, his number 39 jersey draped over the right wheel. As promised, he was presented with his old locker and an urn filled with dirt gathered from behind home plate. Campanella never really wanted to go west to Los Angeles. He said New Jersey was as far west as he cared to go. His heart was in Brooklyn and Ebbets Field. Despite all the racism from the time in which he played, Campanella said not once was a racial slur ever directed to him at Ebbets Field. As fate would have it, Campanella would always be strictly a "Brooklyn" Dodger, for the auto accident that paralyzed him on January 28, 1958 (just four months after he appeared in the last game at Ebbets Field) would cut short his career and prevent him from ever being a "Los Angeles" Dodger.

* * *

After finally wearing out his welcome with Cardinals owner Sam Breadon, Branch Rickey arrived in Brooklyn to oversee the continuation of the Dodgers success that Larry MacPhail had begun. The 61-year-old Rickey came with a colorful resume: grade-schoolteacher, college baseball-basketball-football-coach-athletic director, U.S. Army major, lawyer, Major League catcher-scout-manager-general manager, etc., etc. All that aside, what he was chiefly known for was his brilliant management of the St. Louis Cardinals franchise, with his innovation and leadership building the Cards into a model of efficiency and success that would result in three decades of domination. Rickey was known as a well-read and very thoughtful man—a deeply religious, Bible-quoting beacon of human morality. He was also known to be a cheap, cut-throat, sometimes under-handed—and sometimes scheming—general manager. He was a world-class orator in the eyes of many—a blowhard in the eyes of others. As contradictory as these characteristics seem to be, Rickey did, in fact, somehow manage to legitimately embody all of these traits.

As feared, the war years were not kind to the Dodgers. Rickey, in a money-saving move, cleared out many of the veteran players upon his arrival, and that was followed by the loss of many other key players to the war effort. The Dodgers dropped to third place in 1943, then plummeted to seventh in 1944. Their star-depleted roster was a shell of its former self. Just as Babe Herman had been the poster child of the Daffiness Boys, second baseman Eddie Basinski became the face of the wartime Dodgers. The slender, glasses-wearing Basinski looked more like a handsome professor rather than a rough-and-tumble ballplayer. In fact, he held a degree in chemical engineering from the University of Buffalo and was a violin player in the Buffalo Symphony Orchestra. But he was also a fine ballplayer, so Dick Fisher, a local Buffalo bird dog scout, convinced the Dodgers to take a look at Basinski. The Dodgers liked what they saw in Eddie. In a statement showing how desperate big-league teams were for healthy bodies in 1944, they signed Basinski and brought him straight from the Buffalo sandlots to the big-league club for a trial. When finally given a shot to play after two weeks on the bench, Basinski tripled off the Crosley Field wall in his first at-bat and played crackerjack defense at second. Manager Leo Durocher was impressed and began calling Basinski "Bazooka" because of his cannon arm.

Despite playing solid baseball for the wartime Dodgers in 1944 and 1945, players and the press were obsessed with the fact that Basinski was a concert violinist and did not look the part of a ballplayer. Durocher's needling of Basinski finally led to a showdown where Leo offered to purchase Eddie a new suit if the kid would play his violin for the players in the clubhouse. A fierce competitor, whether it be on the ballfield or in an orchestra chair, Basinski brought his violin to the clubhouse and gave a virtuoso performance. Stunned, Leo said, "Well, I'll be a son of a bitch—the kid can play! What kind of suit do you want?" It was well known that

Durocher was one of the best-dressed men in baseball and wore only the finest suits. Basinski's reply was that he'd take a suit from wherever Durocher got his suits, meaning Leo would have to buy Eddie a suit that cost at least five times as much as any suit Basinski had ever purchased.

It was funny, but Basinski's ballplaying was no joke. Despite a brief stint with the 1947 Pittsburgh Pirates, it was in the minor leagues where Eddie Basinski would become a star, most notably in the highly competitive Pacific Coast League from 1948 through 1959. "A lot of people think musicians are pantywaists," Basinski said. "That's a bunch of nonsense." Mostly, though, Brooklyn fans thought Eddie fit right in with their assorted mix of characters.

* * *

Former Dodgers outfielder Tommy Holmes was present at the demolition-day ceremony. Holmes spent just one season with the Dodgers—1952, the last campaign of an 11-year career in which he batted .302 lifetime—but he had as much reason as anyone in attendance to be saddened by the razing of the old ballpark. Holmes was born and raised in Brooklyn. He attended Brooklyn Technical High School and had fond memories of going to Ebbets Field as a kid. "I was a Dodgers fan growing up," Holmes said. "Many times, three of us would get 55 cents together, we'd go over to Ebbets Field, and one kid would go through the turnstile and the other two would sneak under after him. I'd get to see a ballgame for under 20 cents." As an adult, Holmes played the first ten years of his career with the Boston Braves, so he had many additional fond memories of Ebbets Field where he collected quite a few hits as a visiting player. Holmes put together a National League record 37-game hitting streak in 1945, with four of those games coming at Ebbets Field from June 22–24. Overcome by emotion, Holmes turned away after the wrecking ball struck the first blow on the roof of the visitors dugout and later revealed, "I said to myself, 'Let me get the hell out of here. No one wants to see this.' And I left."

* * *

With World War II in the rear-view mirror, most big league ballclubs were back at full strength just in time for the 1946 season. There was new blood on the Brooklyn team—plum products of Branch Rickey's booming Dodgers farm system—and the club returned to its pre-war winning ways, finishing in a hard-fought tie with the Cardinals at season's end. The club also returned to the tough-luck legacy it began forging in 1941 with its heartbreaking loss to the Yankees in that year's World Series. This time, however, they didn't even make the Series—instead losing out on the pennant by getting swept by St. Louis

Introduction

in a best-of-three playoff for the N.L. flag. Like Mickey Owen in 1941, it was Dodgers first baseman Howie Schultz who took the blame this time. Despite dropping Game One of the playoffs, Schultz had been a bright spot in the game, going two-for-three with a home run and two RBIs.

But things didn't go so well for Schultz in Game Two when Leo Durocher sent him in to pinch-hit with two outs and the bases loaded in the ninth inning, Dodgers trailing, 8–4, at Ebbets Field. Schultz told writer Peter Golenbock:

> I remember hitting the first pitch down the leftfield line, and it hit just outside the chalk mark, and after that the count went to 3-and-2. The bases were loaded, the fans were going crazy, and Harry Brecheen threw me a letup screwball—and I almost fell down swinging at it. Missing. And so that's how you go from hero to goat in one day. So before God and 30,000 fans, I struck out with the bases loaded to end the Dodgers' playoff in 1946.

* * *

Rounding out the small group of former Dodgers players attending the demolition-day ceremonies was hard-throwing right-hander Ralph Branca. One of the nicest men ever to bear such a singular burden for losing a pennant, Branca was the unfortunate Dodgers pitcher who surrendered the game-ending, pennant-clinching home run to the Giants' Bobby Thomson in 1951. Thomson's "Shot Heard Round the World," as it came to be known, had been discussed non-stop and the film clip replayed continuously in the nine years that had elapsed leading up to Ebbets Field demolition-day in 1960, but Branca had been heroic in the strong way that he carried the weight of the defeat in those years. In introducing Branca to those attending the razing ceremony, public address announcer Tex Rickards said, "Ladies and gentlemen, now coming in to pitch for the Dodgers, No. 14, Ralph Branca." It didn't matter to knowledgeable Dodgers fans that Rickards erred—Branca never wore No. 14. Everyone knew Ralph wore No. 13, a number that many superstitious players refused to wear. Branca wasn't superstitious, though, and proved it on a Friday-the-13th in April of 1951 as he playfully posed for photographers. Branca smiles in the picture, his back turned so as to make the "unlucky" No. 13 clearly visible. To cap his good-natured mockery of the concept of "luck," Branca holds a black cat on his shoulder. The next time anyone paid that much attention to the No. 13 on his back was in photos snapped in the clubhouse following Thomson's home run, photos where Branca was seen weeping over the epic failure. Not one to tempt fate again, he jettisoned the No. 13 jersey in 1952 and switched to No. 12.

So, no, the Brooklyn fans there didn't mind Rickards' mistake—it's what they'd come to expect with their Dodgers, and it's part of the reason they so adored them. They simply appreciated Rickards' sentimental nod to Branca, a fine pitcher who'd probably endured an excessive amount of negative attention for the unfortunate outcome of the 1951 playoffs. Following Rickards' introduction, Branca, now an insurance salesman, stepped out of the crowd and smiled as the spectators and Avirom workers cheered. Despite the pain he carried, Branca preferred to recall the joy, saying, "The Brooklyn baseball community was like no other; Brooklyn Dodgers fans were the most knowledgeable. The Brooklyn ballpark was like no other. These were the things I loved with all my heart: this proving ground, this social transformation, this extraordinary community."

*   *   *

Ralph Branca knew exactly what he was talking about when he mentioned Brooklyn's "extraordinary community" as a key ingredient in what made the Brooklyn Dodgers special. The colorful players and memorable on-field events of the Brooklyn Dodgers would alone be more than enough to make them a franchise worthy of continued recollection for as long as baseball history is recounted. But on-field events are just part of what builds a legacy of the scope and complexity of the Brooklyn Dodgers. It's Brooklyn's vibrant and interesting community and fans that elevate the legend of the Brooklyn Dodgers higher than that of most big-league franchises.

A "community" the size of 20th-century Brooklyn is too large and complex to be boiled down to a simple, homogenous description. In fact, Brooklyn was so large that it would have instantly been the third-largest city in America had it been separated from New York City. Despite its size, however, Brooklyn existed in the shadow of Manhattan, and was viewed as second class when compared to its more upscale neighbor. This assaulted the pride of the citizens of Brooklyn and placed a chip squarely on their collective shoulder. They developed an underdog's mentality, which created a strong community bond amongst those in the borough. They had a great sense of humor about who they were, and no one was better at poking fun at Brooklynites than Brooklynites themselves—but woe to the outsider who dared to insult them. Those outsiders who ventured into that territory quickly became the focus of a unified Brooklyn retaliation. The citizens of Brooklyn might be comprised of many varied ethnicities, incomes, and religions, but they were united as Brooklynites. They might have their issues with each other, but they were united against outsiders. And at no time was this unity more visible than when viewed through the lens of the Brooklyn Dodgers.

For six months a year, Brooklynites, going about their daily business in the borough, would enthusiastically discuss the previous day's Dodgers game.

> Did you see dat clown Hoiman [Babe Herman] yesterday? A fly ball nearly conked him right on his bean. My mudda coulda caught dat can o' corn! But he sure can moida [murder] da ball. ... How about dat Munga [Van Lingle Mungo]? What a crazy boid [bird] he is, but you shoulda seen him whiff dem seven straight Reds yesterday! ... Holy cow, Robinson sure had da Cubs eatin' outta his hand yesterday. One minute it's a nail-biter, den Ramsdell [Willie Ramsdell] reaches down to scratch his balls and—BOOM—Robby steals home on him! Da wheels came off da cart for da Cubs after dat. ... You shoulda been at da park yesterday. Ol' Skoonj [Carl Furillo] did it again. Queen's [Mel Queen] lucky enough to squeak a single into right, but Skoonj guns him out at foist [first] base! What a rifle dat kid's got.

The bond between the Brooklyn Dodgers and their fans was formed in an age before exorbitant salaries and television-created superstardom. Many players lived in the community and walked to and from Ebbets Field. Kids in the neighborhood would walk with them, talking and getting to know each other. Other teams represented a city—the New York Yankees, the Chicago Cubs, the Boston Red Sox. The Dodgers represented a community—Brooklyn—so they were a more local entity, and therefore their relationship to their fans was more intimate. This relationship spawned a fan base that was so unique that many of these fans became celebrities in their own right.

There was the unidentified fan who, as columnist Tom Meany wrote, always made a sandwich of his epithets by placing a pronoun before and after them, such as, "Ya bum, ya!" or "Ya dope, ya!" when directed at an individual player, or "Yez bums, yez!" when directed at the whole Dodgers team. There were the men who made up the top-hatted rag-tag Dodgers Sym-phony band. Using a minimal instrumental lineup that usually consisted of bass drum, trumpet, trombone, saxophone and crashing cymbals, the Dodgers Sym-phony band created a cacophony designed to amuse the fans and humiliate opposition players. A perfectly timed cymbal crash just as an opposing player's backside landed on the bench after coming up hitless in an at-bat is a perfect example of how the band taunted visiting players.

There was Eddie Battan and his tin whistle that shrilled "peep-peep-peep-peep" throughout home games. There was Jack Pierce, number-one fan of Dodgers third baseman Cookie Lavagetto. Pierce, who came to games with balloons bearing Lavagetto's name, would spend the whole game screaming "Cooooookie, Cooooookie,

Coooooookie!" while handing out cards featuring slogans like "Cookie for President. Always good in the clutch."

The most famous Dodgers fan of them all—and arguably the most famous baseball fan of all time—was Howlin' Hilda Chester. She began her relationship with the Dodgers in the 1920s as a peanut sacker for concessions moguls the Stevens Brothers, but she achieved her fame later as the round, pink-faced, gray-haired lady in the centerfield bleachers—the one who yelled at everybody with a voice that cut through the noise of the ballpark like a chainsaw. Warned by doctors that continued hollering could be lethal because of a heart condition, Hilda began banging a frying pan with an iron ladle at games—but she still kept hollering. Later, when her fame grew even greater, the Dodgers presented her with a brass cowbell, and it's that image—Hilda hollering while ringing her brass cowbell—that lives on.

Hilda embodied the spunk of Brooklyn fans, and continued to do so even after the club abandoned her for Los Angeles. Appearing on the CBS television show "Be Our Guest" just a few days before the razing of Ebbets Field in February of 1960, gravel-voiced Hilda asked show host George Dewitt if the program was being broadcast in color. When told no, it would be shown in black-and-white, Hilda said she was disappointed because she had died her hair especially for the occasion. Hilda then joined the Dodgers Sym-phony band for a rousing rendition of "Give My Regards to Broadway," with customized lyrics that said, "Give our regards to all Dem Bums, and tell O'Malley 'Nuts to you!'"

* * *

The Avirom crane continued to drop the baseball-wrecking ball on the Ebbets Field visitors' dugout, smashing it to rubble. According to Newsday's *Jack Mann, the crane operator—a 52-year-old guy named Mike Catusco—was a "muscular, middle-aged, Brooklyn-Italian man with abundant chest hair and a stinking black-rope cigar. A prototypical fan from Bensonhurst, who had suffered through all those 'next years' before the Dodgers got good, [Mike] would have to pull the lever to bury them. The strong man would weep, surely." However, when asked if smashing Ebbets Field saddened him, Mike said, "I can't truthfully say yes. I never cared much about baseball." Demonstrating a blunt-force sense of humor not uncommon to Brooklyn, Mike added, "I'm just a frustrated kid. When I was little I got spanked for breaking things; now I get paid for it." While most of Brooklyn did, in fact, mourn the loss of the Dodgers and the destruction of Ebbets Field, Mike Catusco was proof that Brooklyn was also a place of individuality, a place where the unsentimental could coexist with the sentimental. With that, Mike slammed the wrecking ball*

Introduction

into the dugout one final time before turning his attention to other sacred, nostalgia-soaked targets.

* * *

With the tough-luck events of 1941 and 1946 having begun the writing of a new narrative for the Brooklyn Dodgers, it was the 1947 season that would kick that narrative into overdrive, for the '47 Dodgers would return to—and lose—a tough World Series. But, more significantly, that year they undertook what was perhaps the most significant endeavor in the history of modern major league baseball—the single most important thing for which the Brooklyn Dodgers would be forever remembered—the integration of the game with a 28-year-old "negro" infielder named Jackie Robinson.

Brooklyn Dodgers general manager Branch Rickey had been laying the groundwork for bringing a black player to his ballclub since baseball commissioner Kenesaw Mountain Landis died on November 25, 1944. As baseball commissioner since 1921, Landis had been the single most powerful obstacle to earlier integration of the game. Personally, he was all for continued segregation of the game, but make no mistake—in keeping black players out of "organized baseball," he was only doing what most owners wanted. He constantly deflected the issue when queried about it, saying there was no rule against a black man playing in the major leagues. The reality was that it was an off-the-record gentleman's agreement between team owners that kept the major leagues segregated, an agreement that turned out to be ironclad despite the occasional challenge from the game's rare forward-thinking men.

Landis' successor, Happy Chandler, however, let it be known soon after he took over as commissioner that he was a proponent of the integration of baseball. That was the opening Rickey needed, and he immediately began looking for the right player to integrate the Dodgers. Years after his successful endeavor to integrate the game with Robinson, many still dislike giving Rickey any credit for doing anything other than integration for the ultimate goal of financial gain. In other words, integration would create better Dodgers teams and therefore earn Rickey more cash. Rickey certainly hoped that a good financial scenario would play out following integration, but there's simply no denying that he wanted to be part of the desegregation of baseball on a moral level. He believed in his heart it was the right thing to do—and he wanted to be the one to make history doing it.

On the field, it was Jackie Robinson who actually did the difficult work of integrating the game. Rickey believed Robinson was the perfect man to undertake the mighty task of being the first black player in baseball, a man who could stand tall in the face of vicious racism *without* fighting back. Rickey felt that constantly battling the racists would undermine the cause—at least in the first year of the great experiment. Robinson grew up in California where many different races coexisted and, importantly, played integrated sports—but there was still racism to deal with there, so he was conditioned to it. He was college educated, a military veteran, and a soon-to-be husband—things Rickey believed helped build character. He didn't smoke or drink, two major points of merit for the pious Rickey. As a player, Robinson had all the necessary tools to be great, but there was trouble from the start. Sure, there was expected opposition from all manner of outside sources—basic American citizens not ready for integration of any kind; baseball fans who wanted to maintain the status quo; other teams who were not ready to play against a ballclub with a black player; flat-out racists; etc. But the most challenging opposition came from within—the Dodgers players themselves.

Like American society in general, the Dodgers were comprised of men from many different backgrounds, and a good deal of those men came from places steeped in segregation. A group of these players expressed their opposition to playing with Robinson by signing a petition during training camp. Rickey and Durocher came down hard on them, threatening the release or trade of any player who refused to go along, and the petition was crushed. The incident shed light on the fact that what the Dodgers were undertaking would be difficult, possibly undermining their chances for success in 1947. But, just like the people of the Brooklyn community in which they played, the Dodgers grew closer and more unified in the face of their difficult task. Their various beliefs on race and integration were left behind when they stepped on the ballfield, and they played selflessly for each other and team success.

Even Dodgers players who'd struggled to accept integration found themselves rallying behind and defending Robinson. At no time was this more apparent than when Phillies manager Ben Chapman led his team on an over-the-top racist verbal assault of Robinson during a series early in the 1947 season. Watching their teammate suffer unimaginable taunts—and knowing he was ordered not to fight back—only served to coalesce team support for Robinson, and they eventually came to his defense, fighting the battles he was forbidden to fight for himself.

Introduction

Instead of causing the ballclub to struggle, the added tension of the team's integration seemed to increase focus and determination—and the results were amazing. After a slow start, Robinson thrived in the pressure cooker, batting .297 with 12 home runs. He delivered regularly in the clutch and tortured opposition pitchers by stealing a league-leading 29 bases. He also led the league in sacrifice hits while finishing second in runs scored. When the season was over, he was named National League Rookie of the Year. But more importantly, he helped lead the Brooklyn Dodgers back to the World Series. The Dodgers came up short again, however, losing a seven-game thriller to the Yankees—*wait till next year!* Failure, yes. But on a macro level: success—because going forward, *next year*, and many after that, would happily include Robinson, with no more petitions of dissent.

Everyone on the club knew he could help them win pennants, and that put cash in their pockets—something that often trumped racism in the final tally. Georgia-born Dodger Dixie Walker was at the forefront of the effort to block Robinson prior to the 1947 season, but he was a card-carrying convert by the end of the campaign. "He is everything Branch Rickey said he was when he came up from Montreal," Walker said. Walker gained the utmost respect for the way Robinson handled himself in the face of the racism he encountered. "He's as outstanding an athlete as I ever saw," added Dixie. Most of Brooklyn agreed.

* * *

Following the destruction of the visitors dugout, Mike the crane operator drove his carnage machine out to the iconic centerfield wall. The once-beautiful Ebbets Field grass—often described by Brooklyn fans as the greenest grass they'd ever seen—was already torn up and rutted by all the heavy equipment activity that had preceded demolition day. Nonetheless, the crane's heavy treads wreaked further havoc on the field, churning up hallowed ground as Mike drove slowly to center. Soon, his wrecking ball was slamming into the centerfield wall at the 376-foot mark, territory recently patrolled by Duke Snider and Pete Reiser before him. Reiser, whose career was shortened by his penchant for crashing into concrete centerfield walls—including the one Mike was currently destroying—commented prior to the demolition that "they should have no trouble with the centerfield wall—I softened it up for them." Reiser was right—they had no trouble. Gay Talese of the New York Times *recounted the centerfield demolition best when he described the wrecking ball "spinning toward the wall and, after a few shots, there was a hole the size of Hugh Casey."*

* * *

Introduction

The Dodgers of 1948 through 1954 continued their legacy-building by winning more games than any other National League team during that period—but continuing to lose pennants and World Series in spirit-killing fashion. After finishing in third place in 1948, Brooklyn rebounded to win the 1949 pennant—but brought disappointment once again by losing the World Series to the hated Yankees. The Dodgers dropped Game One in agonizing style at Yankee Stadium. Star rookie right-hander Don Newcombe pitched eight brilliant scoreless innings, but surrendered a game-ending solo home run to Tommy "Old Reliable" Henrich to open the ninth. Following the completion of his fine ten-year big league career, Newcombe would say, "They didn't call him 'Old Reliable' for nothing. That was the best game I ever pitched, even though I lost it."

Newcombe, along with Brooklyn's star catcher Roy Campanella, had joined Jackie Robinson as part of the core of superb black players who would help make the Dodgers great for the rest of their time in Brooklyn. But being a Brooklyn Dodger meant that you were going to endure heartbreak whether you were white or black, and Newcombe would shoulder more than his fair share. The Dodgers won Game Two behind a complete game 1–0 shutout from their colorful left-hander, spitballer Preacher Roe, but failed to hit enough to win another game and lost the Series four games to one.

There was high drama for the Dodgers in 1950 as the battle for the N.L. pennant went down to the last day of the season at Ebbets Field. The Dodgers, trailing the Phillies by one game in the standings, needed a win to force a tie for first place and a subsequent playoff for the flag. Back on the hot seat for the Dodgers, 19-game winner Don Newcombe was given the ball for the must-win showdown. Robin Roberts, the Phillies' young 20-game winner, would be on the hill for Philadelphia. Both men were amazing and the game was deadlocked at 1–1 after nine complete. The Dodgers missed a great opportunity to win the game in the bottom of the ninth on a play that is still discussed. With the less-than-speedy and seldom-used Cal Abrams on second base and none out, Duke Snider singled to center. Abrams hesitated, then took off. Knowing Phillies' centerfielder Richie Ashburn had an average throwing arm at best, Dodgers third base coach Milt Stock waved Abrams home. Abrams would later say it was a less-than-confident, half-hearted "go" sign from Stock—but Abrams did as he was told nonetheless. Abrams took a wide turn rounding third; Ashburn made a perfect throw; and Abrams was out by 30 feet. The letdown of this failure may have contributed to

Introduction

events in the top of the 10th inning when the Phillies' Dick Sisler connected for a three-run homer off Newcombe. The Dodgers went down one-two-three in the bottom of the 10th, once again snatching defeat from the jaws of victory.

As hard as it is to believe, the Dodger heartbreak of 1950 was topped by the heartbreak of 1951, again on the last day of the season. The Dodgers and Giants finished the regular season in a tie following a late-season collapse by Brooklyn and a hot-streak by New York. After splitting the first two games of a three-game playoff for the pennant, Brooklyn appeared headed for the World Series as they entered the bottom of the ninth of game three protecting a 4–1 lead. Newcombe was again the man on the big stage for the Dodgers in the do-or-die contest, and he'd again been great through eight innings. But the Giants rallied off big Don in the ninth and pushed a run across before Dodger manager Charlie Dressen, with two on and the tying run coming to the plate, replaced Newcombe with Ralph Branca.

Second guessing has gone on ever since—should Newk have been pulled? Should Dressen have gone with Carl Erskine instead of Branca? Was Branca tired? Did Thomson have Branca's number? Should Thomson have been intentionally walked to set up a double-play? Were the Giants stealing signs with a telescope from behind the scoreboard? Whatever the case may be, the Dodgers' season went down in flames when Bobby Thomson knocked a game-ending three-run round-tripper into the Polo Grounds' leftfield stands.

The Dodgers returned to the World Series in 1952 and 1953, but in an all-too-familiar scenario lost both Series to the Yankees. A great ballclub had been built in Brooklyn, constructed around a nucleus of excellent players—Jackie Robinson, Pee Wee Reese, Gil Hodges, Roy Campanella, Duke Snider, Carl Furillo, Carl Erskine, Preacher Roe, Don Newcombe, etc. Fine complementary players were constantly added—Joe Black, Billy Loes, Clem Labine, Billy Cox, George Shuba, Jim Gilliam, etc. Yet the Dodgers continued to come up short in the spotlight.

The Dodgers brought in new managerial blood in 1954 when they promoted Walter Alston from their Triple-A affiliate in Montreal, but they finished the 1954 season in second place—out of the World Series picture. Brooklyn fans couldn't help but worry that the window of opportunity might be closing on this group of Dodgers and their chance to win the World Series.

* * *

Introduction

Long-standing Brooklyn Dodgers fan Vincent Monahan attended the demolition day ceremonies. He'd seen enough annihilation by the time the baseball-wrecking ball started in on the centerfield wall, so he glumly left the stands and made his way to the rotunda where longtime Ebbets Field concessionaires, the Stevens Brothers, were catering their last-ever Ebbets Field event. "Another landmark gone," Monahan said to Frank Sullivan, a bartender working the affair. "That's progress," commented Sullivan with the philosophical insight bartenders often possess. "If that's progress, they can have it," replied Monahan with the cynical insight Brooklynites often possess.

* * *

The Brooklyn Dodgers famously had more than their fair share of colorful players and memorable on-field events. They also enjoyed a vibrant and interesting community and fans beyond the norm of most franchises. For players and fans this extraordinary, a unique ballpark was needed in which they could come together. Charles Hercules Ebbets had known this even before he became the principal owner of the franchise in 1905, but it would be eight years after that before he would be able to complete his dream of building the Dodgers a home worthy of the Brooklyn fans. But it was worth the wait, and in 1913 Charlie Ebbets opened the doors to Ebbets Field, and what unfolded there for the next four-and-a-half decades was truly special.

The Brooklyn baseball team had played in a number of different home ballparks since Ebbets began his association with the ballclub in 1883. They'd settled into a wooden stadium called Washington Park in 1892, but Ebbets always had a grander vision for the home of the Dodgers. He began scouting the borough for a suitable place to build his vision. He settled on a four-and-a-half-acre plot of land in Flatbush. The area was a shanty-covered slum whose center was a rancid pit where the poverty-stricken citizens and squatters would dump their garbage. Local farmers would let their pigs feed on the fetid trash pit, a dubious tradition that earned the area the not-so-flattering name Pigtown. After deciding that Pigtown was the perfect spot for his dream ballpark, Ebbets meticulously acquired the land, hired architect Clarence Randall Van Buskirk to design the stadium, had the plot cleared and prepped for construction, and broke ground in a ceremony on March 4, 1912.

A little over a year later, on April 9, 1913, Brooklyn lost to the Philadelphia Phillies in the first official game played at Ebbets Field. The 10,000 fans who attended the game entered a park appointed in luxury, a stark contrast to the Pigtown dump that occupied the location just one year earlier. Former New York City planner and architecture expert Daniel Campo gave a great description of Ebbets Field:

> Like the new ballparks of its rivals, Ebbets Field was a two-tier concrete pavilion concentrating seating around home plate, which was strategically placed near the block's narrower southwest corner. With its gracefully arched brick window bays, pilasters, Corinthian columns, and roof ornament, Ebbets Field was one of the more elegant ballparks constructed during this era. Its entry rotunda at the corner of Sullivan Place and Cedar Place (later McKeever Place), featured marble wall treatments, gilded ticket cages, and a marble mosaic floor inlaid with a stitched baseball pattern at its center, while a 12-arm "bat-and-ball" chandelier hung from the stuccoed ceiling above. But like its counterparts in Philadelphia, Pittsburgh, St. Louis, Chicago, and Detroit, Ebbets Field was less an architectural gem and more of a utilitarian structure that could be incrementally expanded as the team's market grew. Starting with an initial capacity of 18,000, additions to the stadium over the years—enlarging bleachers and extending the upper deck around the lower seating bowl—brought the park's capacity to 34,000 by 1937 and filled out its footprint with all but its leftfield bleachers, covered in two decks.

The changes Ebbets Field underwent over the early years of its existence transformed it from a pitcher-friendly stadium to one of the best hitters' ballparks in the major leagues—especially for left-handed batters. Duke Snider, who spent 11 years of his 18-year big league career playing in Brooklyn, found Ebbets Field's short 297-foot right field dimension tailor-made for a left-handed pull-hitter like himself. Despite a 19-foot screen mesh that topped the right field wall, Snider still ended up hitting 175 of his career 407 home runs at Ebbets Field, and, in fitting fashion, hit the last Ebbets homer on September 22, 1957.

In his book *Twilight Teams*, Jeffrey Saint John Stuart gave a detailed description of Ebbets Field.

> The roof and double-decked grandstand extended all the way down the right and leftfield foul lines providing upper and lower deck seating. There was bleacher seating beyond the leftfield wall. The field dimensions measured 348 feet from home plate to the fence along the leftfield foul line. It was 297 feet down the line in right, and 389 feet to the fence in dead centerfield. Balls hit into the screen above the 10-foot high concrete wall in left were in play. Caroms off the 19-foot concrete wall in right field were unpredictable because the lower half of the concave barrier sloped away from the field at a 45-degree angle. The right field wall was topped by nineteen feet of screen mesh. At the junction with the centerfield fence, a large scoreboard, topped by a large S[c]haefer Beer sign and a Bulova clock, stood five feet in front of the wall. The "h" and the "e" in the S[c]haefer sign would light up to indicate a hit or an error.

Introduction

The unpredictable caroms off the right field wall was part of the charm of Ebbets Field—unless one was asking the opinion of opposition right fielders who never had the time Brooklyn right fielders had to master the wall's idiosyncrasies. Of all the Brooklyn right fielders, Carl Furillo was the best at playing the right field corner—a corner that *Green Cathedrals* writer Philip J. Lowry said could provide 300 angles of rebound after a ball hit different parts of the wall out there. Furillo took thousands of practice balls off the wall in right, but he boiled his approach down to the following when interviewed by Peter Golenbock for his book *Bums*:

> Will it hit above the cement and hit the screen? Then you run like hell toward the wall, because it's gonna drop dead. Will it hit the cement? Then you gotta run like hell to the infield, because it's gonna come shooting out. I can't even tell you if it's gonna hit the scoreboard. The angles were crazy.

The outfield wall at Ebbets Field wasn't just the source of crazy bounces, it was covered with a plethora of colorful advertisements that are stamped into the recollections of fans who attended games there. The advertisers changed over the years, but some of the best remembered signs were those for Gem Razors, Ever-Ready Safety Razors, Mennen for Men, Esquire Boot Polish, Sani-White Shoe Polish, Mobilgas, Tydol Flying "A" Gasoline, Botany Ties, Van Heusen Shirts, Stadler's Florsheim Shoes, Clysmic Water, Hygrade's All-Beef Frankfurters, Luckies, Philip Morris, Fatima Cigarettes, "Bull" Durham Tobacco, Johnson Brothers Lumber, Michaels Furniture, Green River Whiskey, Imperial Beer—and the list goes on. The best remembered sign of all, however, was the three-foot-tall by 30-foot-wide yellow Abe Stark sign at the base of the scoreboard. The sign touted Abe Stark as "Brooklyn's Leading Clothier," but the chief element that made the sign memorable was a clever gimmick—a black arrow on the sign that featured the words, "HIT SIGN, WIN SUIT." It was genius in that it was almost impossible for a fly ball to hit the sign because the sign was at the base of the wall in a spot where, because it was shallow in that spot of the outfield, the right fielder was always within a few strides. Most fans and players never saw the sign hit, but there are some who claimed that New York Giants slugger Mel Ott was the only one to hit the sign on the fly—not once, but twice!

Longtime New York sportswriter Tom Meany covered countless games at Ebbets Field, so he knew better than most what Ebbets Field meant to Brooklyn. Writing about the 1960 demolition, Meany said,

Introduction

It's always a wrench to see an old friend go, even an old friend of stone, concrete, and steel. As a kid of nine, my father took me to Ebbets Field to see the infield being sodded down by Mike Daly in March of 1913, a month or so before the ballpark opened. A decade later I was covering the Dodgers for the *Brooklyn Daily Times*. In 34 years I must have passed through the press gate about 3,000 times. There were great doings on the field, including three men on third base in August, 1926, when Babe Herman doubled into a double-play. There was a fight between Dixie Walker and assorted Cubs; Hack Wilson, then a Giant, being mobbed by fans in 1924; Cookie Lavagetto's double which deprived Bill Bevans of a World Series no-hitter in 1947; the second of Johnny Vander Meer's consecutive no-hitters in 1938 when the lights shone on Ebbets Field for the first time.

There were great doings off the field, too, such as Larry MacPhail trying to bar [*Brooklyn Eagle* sportswriter] Harold Parrott from the press box in 1938, and a couple years later wrestling [*New York Herald-Tribune* sportswriter] Red Patterson on the floor of the press room. There was the fan who rushed out on the field in 1940 and assaulted umpire George Magerkurth after a game. The fan [21-year-old Frank Gernano], a parolee with a build like a beer barrel and a heavy blue beard, was hauled into court and Magerkurth was asked if he wished to press charges. "No," was Magerkurth's answer to the magistrate, "I'm the father of a son myself." There was Hilda Chester and her cowbell, and the Dodger Sym-phony with its cacophony. All in all it was quite a place. Brooklyn will never be the same without it. In fact, Brooklyn was never the same with it.

*　*　*

At the conclusion of the demolition day ceremony, the American flag was taken down from the Ebbets Field centerfield flagpole for the final time. The flag had first flown on that same pole on April 5, 1913, when Ebbets Field hosted its first game—a rehearsal/exhibition game between the Superbas and the New York Yankees. "The American flag must be raised on the huge flagpole in deep centerfield," said owner Charles Ebbets before the game. But, like the upside-down flag-raising ceremony on demolition day, Ebbets' stadium-opening flag-raising ceremony had its own glitch. "Mrs. E.J. McKeever," reported the New York Tribune, *"whose husband is now associated with Mr. Ebbets in the ownership of the Brooklyn club, walked across the field [to the flagpole], flanked on one side by the smiling Charlie Ebbets and the other side by her husband. And then it was discovered that the flag had been forgotten! A boy rushed frantically across the field and soon came staggering out with a monster piece of bunting. He arrived at the scene of operations in due time. And then, as the band played* The Star Spangled Banner *and the crowd stood with bared heads, Mrs. McKeever struggled valiantly with the halyards, and finally, with a little assistance, hoisted Old Glory to the top of the pole."*

Mercifully, the esteemed flagpole would not end up in a pile of

Introduction

Ebbets Field rubble. Later, without fanfare, the flagpole was removed and donated to the Veterans of Foreign Wars where it was slated to be installed in front of the VFW post in East Flatbush. It would no longer oversee history-making events at Ebbets Field, but would instead watch over the ordinary comings and goings of Brooklyn folks in and around 1405 Utica Avenue where the VFW was located—far from sunny Chavez Ravine.

* * *

The year 1955—it was an unforgettable one in the lives of Brooklyn Dodgers fans. Like a bolt out of the blue, the Dodgers snapped out of their malaise of 1954 and delivered Brooklyn their long-awaited World Series championship. Only it wasn't fate that stepped in and saw the Bums through—it was Dodgers skipper Walt Alston who came through, expertly balancing a roster of age and youth for maximum efficiency. Veteran Dodgers position players like Campanella, Furillo, Hodges, Snider, Reese and Robinson were still the key components, as were veteran members of the pitching staff like Newcombe, Erskine, Loes and Labine.

But younger Dodgers position players like Jim Gilliam, Sandy Amoros, Don Zimmer, and Don Hoak made invaluable contributions, as did baby-faced pitchers like Johnny Podres, Ed Roebuck, Karl Spooner, Don Bessent, Roger Craig, and Sandy Koufax. Brooklyn fans couldn't believe it—they were finally champions. No more "wait till next year."

The 1955 World Series victory was made even sweeter because it came against the New York Yankees. After enduring so much disappointment at the hands of the Yankees, it was supremely satisfying for the Dodgers to finally exact a measure of vengeance against New York. The Series was a thriller, going the full seven games. Young Podres was the Series' Most Valuable Player. After dropping the first two games, the Dodgers were desperate for a win in Game Three—and Podres turned out to be just what the doctor ordered, pitching a complete-game 8–3 win at Ebbets Field.

Later, with the Series deadlocked at three games apiece, Alston again turned to Podres—and Podres again delivered, pitching a complete-game shutout to clinch the Series at Yankee Stadium. The Game Seven victory turned on a play in the bottom of the sixth, the kind of play that always went against the Dodgers in the past—but not in 1955. With two on and none out, Yogi Berra hit a sinking liner into the leftfield corner. It looked to be a sure RBI hit, but Amoros made a spectacular running catch, then threw the ball in to double Gil McDougald at first base. The play killed the Yankee rally and ultimately sealed the Brooklyn win.

33

Introduction

The Dodgers and the Yankees faced off again in the 1956 World Series, but things returned to the status quo when New York won the Series, four games to three. The everlasting image of the '56 Series is that of Yankees catcher Yogi Berra leaping into the arms of teammate Don Larsen at the conclusion of Game Five. The reason for the celebration—Larsen had just tossed the only perfect game in World Series history.

Game six provided the last big World Series moment in Brooklyn Dodgers history when Jackie Robinson broke up a scoreless pitcher's duel with a game-ending, run-scoring 10th-inning single at Ebbets Field, giving Labine an impressive complete-game win. But Brooklyn's joy was short-lived when the Yanks cruised to a 9–0 victory in game seven at Ebbets Field. Facing Yankee right-hander Johnny Kucks with two out in the ninth, Jackie Robinson struck out to end the game. Little did Brooklyn fans know that it also ended an era.

* * *

On April 24, 1960—ten weeks after it began—the demolition of Ebbets Field was near its completion. But the old ballpark had one last public moment to play out—an auction of various Dodgers items left behind when the club lit out for Los Angeles. Bats, balls, bases, pennants, chairs, bricks and photos were just some of the items sold by auctioneer Saul Leisner. The item that garnered the most interest was the Ebbets Field cornerstone. Suspense filled the air when the giant cornerstone was brought out to the auction block. The crowd had been informed that the cornerstone was filled with items that had been enclosed within it when it was laid in place on July 3, 1912. A time capsule, if you will, containing items that Charlie Ebbets thought might be interesting to anyone opening it in the far-off future. With much fanfare, the cornerstone was struck with a hammer and—BOOM!—an explosion ensued. Then, out of the smoking cornerstone popped five clowns—three of whom were midgets dressed in tiny Dodgers uniforms. The gag added to the inappropriate circus atmosphere that had come to define what was at its core a truly somber event in the lives of Brooklyn Dodgers fans.

When the smoke cleared, the real cornerstone was brought out and set in front of the crowd of 150 or so collectors in attendance. What they saw was a rather plain stone, approximately two feet tall by four feet wide by eight or so inches deep, upon which was inscribed EBBETS FIELD 1912. Originally located on the right field side of the rotunda, the cornerstone might have been smashed to bits by the baseball-wrecking ball were it not for a timely call to the Avirom offices from Edward A. Duval, a 63-year-old inspector for the Department of Water Supply, Gas, and Electricity. Duval had been present at the Ebbets Field cornerstone-laying ceremony back in 1912, and he informed the Avirom people that the cornerstone included a time capsule. It was on that morning that Charles Ebbets swore he'd never leave the place until his team won a world's championship. Ebbets never lived to see his dream realized, unfortunately, passing away in 1925—five years after the Dodgers had suffered their second World Series defeat.

"I was 15," Duval told reporters at the auction. "It was a rainy day, I think, and there were about as many people here then as there are now. But not as many photographers." Duval told of how the dignitaries on hand that day had filled a copper box with newspapers, baseball publications, a 1912 calendar, pictures, coins, rosaries, Stars of David, and other items of interest from the day—including a copy of Admiral Peary's 1909 wireless message announcing that he had flown the Stars and Stripes over the North Pole. Onlookers were also invited to drop in their own personal calling cards and messages if they were so inclined. "I had a card," Duval said, "because it was the custom of young fellows in those days to make one up to impress the girls." Duval dropped his card in the copper box. When all were completed dropping in their items, the copper box was sealed, enclosed within the cornerstone, and set in place where it remained for 48 years.

Standing behind Charlie Ebbets' uprooted cornerstone, auctioneer Leisner announced that a bid of $600 had already been phoned in for the relic. When nobody offered to top the bid, Leisner announced that the buyer was none other than National League president Warren Giles, who would subsequently turn the stone over to the Baseball Hall of Fame in Cooperstown, New York. Now all that was left was to open the vault and enjoy viewing its contents. With all the delicacy of the clichéd bull in a china closet, Avirom worker Maxie Rosenfeld, swinging a sledgehammer from the left side, bashed away at the stone until a large chunk was knocked out of the top center. The vault was lifted out of the stone and opened. Much to everyone's disappointment, the vault's seal proved to be unsound, allowing decades of water to seep in. Seymour Goldsmith, an official from the Kratter Corporation, fished out the contents only to watch them fall apart in his hands. The fun over, workmen picked up the stone and hauled it away—but not before Duval looked through the ruins of the vault and found his old card. It seemed to be a fitting conclusion.

* * *

There was uncertainty in the air when the 1957 season began. The core Dodgers were aging and there was fear that their best days might be behind them. More unsettling, however, was the uncertainty about the future of the Brooklyn Dodgers. In a hostile takeover, Walter O'Malley ousted Branch Rickey and became the owner of the Dodgers in 1950. By the middle of the decade O'Malley had made it clear that he needed a new stadium in order to be financially competitive in Brooklyn. His demands had him at odds with city officials, and this conflict reached a fever pitch by 1957, and Brooklyn fans were now living with the very real possibility that their beloved Dodgers could, in fact, leave for greener pastures in California should the city of Brooklyn not meet O'Malley's demands. It was under this pall that the Dodgers began what would turn out to be their final season in Brooklyn.

ONE

Preseason

January

While talk of the Dodgers leaving Brooklyn had been going on for the previous few years, it would escalate to new heights in 1957 and hang like a black cloud over the entire season. Brooklynites, still recovering from their New Year's Eve celebrations, opened their morning newspapers and were immediately reminded of the ongoing battle for a new ballpark being waged between Dodgers owner Walter O'Malley and Brooklyn city officials. What would normally be viewed as a minor story of little significance, the Dodgers were announcing that they had purchased a twin-engine transport plane from General Dynamics Corporation. The plane could seat 44 passengers—just enough to carry a team of ballplayers, coaches, trainers, writers and club executives. It also had plenty of cargo space—perfect for luggage and—whaddaya know—large quantities of baseball equipment.

While franchises were delving more and more into air travel as an alternative to train travel for their ballclubs, no franchise had yet committed to flying enough to consider buying their own plane—until now. When it was suggested that owning a plane could prove useful were an East Coast ballclub to relocate to the West Coast, O'Malley told reporters, "If any club should go to the West Coast, it would have to fly and it would have to own an airplane. But our future—for the time being—is in Brooklyn." It was not exactly a happy way to ring in the New Year for Dodger fans in Brooklyn.

A mid–January tidbit in the papers served as another red flag to those who feared the Dodgers were gearing up to leave Brooklyn. The article informed that the Dodgers had sold Ebbets Field to real estate developer Marvin Kratter, who planned to eventually replace the ballpark with an apartment complex. The Dodgers would lease the park back from Kratter for three years, but it was unknown as to what would happen after that—or even if the Dodgers would still be in Brooklyn at the time the three-year lease expired.

Farewell to Flatbush

The annual drama of contract signings played itself out as January ticked by. The first Dodgers to sign contracts were Pee Wee Reese and Don Newcombe. Next was the Dodgers hero of '55, 24-year-old southpaw Johnny Podres. Fresh out of the Navy after being discharged for a back ailment, Podres agreed to sign for $18,000 on a phone call with General Manager Buzzie Bavasi. By the end of the month only three Dodgers remained unsigned—outfielder Sandy Amoros (another hero of '55), infielder Chico Fernandez, and right-handed pitcher Bob Darnell. Fernandez played briefly with Brooklyn in 1956, but he'd be traded to the Phillies days before the '57 season opened. Darnell spent short stints with Brooklyn in 1954 and '56, but he'd never again be called up the majors. Amoros, holding out for a $1,000 increase, finally got his raise and inked his contract at training camp in Vero Beach, Florida, on March 2.

Also playing itself out in the January newspapers was the complicated retirement of 38-year-old Dodger icon Jackie Robinson. Back on December 13, 1956, it was announced that the Dodgers had traded Robinson to the rival New York Giants. While the idea of Robinson wearing a Giants uniform and playing *against* the Dodgers was shocking to many baseball fans, it was not altogether surprising to people who followed Brooklyn that Robinson would be dealt. Robinson was a Branch Rickey man, so there was some tension with Walter O'Malley once O'Malley replaced Rickey. And Robinson's relationship with Walter Alston, O'Malley's most recent managerial choice, was strained to say the least. In fact, the two nearly came to blows once on the team bus!

For two years Robinson had a secret deal with *Look* magazine to provide the exclusive scoop of his retirement whenever he decided to hang up his spikes. According to Robinson, he'd begun discussions with *Look* for his retirement story just days prior to his trade on December 13, but just a few hours after the trade was made the news was leaked to the press. Robinson refused to accept the trade, retiring instead—then wavering on his decision. The whole public drama left more than a few players, newspapermen, and team executives feeling burned. Robinson wrote a letter of voluntary retirement to New York Giants owner Horace C. Stoneham; then the letter was forwarded to the National League office. The letter voided the trade, ensuring that Robinson would retire a Dodger, but that was the last thing on the minds of everyone involved when the mess was finally concluded. In his letter Robinson said,

> After due consideration I have decided to request to be placed on the voluntary retired list as I am going to devote my full time to the business opportunities that have been presented. My sincere thanks to you and Mr. [Chub]

Feeney for your wonderful cooperation and understanding in this matter. I assure you that my retirement has nothing to do with my trade to your organization. From all that I have heard from people who have worked with you, it would have been a pleasure to have been in your organization. Again my thanks and continued success for you and the New York Giants—Sincerely, Jackie Robinson.

Although Robinson was out of playing shape with legs that were spent, many people hoped he would change his mind and return to the Dodgers. But by rule his letter of voluntary retirement required that he would not be eligible to return until 60 days after the beginning of the 1957 season. His retirement letter seemed definitive, but Robinson, always a complex character, seemed to leave the door open to a return when a reporter asked him if he could get in shape by June. "Yes," Robinson replied, "I could get in shape, let's say if I decided in May that I wanted to play."

Considering what he'd accomplished in his career, who could doubt him? Sal Maglie, for one. For years with the Giants, right-handed pitcher Maglie was a hated rival of the Dodgers. But he'd joined Brooklyn in 1956 and won many key games in their road to the pennant. He was back with Brooklyn for 1957, and he was not speaking very highly of Robinson when asked by reporters for his thoughts about the retirement drama. Maglie said that Robinson was "out of shape" during the previous year's pennant race, but that

> for the last month he played every day and never said a word. Before that Robinson didn't want to play and you had to ask him every day if he would. If he got in shape, I think he could play another year or two. But I used to play against him, and last year he didn't compare with what he was years ago. His reflexes were gone and he was slower.

February

As January gave way to February, most news about the Dodgers continued to center on whether 1957 would be their last year in Brooklyn. Brooklyn fans were interested in watching baseball, not the battle being waged by their multi-millionaire team owner against clueless city officials. But that's what they'd be forced to endure all season long in '57. For good reason, Walter O'Malley wanted a new ballpark—in Brooklyn—for the Dodgers. And he was willing to pay for it with private, not public, funds. Ebbets Field was small, falling apart, and lacked suitable parking for a fan base that now needed it, following a decade-long exodus to the suburbs. City officials countered O'Malley's demands with their own propositions, none of which were suitable to the Dodgers owner—and Brooklyn fans had to be reminded of this every day of the season in the sports pages as the on-field exploits of the '57 team were positioned side-by-side with O'Malley's battles with the city.

Early February saw the Dodgers announce a major signing. A new pitcher? A slugger? No, a clown. Emmett Kelly, the famous former Ringling Brothers and Barnum & Bailey Circus clown, had joined the Dodgers and would perform his "Chaplinesque" pantomimes at Ebbets Field and with some Brooklyn farm clubs. Kelly, with his hobo-rags-outfit and sad-faced-five-o'clock-shadow make-up, already bore a striking resemblance to cartoonist Willard Mullin's "Bum" who had been featured on so many Dodgers programs and scorecards of the 1950s, so he seemed to be a natural fit for Brooklyn. Reporters, however, suspected more to the story and asked O'Malley why he'd signed the clown. "Oh," O'Malley said, vaguely, "just to ease the tension at Ebbets Field."

One thing that wasn't helping ease tension at Ebbets Field was a blurb in the newspaper reminding folks that the '57 Dodgers would again be playing some of their home games at Roosevelt Stadium in Jersey City, just across the Hudson River from lower Manhattan. Roosevelt Stadium opened in 1937 and quickly began building a rich tradition of minor league baseball, but attendance there had dwindled in the post-war years when the automobile boom made it much easier for Jersey City fans to drive to New York to see big league baseball instead of giving full support to the local minor league team. The Dodgers drew well at Roosevelt Stadium in 1956, averaging 21,196—about 5,400 more than for the games played at Ebbets Field that year. O'Malley wasn't overwhelmed, though—he'd hoped for sellouts at each game. But he was hoping for increased traction of the experiment in 1957, and that just served to remind Dodger fans of how unhappy O'Malley was with the situation at Ebbets Field.

A planeload of Brooklyn players and executives arrived at Dodgertown in Vero Beach on February 20, signifying the official opening of spring training. Aboard the plane among others were catchers Roy Campanella and Joe Pignatano, and pitchers Sandy Koufax, Johnny Podres, and rookie left-hander Marty Stabiner. There were position players there early, but manager Walter Alston laid down the law with them, saying,

> It's all right with me if such other fellows as Gil Hodges, Carl Furillo, and Randy Jackson want to work out with the pitchers and catchers. But if they want to join the workout, I want them to go all the way through it. I don't

want them working a little then quitting. It's a bad example for the rest of the squad who are going through the full workout.

A changing of the guard was in the works for the catcher position. Roy Campanella had started to slow down from age and injuries, but he still planned on handling the bulk of the catching duties for the 1957 Dodgers. Apparently unthreatened by the potential loss of his starting job, Campanella spent much of spring helping to train the Dodgers' catcher-of-the-future, John Roseboro. Originally signed as an outfielder and first baseman, Roseboro shifted to catcher after doing a stint in the Army. Campy helped school Roseboro on defensive positioning, footwork, blocking the plate, and quick-release throwing. Roseboro wouldn't get many opportunities to use Campanella's tips in 1957, but he'd put that knowledge to use for many years in the future after he took over catching duties from Roy following Campy's career-ending automobile accident in the winter of 1958.

Late February saw the release of a poll in which sportswriters, broadcasters, managers and coaches ranked ballplayers against their teammates in categories not found on a stat sheet. On the Dodgers, Pee Wee Reese placed first in the following categories: best student of the game; most relaxed on the field; most helpful to rookies; has done most for the team; best two-strike hitter; best at hit-and-run; best at sacrificing; best at bunting for a hit; best at hitting behind the runner; infielder best at decoying; best at taking extra base; best at getting jump to steal; and best at sliding. It spoke volumes about Reese, and no other Dodgers player came close to winning as many categories. Other results of particular interest were: Sandy Amoros—most nervous on the field; Don Newcombe—best bench jockey; Duke Snider—most graceful batting form; Sandy Amoros—most unorthodox batting form; Jackie Robinson—toughest to retire in a rundown. There was no mention as to whether the poll was conducted before or after Robinson's retirement rundown between the Giants and Dodgers.

March

Pee Wee Reese had good reason to be at the top of so many categories in the sportswriters/broadcasters/managers/coaches poll. He did everything right on the field and conducted himself in a manner that made him hugely popular with teammates and opponents—and fans, of course. But the 38-year-old Reese was slowing down by spring training of 1957, and he was dogged by annoying injuries and illness as March unfolded. First, he was felled with a flu that was running rampant through camp in early March. Then, he fouled a ball off his shin resulting in a deep bone contusion that sidelined him for a week. Reese, though, had the special ability to be whimsical even in the face of trying times. Sitting on the trainer's table with a black-and-blue knot the size of an egg on his shin, Reese said to Gil Hodges, "If this happened to an ordinary man, he'd go to the hospital."

Hodges, on cue, then skillfully recited the line he knew was supposed to deliver: "But you, indomitable one, intend to play ball." Reese finished the shtick by saying, "Not me—I'm going to the hospital!" It was another hit for the old team captain.

There were some special guests drawing lots of attention as the workouts of March 1 got underway. The Dodgers had invited two Japanese players from the Tokyo Giants to train with them—22-year-old catcher Shigeru Fujio and 21-year-old right-handed pitcher Sho Horiucho. They were there with their manager, Shigero Mizuhara, and an interpreter. They weren't trying out for the team—they were there in a reciprocal gesture of hospitality following the Dodgers' tour of Japan in the fall of 1956—but everyone seemed to enjoy watching them play in practices and squad scrimmages.

The Japanese contingent broke camp on March 21 and headed to New York. From there they would fly to San Francisco, then home to Japan. While in New York they visited Ebbets Field to see where their new Dodgers friends played. They were received by Dodgers employee Matt Burns who took them on a tour of the ballpark. The thing that impressed the Japanese group most was the lush green grass at Ebbets— the same thing that had impressed Brooklyn's fans for decades. Japanese players were unaccustomed to grass fields as their diamonds back home were of the all-dirt variety. While these players had already enjoyed the green grass on the fields at Vero Beach, what they saw at Ebbets Field was stunning to them. Despite being dressed in suits and ties, they couldn't resist the temptation to break out the bats, balls, and gloves. With manager Mizuhara pitching, Fujio and Horiucho took their swings. Fujio won bragging rights for the longest drive—a 300-foot clout to left-center.

Meanwhile, fans and teammates were still getting to know the pitching style and sense of humor of 20-year-old right-hander Don Drysdale, just beginning his second season in the big leagues. Drysdale enjoyed the company of the Japanese players at camp, just like he'd enjoyed them back in the fall in Japan. It was in Japan where teammate Jim Gentile got a lesson in Drysdale's sense of humor, with the Japanese players providing the inspiration for Don's prank. Gentile, Drysdale's roommate, thrilled the Japanese fans by hitting more home runs than any other Dodger, but he was embarrassed one day when he struck out four times against a Japanese lefty with a slow curve.

Following their return to the hotel, Gentile went up to their room while Drysdale secretly called Jim from the hotel lobby. Doing his best imitation of a Japanese reporter, Drysdale asked, "You hit no home run today, no? Why not, please?!"

"A guy can't hit home runs every day," snapped Gentile. "It was one of those days."

"Our pitcher left-hand throw slow curve," said Drysdale, the imitation Japanese reporter. "Slow curve maybe reason no home run, please?!"

The imitation Japanese reporter pressed Gentile for several minutes, with Jim growing madder by the second. Finally, Gentile hung up and Drysdale returned to their room. "These newspaper men are the same the world over," Jim said to Don. "This guy wants to know why I didn't hit a homer today—the so-and-so!" Drysdale made no comment, just listened with mock sympathy.

As for getting to know about Drysdale's pitching style, players and fans were quickly learning that Don didn't mind throwing blistering brushback pitches, some of which happened to hit batsmen. Upon his retirement from the game, Drysdale's 154 hit batters was a modern National League record, but Don was still new to throwing inside in 1957—and it was teammate Sal "The Barber" Maglie who deserves a lot of credit for teaching Drysdale one of baseball's fine arts. Maglie, a New York Giant for seven seasons, had given many Dodgers a close shave (hence the nickname "The Barber") over those years, but now he was dishing out shaves on behalf of the Dodgers—and passing the art on to youngsters like Drysdale.

"I never brushed back a hitter until last year," Drysdale told *New York Times* reporter Roscoe McGowan in early March.

> That was in a game where our fellows were being knocked down pretty regularly. It steamed me up a little, and I guess I retaliated. Sal Maglie had talked to me and told me that I couldn't let all those hitters dig in against me, that I had to make 'em respect me. I think he's right. I don't think Sal ever tries to hit a man, but he sure can make 'em think so with that high-and-tight pitch. It's not attempted mayhem, it's just psychology.

Farewell to Flatbush

It wasn't just Sal Maglie who was trying to teach Drysdale the finer points of pitching. Drysdale was as promising a young pitcher as there was in all of baseball, and it was Dodgers pitching coach Joe Becker who had the responsibility of taking Don from raw power-thrower to complete pitcher. Becker learned volumes about pitchers and pitching while catching for 17 years in organized ball—two of which were in the big leagues with the 1936–37 Cleveland Indians. After managing in the minors for a few years, Becker joined the Dodgers coaching staff in 1955. His approach to pitching and training was an immediate benefit to a staff that would pitch the Dodgers to a World Series championship that season. So much better was the '55 staff that *Life* magazine wrote about it in May:

> The pitching staff is the main reason for the Dodgers' improvement this year, and the main reason for the state of the pitchers is a leather-faced old catcher named Joe Becker. His job is to keep the pitchers in shape. He began running Dodger pitchers last spring and has never stopped. Before each game Becker makes the pitchers sprint in the outfield. He has the knack of hitting fungoes just beyond their reach, causing them to run harder. "You see, legs are very important," says Joe mildly. "Everyone thinks that if a pitcher has a good arm that's all he needs." The increased stamina of the staff is a natural result of Becker's work. "It's not that nobody ever thought of running pitchers before," says pitcher Carl Erskine. "It's just that Becker really made us stick to it."

It wasn't just conditioning that made Becker an effective pitching coach, he also had a thorough understanding of how to maximize a pitcher's repertoire. Johnny Podres was one of the pitchers who took a major step forward in 1955 under Becker, culminating in an amazing performance in the World Series. Podres already had a devastating change-up thanks to the teaching of former Dodgers manager Charlie Dressen in 1953, but Becker helped Podres refine his off-speed pitch, in addition to working on his rhythm and coordination. The results were impressive to say the least—a World Series championship for Brooklyn and a Series M.V.P. award for Johnny. Now, it was Drysdale who was learning Becker's change-up. Drysdale described the screwball-like change-of-pace: "I don't really give my wrist a twist the way Carl Hubbell did it. I just sort of let it spin off my fingers. It doesn't really break, but since I throw it with the same motion and from the same spot I throw the fast one, it works pretty well as a change-up." Drysdale would have a breakout season in 1957, jumping to 17 victories after winning just five in 1956. When asked how he did it, he gave much of the credit to Joe Becker.

Brooklyn opened the exhibition season with a 3–2 victory over

1957
𝓑𝓻𝓸𝓸𝓴𝓵𝔂𝓷
DODGERS

JOE BECKER
PITCHING COACH

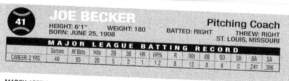

	41	JOE BECKER							Pitching Coach					
		HEIGHT: 6'1" WEIGHT: 180						BATTED: RIGHT	THREW: RIGHT					
		BORN: JUNE 25, 1908							ST. LOUIS, MISSOURI					

	Games	At Bats	Hits	2B	3B	HR	HR%	R	RBI	BB	SO	SB	BA	SA
CAREER: 2 YRS	40	83	20	5	2	1	1.2	8	13	8	8	0	.241	.386

MARCH 1957: In preparation for a long hard campaign, pitching coach JOE BECKER stressed conditioning as spring training moved into early March of '57. A catcher for 17 years in organized ball, two in the majors with the Cleveland Indians, Joe knew volumes about pitching – and conditioning was one of his top priorities. Joe joined the Dodgers as a coach in 1955 and his input yeilded immediate results – the staff had a great season and pitched the Bums to a World Series championship. The staff pitched great again in 1956 under Joe, leading the National League in shutouts, a category in which they would again be tops in 1957.

GO AHEAD AND BE STUBBORN – I GOT ALL DAY!

JOE TRAINED MULES IN THE OFFSEASON AT HIS ARKANSAS HOME!

the Milwaukee Braves on March 9. Rookie third baseman Dick Gray, 25 years old, was the hero with a game-ending solo homer in the ninth inning. Don Zimmer kicked off what would be a hot spring for himself by going one-for-three, while knuckleballer Fred Kipp pitched three strong innings of relief to pick up the win. Despite the positive start, the month of March for Brooklyn would come to be defined by injuries and illness. Half the team seemed to be battling mumps and flu, while a raft of others were dealing with assorted injuries. Reese had his bad shin. Carl Furillo was dealing with a sore elbow on his legendary throwing arm. Pitchers Don Newcombe, Karl Spooner, Don Bessent, Carl Erskine and Ed Roebuck were also suffering from sore arms. Roy Campanella had a pulled leg muscle and a bad ankle, and Randy Jackson had an infected boil on his neck. Ironically, Zimmer, who had suffered a broken cheekbone in a 1956 "beaning," was immune to all the maladies. "I've never felt better in my whole life," said Zip. "If I felt any better they'd probably put me in a hospital!"

March ended on a sad note for the Dodgers as they gave up on Spooner's attempted comeback from an injured shoulder. Spooner, a hard-throwing left-hander, exploded on the scene back in 1954 in his first two big league appearances. He made his major league debut by pitching a complete-game shutout against the Giants on September 22. He struck out 15 batters that day, setting a record for most strikeouts by a pitcher in his first major league outing. Spooner made his only other appearance of the season four days later. This time it was the Pirates who he shut out while fanning 13. Spooner's meteoric start had Dodgers fans drooling over the possibilities for Karl in 1955, but it all came crashing down when Spooner injured his shoulder during spring training. He labored to eight wins for the '55 Dodgers, but he wasn't the same. He pitched in just four minor league games in 1956 and hoped to make a comeback in 1957—but his shoulder just wouldn't respond. Spooner was mad when told he was being "designated for assignment," but, according to Dodgers general manager Buzzie Bavasi, Karl "slept off his anger" and admitted there was nothing he could do to help the ballclub. Spooner traveled back to New York for a medical evaluation, but he never again pitched in the majors, and was out of baseball by 1959 at the age of 28—a cautionary tale of how fleeting success can be when predicated on the unpredictability of flesh and bone, an imposing reality every ballplayer lived with on a daily basis.

Two

April

Brooklyn fans were hoping that their beloved Carl Erskine wasn't heading for the same sad ending that had just befallen Karl Spooner, but things didn't look so good for Oisk as April began. Like Spooner, days before him, Erskine decided to leave camp and head back to New York for more medical examinations on his ailing right throwing shoulder. If the doctors couldn't figure out what was wrong, the nine-year veteran said he would end his career. Erskine, unlike Spooner, was no flash in the pan. Erskine had won 113 games for Brooklyn since he'd broken in with them in 1948. Along the way he'd tossed two no-hitters and was the author of two brilliant World Series wins—including one in which he struck out 14 Yankee hitters. And he'd done it all while dealing with a bad shoulder which he'd injured as a rookie in '48—but the situation now seemed worse than ever to Erskine.

"This thing won't be ready in May," a glum Erskine told reporters after what turned out to be his final appearance in his now-truncated spring training. "I could hang around longer, but I don't feel I'm able to give the club an honest effort—and that's what I always want to give. It's not that I have pain in the arm—which I have. A lot of fellows pitch with pain. But I just haven't got the stuff I need." Because of his shoulder soreness, Erskine made just two appearances in the spring. His last appearance, a one-inning relief stint on March 31, went poorly, and it showed Erskine that he couldn't pitch through it this time as he'd done so many times before. "In that one inning I felt that if I just had that little bit more, I'd have done all right. But I didn't have it." All of Brooklyn was pulling for Oisk. He was symbolic of them—an underdog who over-achieved through smarts, grit and determination. Erskine had been there for nearly all of Brooklyn's ascension to greatness (1947–56), so he would forever be linked to those glory days. Seeing the possible end of Erskine's career reminded fans of the possible end of the Brooklyn Dodgers, hanging over their heads like a dark cloud.

Farewell to Flatbush

The struggle to keep the Dodgers in Brooklyn was raging up in New York while the Dodgers continued their training in April. Abe "Hit Sign Win Suit" Stark, now the City Council president, had waded into the fight and really stepped in it when he suggested that a new stadium be built for the Dodgers on the site of the Brooklyn Parade Grounds. The Parade Grounds was a nearly 100-year-old 40-acre tract of sandlot playing fields in the Flatbush section, just a long Furillo throw away from Ebbets Field. It had produced many big-league players, including Sandy Koufax and Joe Pignatano of the 1957 Dodgers. While Stark thought he was doing what the people of Brooklyn wanted—trying anything to keep the team in the borough—he quickly found out that there was one thing the locals loved more than their Dodgers—the kids of Brooklyn. The locals were outraged at the suggestion of wiping out the Parade Grounds, and they loudly voiced their opposition. Backpedaling, Stark said that any plan to build a new ballpark on the Parade Grounds would include plans to construct a new sandlot complex elsewhere. It didn't matter. O'Malley rejected Stark's plan anyway, and the battle moved to new territory.

On April 4 the Dodgers left Florida and began a winding journey north where they would open the 1957 season in Philadelphia on April 16. They would stop in Texas, Oklahoma and Missouri for exhibition games against the Milwaukee Braves along the way. First, they played in front of an overflow crowd at Mission Stadium in San Antonio. The next day they were in Houston, and it was there that the right-hand swinging Gil Hodges surprised the fans by taking his batting practice from the left side. Asked when he had become a switch-hitter, Hodges, noting the wind blowing to right, said, "Today." He then lined one sharply into right field, turned to the reporters and announced that he would hit the next one over the wall. He nearly made good on his prediction, too, as his next drive ricocheted high off the wall 345 feet away.

Dallas followed, then a game at Ft. Worth where the hot-hitting and healthy Don Zimmer finally got unhealthy when he was hit on the knee by a line drive off the bat of new teammate Elmer Valo. Zimmer, hobbled but still playing, was in the thick of things four days later when the Dodgers played the Athletics in an exhibition game in Kansas City. Zip, who had one of the strongest arms on the club, drilled A's base-runner Vic Power right between the eyes with a throw while attempting to turn a double-play. Power was unconscious for 15 minutes and sent to the hospital—and the A's were mad as hell. The next time up, A's hard-throwing right-hander Virgil Trucks flipped Zimmer with a heater up and in. Fearless in spite of his serious beaning the previous season, Zimmer bounced up and drove the next pitch 387 feet for a long, loud out. Still angry, Trucks knocked down Gino Cimoli, but cooler heads then prevailed and the rest of the game was played without incident.

The Dodgers wound up their Grapefruit season with home-and-home exhibition games against the Yankees on April 13 and 14. The lineups were very similar to the lineups each team played with six months earlier when they met in the World Series, with a few minor exceptions. The Yankees won the first contest, 5–4, in front of 7,742 frozen fans at Ebbets Field, then the Dodgers won the next day in front of an equally-frozen 7,897 fans at Yankee Stadium. Most importantly, the teams escaped relatively healthy—except Zimmer, who, in an effort to further undermine his early-spring statement that he never felt better in his whole life, missed the finale after fouling a ball off his ankle in batting practice.

April 16: Opening Day 1957

With lingering doubt as to whether 1957 would be their last year in Brooklyn, the Dodgers kicked off the season with a 7–6 win over the Phillies at Connie Mack Stadium in Philadelphia. Baseball commissioner Ford Frick and American League president Warren Giles were on hand for a pregame ceremony where a statue of baseball lifer Connie Mack was unveiled in a small park across the street from the stadium named in his honor. Mack was known for owning and managing the A.L. Philadelphia Athletics for 50 years, yet just four years after he managed his last game in 1950, the Athletics were uprooted and moved to Kansas City. The similarities to the situation in Brooklyn were not lost on those in attendance.

As for the game on the ballfield, it was a seesaw battle that Dodger rookie leftfielder Gino Cimoli broke open in the top of the 12th inning with a solo homer that proved to be the game winner. Right-hander Clem Labine, in relief of Don Newcombe, picked up the win for the Dodgers by tossing five shutout innings. Right-hander Robin Roberts, amazingly, went the distance for the Phils despite giving up seven runs and three long balls. Gil Hodges tried his best to knock Roberts out of the game with a game-tying bases-empty homer in the eighth, but Roberts was still in there when Hodges returned to the plate in the tenth with the game still tied. This time Hodges tried a different tact, drilling Roberts in the chest with a screaming line drive. Roberts picked up the ball, threw Hodges out, and then collapsed. It was a scary moment, but Roberts, a true gamer, recovered and resumed pitching to the wild cheers of the sell-out crowd. Their joy turned to sorrow in the 12th, however, when Labine retired the Phillies in order following Cimoli's homer, buttoning up the opening day win for Brooklyn.

While "Gino Anichletto Cimoli" sounds like the name of a guy who could have been born right in the heart of Brooklyn, the 27-year-old Dodger leftfielder was actually born in faraway San Francisco, in the predominantly Italian-American North Beach section. An all-around athlete who was offered a basketball scholarship to the University of San Francisco, Gino passed on it, thinking he was too small at six-foot-one to make a career of it. His sports career, it turned out, would come in baseball after impressing scouts at the Hearst Sandlot Classic at the Polo Grounds in 1948. The Hearst Sandlot Classic pitted sandlot all-stars from a national team against a New York squad. Brooklyn scout Howie Haak liked the potential he saw in Gino and signed the youngster after four days of all-night drinking and coercion with Gino's father, Abramo Cimoli. Making no progress despite hours of time and many bottles of Ancient Age Bourbon, Haak finally asked Abramo, "Who wears the pants in this family?" That did it. Abramo immediately woke up his wife Stella and their son and had Gino ink his name on a contract for $15,000.

Now, nearly ten years later, Cimoli was getting his first real shot at a full-time job with Brooklyn—and making the most of it from the start with his big opening day round-tripper. He'd broken in with Brooklyn in 1956, but had appeared infrequently, usually as a defensive replacement, and had only 36 at-bats. Cimoli continued to make good on the chance given to him by manager Walter Alston in 1957. Cimoli was batting .314 by the all-star break whereupon Alston—also the N.L. All-Star manager—named Gino to the all-star team. Cimoli would play ten years in the majors, but 1957 would always rank as one of his best seasons as he finished with a .293 batting average, ten home runs and 57 RBIs, while scoring 88 times himself. One of those 88 runs scored would be the last run ever scored at Ebbets Field—September 24, 1957.

1957
Brooklyn
DODGERS

GINO CIMOLI
OUTFIELDER

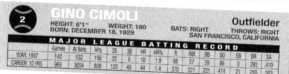

GINO CIMOLI

2

	HEIGHT: 6'1"		WEIGHT: 180						**Outfielder**				
	BORN: DECEMBER 18, 1929					BATS: RIGHT			THROWS: RIGHT				
									SAN FRANCISCO, CALIFORNIA				

				MAJOR LEAGUE BATTING RECORD									
	Games	At Bats	Hits	2B	3B	HR	HR%	R	RBI	BB	SO	SB	BA	SA
YEAR: 1957	142	532	156	22	5	10	1.9	88	57	39	86	3	.293	.410
CAREER: 10 YRS	969	3054	808	133	48	44	1.4	370	321	221	474	21	.265	.383

4-16-57: Amid rumors that the Brooklyn Dodgers were going to move to Los Angeles following the 1957 season, the Brooks kicked off the new campaign in style with a 7-6 victory over the Phillies at Connie Mack Stadium. Rookie leftfielder **GINO CIMOLI** already had two hits to his credit when he stepped in to bat in the 12th inning with the bases empty and the score deadlocked. Seconds later Gino smashed a Robin Roberts pitch into the left-centerfield seats for what turned out to be the game winner. There were a lot more highlights for Gino in the 1957 season, including a pinch-hitting appearance for the National Leaguers in the All-Star Game.

THE PHILLIES BULLPEN DUPED GINO WHEN THEY HID A LIVE BALL FROM HIM ON 7-6-57!

April 18: Ebbets Field Home Opener

After a day off following their season opener in Philadelphia, the Dodgers played their home opener against the Pittsburgh Pirates at Ebbets Field on April 18. There were lots of pregame activities to get through before any ball would be played. First, Walter Alston, with an assist from the Marine color guard, proudly raised the 1956 N.L. pennant into the Brooklyn sky. Next, N.L. president Warren Giles presented the team with their 1956 N.L. championship rings—or watches or cuff links or clasps in the case of the few who had chosen those options.

Then came a few individual prizes. Don Newcombe, winner of 27 games in 1956, was presented with the '56 M.V.P. Award from Giles. Big Newk also received the first-ever Cy Young Award, presented to him by Dan Daniel, president of the National Association of Baseball Writers. Don Drysdale also received an individual prize—the first-ever Brooklyn Dodgers Rookie-of-the-Year Award, presented to him by Mike Lee, president of the Brooklyn chapter of the Baseball Writers Association. As fate would have it, it turned out to be the last-ever *Brooklyn* Dodgers Rookie-of-the-Year Award. That was followed by a rousing rendition of the National Anthem as sung by Everett McCooey, son of the late Brooklyn Democratic boss John McCooey, backed by the Fourteenth Regiment Band. Lastly, borough president John Cashmore threw out the first pitch and home plate umpire Tom Gorman shouted, "Play ball!"

The game itself was less eventful than the pregame ceremonies as the Dodgers won easily, 6–1, behind the crisp four-hit pitching of Sal Maglie. The most notable part of the game, perhaps, was the fact that Duke Snider was booed by the Brooklyn fans so early in the season. Snider was generally loved by Dodgers fans, but their relationship could be complicated. Snider was prone to occasional bouts of pouting, complaining and whining, and the fans did not hesitate to voice their disapproval through loud boos. Duke usually turned the boos into cheers with a perfectly-timed homer, and that was the case on this day. After grounding out twice and being called out on strikes, Snider was jeered vociferously as he came to bat in the seventh—but he soon had them cheering madly after he clubbed a 400-foot home run over the scoreboard. The Pirate victim of Snider's blast: rookie right-hander Clarence Nottingham Churn.

Brooklyn fans' stomachs were still churning over the daily articles reporting the not-so-good situation between Walter O'Malley and Brooklyn city officials. Some believed that was the reason that the turnout for the Ebbets Field opener was so low—just 11,202 subdued souls. Certainly, more was expected for the defending N.L. champions first home game of the new season. New Dodger clown Emmett Kelly debuted his act for the Ebbets Field crowd, but his forlorn face seemed to reflect the mood of the fans. One fan was not ready to give up his fight to stop the Dodgers from taking off for California—his name was Henry Modell, and he was the chairman of the Keep the Dodgers in Brooklyn committee. He had a Keep the Dodgers in Brooklyn banner hanging over his box, and there was a gang of teenagers handing out buttons featuring the same slogan. For Modell, the real battle was just beginning.

Brooklyn resumed their four-game home set against the Pirates with a 2–0 win on April 20. Johnny Podres pitched a masterful complete game, his fastball and change performing to perfection. The modest season-opening win streak came to an end the next day as the Dodgers lost the front end of a twin-bill, but then rebounded in the nightcap with a 7–4 victory. Newcombe took the loss in the opener, 6–3, his fate sealed in the third frame when he issued back-to-back-to-back homers by Frank Thomas, Paul Smith, and Dick Groat. Drysdale picked up his first win of the season in the second game with 7⅔ innings pitched.

April 22: Jersey City Dodgers

Walter O'Malley's Roosevelt Stadium experiment continued on this day, April 22, as the Dodgers played the first of eight "home" games they would play in Jersey City, New Jersey, in 1957. While attendance at Dodgers' games in Jersey City was less than O'Malley had hoped in 1956, and fan sentiments there were sometimes not so friendly (it was Giants territory and the Bums were often booed), the '56 Jersey City results were impressive as the Dodgers won six of seven. To boost attendance on this day, the Dodgers had a nice give-away item for the first 3,000 youngsters to pay their way into the park: free glossy prints of the leading Dodgers players (suitable for framing). What they didn't mention, however, was that the photos were also suitable for unframing in the event the Dodgers should abandon Brooklyn following the season.

One of the players featured in the photo pack did a great job helping the Dodgers get a win in the Jersey City opener—pitcher Roger Craig. The lanky six-foot-four-inch right-hander spaced out seven Phillies hits over 7⅓ innings and held a 3–1 lead in the eighth, but Walter

1957
Brooklyn DODGERS

ROGER CRAIG
RIGHT-HAND PITCHER

ROGER CRAIG

3

HEIGHT: 6'4" WEIGHT: 185
BORN: FEBRUARY 17, 1930

Right-Hand Pitcher
BATS: RIGHT THROWS: RIGHT
DURHAM, NORTH CAROLINA

MAJOR LEAGUE PITCHING RECORD

	Games	IP	Won	Lost	Pct	Hits	Runs	ER	SO	Walks	ERA
YEAR: 1957	32	111.1	6	9	.400	102	58	57	69	47	4.61
CAREER: 12 YRS	368	1536.1	74	98	.430	1528	763	653	803	522	3.83

4-22-57: Brooklyn defeated Philadelphia 5-1 in the first of eight "home" games played at Roosevelt Stadium in Jersey City, NJ. 1957 was the second year of the Dodgers' Jersey City experiment. Roosevelt Stadium had a much larger seating capacity than Ebbets Field, and the experiment was aimed at convincing politicians back in Brooklyn that the time had come to build a new ballpark. Unfortunately, Jersey City was mostly Giants territory, so the Dodgers didn't draw very well there — and to add insult to injury, they were often booed. ROGER CRAIG earned his first win of the season on this day by limiting the Phillies to just one run in 7-1/3 innings pitched.

SOME LIKE IT HOT?!

ROGER CAME OUT OF THE PEN TO EXTINGUISH A FIRE AND EARN A BIG WIN ON 9-7-57!

Alston gave him a quick hook following a single by Richie Ashburn and a double by Solly Hemus. Clem Labine took over and buttoned up the win for Craig, and while Roger might have been slightly disappointed at not finishing what he started, he had to be happy about the single he hit off Jim Hearn in the third.

Craig was one of the worst hitting pitchers on the ballclub, so it was a special occasion when he got a knock. Really, though, Craig felt it was always a special occasion when he pitched for the Brooklyn Dodgers, and he was in awe of the team when he first joined them in July of 1955. "They had all those great players," Craig would later say. "I saw Jackie Robinson, Duke Snider, Pee Wee Reese, Roy Campanella, Don Newcombe, Jim Gilliam. It was like an All-Star team, and I said, 'I don't really belong here.'"

But he did belong there. Craig pitched in 21 games for the '55 Dodgers after he was called up that July, posting a 5-and-3 record with a 2.77 ERA. He started and got the win in Game Five of the World Series, later saying, "It was very special; a great experience. I was just fortunate enough to be on the only world championship they won in Brooklyn." Perhaps it was his upbringing that made him so humble and appreciative of his good fortune in Brooklyn. "My dad was a shoe salesman," said Craig. "He was on the road a lot. Raising ten kids, I don't think he made more than $50 a week in his life. I was number eight. My mom worked at Watts Hospital in Durham. She was like the housemother at a nursing home. My parents never really had a lot. It's still amazing they raised ten kids with the little money they made. But we never felt we were poor. We never complained about it." 1956 saw Craig become a regular in the rotation, and he responded with a 12-and-11 record and a 3.71 ERA, but 1957 would play out quite differently.

* * *

The Dodgers and Giants resumed their long-running rivalry on April 24 in front of nearly 23,000 fans at Ebbets Field. When Don Mueller grounded out to Jim Gilliam to end the game, it wasn't Newcombe, Drysdale, or Podres who got the 4–3 win—it was 28-year-old Cuban rookie Rene Valdes. It would be the only big-league win Valdes would ever get. The Dodgers held a 4–2 lead when Valdes took over for Sandy Koufax in the fifth. Valdes was shaky and quickly surrendered a run, but he then settled into a groove that carried into the 8th when ace reliever Labine came in to slam the door on New York. The Dodgers had high hopes for the skinny six-foot-three-inch hard-throwing right-hander after watching him win 22 games for their Pacific Coast League affiliate in Portland in 1956.

Valdes sparkled in spring training with a crackling fastball and a sharp-breaking curve, and he made fast friends everywhere with his ready smile and affable manner. There was only one thing that bothered him, though—no one back home in Cuba believed him when he told them of his success in the minors and at Dodgers spring training. You see, Valdes' full name was Rene Guttierez y Valdes, but, because it was easier to spell and pronounce, the Dodgers had shortened it to Rene Valdes. "When I go home," Valdes said, "my friends ask me how do I do in the United States. I say I won 22 games for Portland, and they laugh. They say, 'We saw no Guttierez winning games anywhere.' And I tell them I pitch under the name of Valdes, and they laugh again." They would have been laughing even harder back in Cuba if they knew the nickname his teammates had hung on him due to his long, skinny legs. "Some American players," he admitted with a wide grin, "call me 'Fungo Legs.'"

Brooklyn had a day off after Fungo Legs' big win against the Giants and then journeyed to Pittsburgh for a third-game series against the Pirates at Forbes Field on April 26, 27, and 28. The Bucs pounded Johnny Podres for five runs in the opener, sending him to an early shower in the sixth inning. Carl Furillo got an early shower, too, as hostile right field fans inexplicably barraged him with Iron City beer cans throughout the game. One possible explanation for their poor behavior was drunkenness, as all the beer cans hurled at Furillo were empty, their contents having been consumed by the Forbes Field rowdies. As the slogan said, "Pirate time is Iron City time!"

Brooklyn bounced back to win game two of the series behind a strong pitching performance from Don Newcombe, who contributed two hits and two RBIs to his cause. No home runs were hit in the game. For an idea of just how big Forbes Field was in centerfield and in the power alleys, look no further than two mammoth drives *held* by the ballpark—a 450-foot Gino Cimoli triple to center and a 440-foot Duke Snider sacrifice fly to right-center. Roger Craig pitched well enough to win in the finale, but the Dodgers couldn't put any runs across on Pirate right-hander Bob Friend and lost, 3–0. Rookie catcher Joe Pignatano, age 27, made his big-league debut pinch running for Roy Campanella in the eighth, but he never got off first base. After losing their seventh straight to Friend at Forbes, the Dodgers were happy to leave Pittsburgh and head back to the more friendly confines of Ebbets Field.

1957

Brooklyn
DODGERS

RENE VALDES
RIGHT-HAND PITCHER

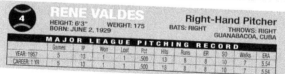

④ RENE VALDES   Right-Hand Pitcher
HEIGHT: 6'3"   WEIGHT: 175   BATS: RIGHT   THROWS: RIGHT
BORN: JUNE 2, 1929   GUANABACOA, CUBA

MAJOR LEAGUE PITCHING RECORD

	Games	IP	Won	Lost	Pct	Hits	Runs	ER	SO	Walks	ERA
YEAR: 1957	5	13	1	1	.500	13	8	8	10	7	5.54
CAREER: 1 YR	5	13	1	1	.500	13	8	8	10	7	5.54

4-24-57: The defending National League champion Brooklyn Dodgers downed their arch rivals the New York Giants 4-3 at Ebbets Field. Taking over for Sandy Koufax to start the 5th inning, rookie **RENE VALDES** got credit for the win after pitching solidly into the 8th frame. It would be the lone win of Rene's major league career as his five games with the '57 Dodgers turned out to be his only time in the big show. The Brooklyn front office had high hopes for Rene after he led the P.C.L. with 22 victories in 1956, but on May 21, 1957, he was optioned to Montreal for more seasoning. Rene was recalled in September after notching 11 wins for the Royals.

¡CUIDADO CON EL LATIGO!

RENE, WHO CALLED HIMSELF "EL LATIGO" ("THE WHIP"), GOT HIS ONLY START ON 9-28-57!

April 30: Home Run Derby

The Dodgers closed out the month by playing a little Home Run Derby against the Chicago Cubs at Ebbets Field on April 30. Campanella led the long-ballers with two circuit blasts. Gil Hodges, Sandy Amoros, and Don Zimmer each chipped in one apiece. Unfortunately, the Cubs were leaving the yard, too, with Gene Baker, Bob Lennon, and Walt Moryn all homering. Amoros' home run was needed in the bottom of the ninth to tie the game and force overtime; then Zip's round-tripper finally ended the three-hour and 35-minute marathon in the 10th—final score, 10–9. Sal Maglie, Rene Valdes, Clem Labine, and Sandy Koufax all got knocked around in the game. When it was over, it was right-hander Don Bessent left standing to collect the win.

The fact that Bessent was standing at all was quite amazing. A star quarterback at Robert E. Lee High School in Jacksonville, Florida, Bessent was courted by the football programs of the University of Florida, Auburn University, and Southern Methodist University. But fearing that his slender, six-foot, 170-pound frame couldn't stand the beating of big-time college football, Bessent, who was also a pitcher with a roaring fastball, signed with the Yankees. Spud Chandler, the fine old Yankee right-hander, schooled Bessent in the fundamentals of pitching in the pros, then the great Ted Lyons taught Don the wonders of the change-up.

As it turned out, it wasn't the beating of college football that would endanger Bessent's career—it was the rigors of baseball. Bessent was tearing it up in the Yankees farm system when one day he felt an electric bolt of pain shoot up his spine while delivering a pitch. He pitched in pain the rest of the season, but then the unimaginable happened. Getting out of bed one morning, he fell to the floor. Two vertebrae had separated, leaving Bessent paralyzed below the waist. He underwent dangerous spinal fusion surgery and the long process of rehabilitation.

The Yankees gave up on him, but the Dodgers took a chance that he could come back and signed him. Not only did he come back, he helped them out of a mid-season slump when he was called up in July of 1955. Working first as a starter and then in the bullpen, Bessent went 8-and-1 in 24 games and didn't allow a run in three appearances in the Dodgers' World Series championship. Being used strictly out of the pen in 1956, Bessent was just as good, pitching to a 2.50 ERA in 38 games. He was the winning pitcher in Game 2 of the 1956 Series after entering a tie game and holding the Yankees to two runs in seven innings. All in all,

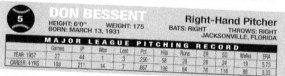

		Games	IP	Won	Lost	Pct	Hits	Runs	ER	SO	Walks	ERA
YEAR: 1957		27	44	1	3	.250	58	28	28	24	19	5.73
CAREER: 4 YRS		108	211	14	7	.667	196	84	78	118	88	3.33

4-30-57: Dodgers relief specialist **DON BESSENT** got his only win of 1957 when teammate Don Zimmer hit a game-ending solo shot in the bottom of the 10th inning against the Cubs at Ebbets Field. Bessent pitched only the top of the 10th, but he was perfect and set down the Cubs in order, fanning Gene Baker and Dave Hillman in the process. It was a good outing for Don, but for the most part 1957 saw him fail to recapture the magic that he possessed in 1955 and '56 when his stellar work out of the bullpen helped the Dodgers win back-to-back N.L. pennants. Of the 27 games in which Don appeared for the 1957 Dodgers, Brooklyn was victorious in only two.

Bessent posted a 1.35 ERA against the Yankees in five Series games from 1955 to 1956.

The year of 1957 would be a tough one for Bessent, though, as his ERA ballooned to 5.73 in 27 games. There were hints that he had developed a serious drinking problem, and maybe that was at the root of his ineffectiveness on the mound. He would later admit as much. A shoulder injury limited him to just 18 games in 1958, and that turned out to be Bessent's last season in the majors. Bessent's star burned bright but brief, but what he did for the Dodgers was not forgotten by his teammates. "Don Bessent won my 27th game for me in 1956," said Don Newcombe. "That save always reminded me Bessent was involved in helping me win the Cy Young Award." Don Drysdale added, "He was quiet in his own way, but he would go to war for you."

THREE

May

The Brooklyn Dodgers were 8-and-3 and in second place in the N.L., one game back of the Milwaukee Braves, as they opened the month of May by finishing their two-game series against the Cubs at Ebbets Field. Don Drysdale coasted to his second win, a complete-game 7-hitter. The St. Louis Cardinals came to town the next day for a three-game series. The Dodgers dropped the opener, 3–2, in a 16-inning marathon, then both teams left town for game two of the set, played in Jersey City on May 3. A temperature of 45 degrees and a driving wind made it feel even colder, prompting Stan Musial to joke, "Don't they ever call a game here on account of cold weather?!" The wind and cold didn't stop 14,470 fans from coming out, however, and Don Newcombe rewarded them by tossing a nifty 6–0 shutout. They completed the series back at Ebbets Field the next day with a 4–2 win, capped off by Charlie Neal's ninth-inning home run. Carl Erskine made an appearance as a pinch runner, but his ailing shoulder would prevent Oisk from taking the mound until mid–June.

May 5: A Rivalry Rekindled

Early on, 1957 was shaping up to be much like 1956—with the Dodgers and Braves battling for the N.L. pennant. A heated rivalry developed as Brooklyn edged out Milwaukee by one game for the '56 flag, and the Braves looked determined to take the next step in 1957. The Dodgers trailed the first-place Braves by two games as Milwaukee came to Ebbets Field for a second-game series. The crowd was ready to renew the battles of 1956 as 26,599 turned out to see the opening game on May 5—but they left disappointed as the Braves out-slugged Brooklyn 10–7. Roy Campanella hit his third home run of the season—but Hank Aaron hit his sixth. A host of Dodgers pitchers surrendered runs to Milwaukee's potent lineup that day, but the one Brooklyn pitcher whose ERA

1957

Brooklyn

DODGERS

DON ELSTON
RIGHT-HAND PITCHER

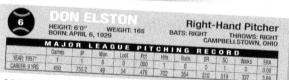

6

DON ELSTON

HEIGHT: 6'0"   WEIGHT: 165
BORN: APRIL 6, 1929

Right-Hand Pitcher

BATS: RIGHT   THROWS: RIGHT
CAMPBELLSTOWN, OHIO

MAJOR LEAGUE PITCHING RECORD

	Games	IP	Won	Lost	Pct	Hits	Runs	ER	SO	Walks	ERA
YEAR: 1957*	1	1	0	0	.000	1	0	0	1	0	0.00
CAREER: 9 YRS	450	755.2	49	54	.476	702	354	310	519	327	3.69

5-5-57: The Dodgers dropped a 10-7 slugfest to the Braves at Ebbets Field. Entering the game to pitch the top half of the 9th was **DON ELSTON**. It was his first appearance in the majors since he'd pitched in two games for the 1953 Cubs. Brooklyn traded for Don prior to the 1956 season, then sent him to St. Paul where he was converted from a starter to a reliever. On this day, Don gave up a lead-off double to Bill Bruton, then retired the next three Milwaukee hitters in order. It proved be the only inning Don would ever pitch in a Dodgers uniform.

* Only statistics from the 1957 Brooklyn Dodgers are displayed. Don played in an additional 39 games with the 1957 Chicago Cubs.

THAT ABOUT SUMS IT UP!

DON WAS TRADED BACK TO THE CHICAGO CUBS ON 5-23-57!

did not rise was right-hander Don Elston. He pitched a scoreless ninth in his first appearance for Brooklyn after being acquired from the Cubs in December of 1955. It would be Elston's only appearance with the Dodgers, however, for he was shipped back to Chicago on May 23 in exchange for four minor leaguers—this in spite of the fact that he'd shown promise by winning 41 minor league games from 1954 through 1956.

Elston would pitch against his former Dodgers teammates six times in 1957 following his trade to Chicago. In two of his best performances against them he helped the Cubs beat Brooklyn on June 30 with eight strong innings of work, then was the hard-luck loser on July 19 when Brooklyn defeated Chicago despite 9⅓ innings of solid pitching from Elston. Chicago eventually converted Elston to a full-time reliever, and it was in that role that he would thrive as the main man out of the Cubs bullpen for many years.

Maybe it was the presence of team captain Pee Wee Reese who made his first appearance of the season after sitting out the first 16 games with a bad back, but the Dodgers gave a spirited performance on May 6 to beat the Braves and split the series. More than anything, though, it was the presence of Gino Cimoli who blasted a game-ending home run in the bottom of the 14th just as the Bulova clock struck midnight. Cimoli was 5-for-7 in the game, but he was shut out in the RBI category until it mattered most. It was the second time of the young season that Cimoli won a game with an extra-inning home run.

* * *

The hottest team in the National League came to Ebbets Field on May 7. It was the Cincinnati Reds and their seven-game winning streak. The wind, rain, and cold had moved out and perfect weather had rolled in—but still just 9,830 turned out for the game. Joseph M. Sheehan of the *New York Times* suggested the low turnout was due to the continuing talk about the Dodgers moving to Los Angeles. Whatever the reason, Sheehan warned, Brooklyn is not supporting the Dodgers. The 9,830 fans who *were* supporting the Dodgers that day unfortunately saw the Reds assault the Brooklyn pitching staff and run their win-streak to eight with a 9–2 victory. Cincinnati won their 10th in a row the next day as they bombed Don Newcombe for three long-balls, the last being an eighth-inning grand slam by Don Hoak. The game was the 1,400th that Gil Hodges had played for Brooklyn, and that moved him into fourth all-time with the Dodgers, behind Zach Wheat (2,318), Pee Wee Reese (2,006) and Carl Furillo (1,525).

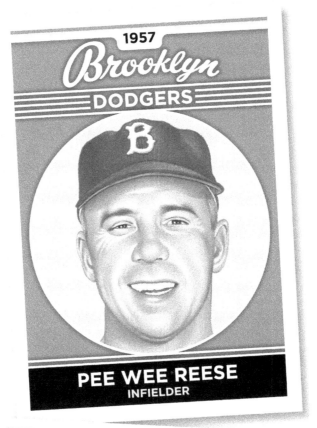

	Games	At Bats	Hits	2B	3B	HR	HR%	R	RBI	BB	SO	SB	BA	SA
YEAR: 1957	103	330	74	3	1	1	0.3	33	29	39	32	5	.224	.248
CAREER: 16 YRS	2166	8058	2170	330	80	126	1.6	1338	885	1210	890	232	.269	.377

5-6-57: Longtime Dodger great PEE WEE REESE made his first appearance of the season as Brooklyn edged Milwaukee 5-4 in extra innings at Ebbets Field. A back injury kept Pee Wee on the bench through the first 16 games, but The Little Colonel battled through the pain and entered this game at shortstop in the 10th inning. He failed to hit safely in his two trips to the dish, but teammate Gino Cimoli bailed out the whole ballclub when he ended the 4-hour marathon with a game-ending bases-empty round-tripper in the bottom of the 14th. Assorted injuries were a repeating theme for the 39-year-old Reese in 1957, limiting him to 103 games.

ANOTHER BLOW AGAINST FATHER TIME!

PEE WEE CLOUTED A GAME-WINNING 9TH-INNING TRIPLE ON 6-22-57!

Hodges celebrated with a three-run homer in the eighth, his fourth of the season, but it was not enough to lift Brooklyn to victory. The Reds win moved them ahead of the Dodgers into second place in the N.L., while the Brooks dropped into third.

* * *

Brooklyn began a 10-game road trip on May 10, beginning with a three-game series against the Giants at the Polo Grounds. Willie Mays had missed a couple of games with a virus, but he was back in time for the series-opener against the Dodgers—and it was Dem Bums who were feeling ill after a 2–1 loss. On offense, Mays drove in one run with a triple, then scored the deciding run off a single by Don Mueller. On defense, the Say Hey Kid held a possible Duke Snider inside-the-park homer to a mere triple, then turned a massive drive by Gil Hodges into a long out in the ninth. Brooklyn lost again the next day, May 11, extending their modest losing streak to four. The game was a 15-inning, four-hour and 39-minute struggle that featured 35 players, but it ended badly for the Dodgers when Giants back-up catcher Valmy Thomas unloaded on Don Bessent with a game-ending solo homer.

May 12: Podres at His Best

Johnny Podres played the role of stopper, halting the Dodgers' losing streak by pitching them to a 5–0 triumph over the Giants in the series finale on May 12. It was Podres' second shutout of the season. Podres enjoyed some success with the bat early in his career with the Dodgers, but for the most part he was not much of a threat at the plate. Still, like a lot of pitchers, Podres hoped to one day hit a big-league round-tripper. Prior to his victory over the Giants, the *New York Times'* Arthur Daley recorded some chatter around the batting cage involving Podres. "See that spot in the upper right field stands," Podres said to Pee Wee Reese, pointing at three sailors who were gathered there. "I hit one up there once."

"I can't see it," said Reese, squinting in the direction where Podres pointed.

"See what?" asked Podres, confused.

"The plaque," replied Reese. "It stands to reason that an event of such earth-shaking significance should be commemorated. I naturally assume that public-spirited citizens would put a bronze plaque on the

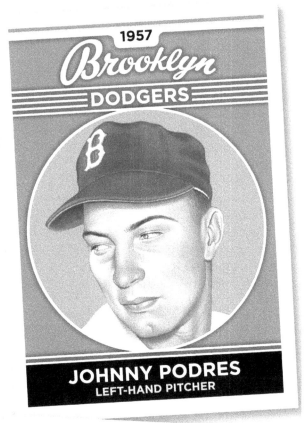

1957

Brooklyn

DODGERS

JOHNNY PODRES
LEFT-HAND PITCHER

JOHNNY PODRES

8

HEIGHT: 5'11"   WEIGHT: 170   Left-Hand Pitcher
BORN: SEPTEMBER 30, 1932   BATS: LEFT   THROWS: LEFT
WITHERBEE, NEW YORK

MAJOR LEAGUE PITCHING RECORD

	Games	IP	Won	Lost	Pct	Hits	Runs	ER	SO	Walks	ERA
YEAR 1957	31	196	12	9	.571	168	64	58	109	44	2.66
CAREER 15 YRS	440	2285.1	148	116	.561	2239	1026	925	1435	743	3.67

5-12-57: Hero of the 1955 world champion Dodgers, JOHNNY PODRES was at his best on this day when he shut out the Giants 5-0 on a 6-hitter at the Polo Grounds. The five runs of offensive support was an unusually large amount for Johnny in 1957 as is evidenced by the fact that he won only 12 games that year but led the N.L. with a 2.66 ERA. He also led all the majors in shutouts that season with six. Johnny always said that he did his best pitching in 1957 in spite of the fact that he had just 12 wins to show for it. Pee Wee Reese understatedly summed it up best for Podres when he said, "You know, Johnny, sometimes you've got to beat somebody 1-0."

BATTERS AWEIGH!

JOHNNY SPENT 1956 IN THE NAVY, THEN TOSSED A SHUTOUT IN HIS RETURN ON 4-16-57!

seat with the inscription, 'This marks the spot where Johnny Podres hit a home run.'"

"Didn't I tell you," said Podres innocently. "I didn't hit it in a game. I hit it during batting practice. I've never hit a big-league homer in my life." Podres would finally get his big-league homer in 1962—then one more in 1963.

Despite battling some elbow problems in 1957, Podres would pitch well in the Dodgers' final season in Brooklyn, further cementing him fondly in the memories of the Flatbush fans left behind when the franchise moved out. In 31 starts, Podres would post a 12-and-7 record in 1957 while leading the league in shutouts (6) and ERA (2.66). Still, it would be the Dodgers' 1955 World Series championship and his role in it that Brooklyn fans would always remember when they thought of Podres. In fact, Johnny felt the same way, too. "Sometimes when I'm home doing nothing, I'll put the video in," Podres told the *Philadelphia Inquirer* 50 years later. "I get the feeling that I'm young again. What a time that was."

* * *

May 14 saw the opening of a two-game series between the Dodgers and Braves in Milwaukee. A large crowd of 34,731 packed County Stadium for the opener to get their first look at the club that had denied them the N.L. pennant in 1956. Brooklyn fans back in Flatbush needed to look no further than the Milwaukee Braves to see a real live example of what could happen to them. The Braves had played in Boston since the late 1800s. They struggled to match the on-field success of their American League counterpart Red Sox, but the Boston Braves had their moments—most notably a World Series championship in 1914 and a N.L. pennant in 1948. Despite dwindling attendance following their appearance in the '48 World Series, the Boston Braves had a devout core of fans. It didn't matter. With the promise of greater riches in Milwaukee, Braves ownership ripped the franchise out of Boston and moved to Wisconsin just prior to the 1953 season. The lesson for Brooklyn fans was simple: baseball was big business as far as the owners were concerned. Nostalgia and sentimentality played no part in the final decision as to whether a franchise would stay or leave a city. It all came down to one thing—where could the owners make the most money?

Thoughts of losing a franchise was the last thing on the minds of the County Stadium fans, though. They were overjoyed at the bounty that had come to them in 1953, a powerful club that now seemed to be on the verge of a National League pennant. And their powerful Braves flexed their muscles by defeating the Brooklyn Dodgers and their ace, Don Newcombe, 3–2. It was the first time Newcombe had been beaten on the road in his last 13 starts, and the loss dropped him to 2-and-3 on the year.

As they'd done a week earlier in Brooklyn, however, the Dodgers salvaged a series split by winning the series finale on May 15. The game was fought tooth-and-nail, as would be the fight for the pennant between these two teams, but on this day it went the Dodgers' way as Don Zimmer belted a tenth-inning solo homer off Lew Burdette to break a 2–2 tie. Clem Labine pitched his third inning of scoreless relief in the bottom half of the 10th to earn the win. Burdette was one of the Braves' best starters, and the spitball was one of his best offerings despite it being an illegal pitch. It's quite possible that Zimmer was listening to Giants slugger Hank Sauer and Newcombe discussing Burdette's famed spitter during pre-game warm-ups before the Dodgers–Giants game on May 12.

"I tried, but I can't throw the spitter," Newcombe said to the gathering of Giants and Dodgers players loosening up. "It won't work for me. Here's the way Burdette does it." Newcombe moistened his fingertips, then reached down for the resin bag. Instead of picking it up with his fingertips, however, Newcombe picked it up with his knuckles.

"Whenever I see him do that," Sauer said, "I step back out of the box and wait for the moisture to dry on his fingers."

Whether or not Zimmer heard this conversation, he nonetheless unloaded on Burdette's first pitch of the inning and deposited a 350-foot homer over the leftfield fence. It was the second time in two weeks that Zimmer had hit a tenth-inning home run to win a game, the previous one coming on April 30 against the Cubs. Small at five-foot-nine and 165 pounds, Zimmer didn't necessarily fit the bill of a big-time athlete, but he was, in fact, an excellent athlete. A fine fielder with a cannon for an arm, little Zip also had some pop in his bat and hit 15 home runs in just 280 at-bats for the 1955 Dodgers. Despite his spring training declarations of great health, injuries slowed him in 1957 and limited him to just 84 games. Still, it could be viewed as a miracle that the 26-year-old Zimmer was still in the game at all in 1957. Laid low by a devastating beaning with St. Paul in 1953, Zimmer suffered a fractured skull which led to a blood clot, leaving him in a coma for 12 days. After two surgeries and five spinal taps, Zimmer returned to the game. Stories circulated that he had a steel plate in his head, but Zimmer corrected the facts by

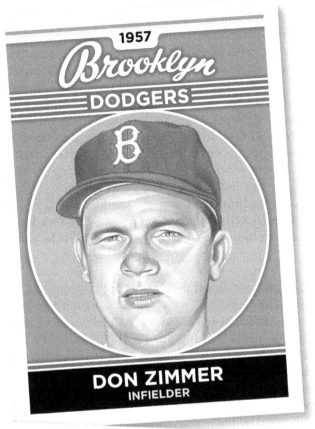

1957
Brooklyn
DODGERS

DON ZIMMER
INFIELDER

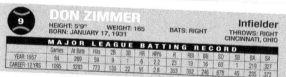

DON ZIMMER

9

HEIGHT: 5'9"   WEIGHT: 165   BATS: RIGHT   **Infielder**
BORN: JANUARY 17, 1931   THROWS: RIGHT
CINCINNATI, OHIO

MAJOR LEAGUE BATTING RECORD

	Games	At Bats	Hits	2B	3B	HR	HR%	R	RBI	BB	SO	SB	BA	SA
YEAR: 1957	84	269	59	9	1	6	2.2	23	19	16	63	1	.219	.327
CAREER: 12 YRS	1095	3283	773	130	22	91	2.8	353	352	246	678	45	.235	.372

5-15-57: On this day, for the second time in the young 1957 season, **DON ZIMMER** hit a home run in the 10th inning to win a game for the Dodgers. The blast, a 350-foot poke over County Stadium's leftfield fence, came as Don led off the top of the 10th against Braves right-hander Lew Burdette. Nicknamed "Popeye" by teammate Roy Campanella because of his strong forearms, Don was compactly built with excellent power and poled 15 homers in 1955. A 1956 beaning cost him most of the season. Don hit for half the cycle in one inning on September 4, 1957, when he tripled and singled in the 7th inning of a 12-3 rout of the Phillies.

YERRRRRR OUT!

HUH?!

DON WAS PICKED OFF DURING A TIME-OUT, THEN EJECTED FOR ARGUING ON 7-11-57!

saying, "I don't have a plate in my head. What I have in my head are buttons, which are like tapered corkscrews in a bottle. Three of them on one side, one on the other side."

Four screws in his head—that was even more impressive than a simple steel plate! And it went a long way to building his reputation of indestructibility, which, unfortunately, would need to be proven again after being drilled in the face by a Hal Jeffcoat fastball on June 23, 1956. The pitch fractured Zimmer's cheekbone and partially detached his retina, effectively ending his season (although he would return for a pinch-running appearance on September 22). Zimmer would spend a lifetime in the majors, playing, coaching, and managing for 14 teams along the way. Still, he was always in awe of his days in Brooklyn. "I'm very proud of playing with the Brooklyn Dodgers," Zimmer told *USA Today*. "Jackie Robinson, Don Newcombe, Roy Campanella, Pee Wee Reese—to think that I played with those guys, I'm the luckiest man in the world."

* * *

The Dodgers continued their road trip, stopping in Chicago where they defeated the Cubs, 3–2, on May 16. Young left-hander Sandy Koufax showed everyone why he was such a top prospect as he pitched a complete game while striking out 13. He also showed everyone why he had yet to achieve his full potential—lack of control—as he walked seven Cubbies. In a perfect scenario, Koufax would have been in the minors working out his control issues, but the Dodgers were forced to keep him on their big league roster since his signing price had exceeded limits established by the league. That made him a Bonus Baby, and he'd been that since December of 1954 when the Dodgers signed him, but the negative repercussion of this was that he did not pitch as many innings as he would have down on the farm and was therefore slow to develop into a finished product. But as of May 15, the Bonus Rule restriction had been lifted from Koufax—so Walter Alston gave Koufax a start against the Cubs in what amounted to a tryout to stay up with the big club. Koufax was a work in progress, but on this day he proved he belonged in the big leagues—something the Chicago Cubs would attest to.

May 19: The Jim Gilliam Show

Rain washed out the rest of the Chicago Cubs series, so the Dodgers got a few days to rest their wounded before opening a series against the Cardinals in St. Louis on May 19. Don Newcombe appeared to be in control as he rolled into the eighth inning leading 3–1, but a two-run homer by Wally Moon knotted the score heading into the ninth. It was then that the Dodgers unleashed their biggest inning of the season as they routed Cardinals pitching for seven runs, then Newcombe bore down in the bottom of the inning to seal the 10–3 victory. Carl Furillo was the Dodger who did the most offensive damage with four RBIs, but it was switch-hitting second baseman Jim Gilliam who pulled off the most interesting feat of the day by doubling twice in the ninth inning—first right-handed and then left-handed. Gilliam's feat did not come as a surprise to the knowledgeable baseball fan, however, because many recalled when he had homered from both sides of the plate (in separate games) against the Yankees in the 1953 World Series.

Jim "Junior" Gilliam was a rookie in 1953, brought up to take over second base as Jackie Robinson was moved to third. He made the most of the promotion, batting .278 with 63 runs driven in and being named N.L. Rookie of the Year. He was a versatile fielder, capable of playing third base and outfield, which he often did. He also had good speed and could swipe a bag when necessary. In spite of his lefty-righty homer achievement in the '53 Series, Gilliam wasn't a power hitter and averaged just four to five round-trippers per season. He wasn't a superstar—just a steady, all-around solid performer. Perhaps that is why every year Gilliam's name was floated as trade bait, or mentioned as the Dodger who would be odd-man-out when each year's opening day lineup was written. But the Dodgers always came to their senses before allowing either of those things to happen, and when it was all said and done, Gilliam spent his entire 14-year career as a full-time player with the Dodgers.

Brooklyn continued to pile on the Cardinals in game two of their series at Busch Stadium on May 20, this time winning by a score of 10–4. Sandy Amoros, Duke Snider and Carl Furillo provided the Dodgers' long-balls in the game, and Don Drysdale pushed his record to 3-and-0. The triumph made it four wins in a row for Brooklyn, leaving them in third place in the N.L., 2½ games behind the surging Reds and a half-game behind the Braves.

* * *

The last stop on Brooklyn's two-week road trip was Cincinnati where the Dodgers would play two games against the first-place Reds.

1957

Brooklyn DODGERS

JIM GILLIAM
2nd BASEMAN

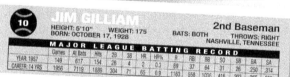

10 | **JIM GILLIAM** | | | | | | | | | | **2nd Baseman**

HEIGHT: 5'10"   WEIGHT: 175
BORN: OCTOBER 17, 1928

BATS: BOTH   THROWS: RIGHT
NASHVILLE, TENNESSEE

MAJOR LEAGUE BATTING RECORD

	Games	At Bats	Hits	2B	3B	HR	HR%	R	RBI	BB	SO	SB	BA	SA
YEAR: 1957	149	617	154	26	4	2	0.3	89	37	64	31	26	.250	.314
CAREER: 14 YRS	1956	7119	1889	304	71	65	0.9	1163	558	1036	416	203	.265	.355

5-19-57: Brooklyn lead-off man JIM GILLIAM chipped in two hits while helping his club to a 10-3 win over the Cardinals at Busch Stadium. The funny thing was that both hits came in the 9th inning. Even funnier was that Jim batted from the right side for the first hit (a double off right-hander Jim Davis), then from the left side for the second hit (a double against right-hander Willard Schmidt). Jim had already proven his switch-hitting ability when he homered from both sides of the plate against the Yankees in the 1953 World Series. Jim's 1st-inning homer on July 1, 1957, helped Don Drysdale to a 3-0 shutout win over the Giants at the Polo Grounds.

STOP! THIEF!

SPEEDY JIM SWIPED TWO BAGS TO RUN HIS STREAK TO 12-IN-A-ROW ON 8-28-57!

The Brooklyn bats stayed hot as they drubbed Cincinnati, 6–1, behind a pair of two-run home runs by Sandy Amoros and Pee Wee Reese. Johnny Podres was masterful on the mound, going the distance to run his record to 3-and-2. The Dodgers' win streak reached six with the victory, but it was snapped the next day as the Reds' exploded for eight runs while holding Brooklyn to a single tally. While the Dodgers drew first blood by scoring their run in the second frame, the Reds were never really in danger of losing as Cincy right-hander Johnny Klippstein got dialed in after that and shut Brooklyn out the rest of the way.

The only real danger that evening was to some spectators behind home plate during pregame warm-ups. A ball had gotten lodged atop the backstop screen whereupon Don Newcombe tried to dislodge it by throwing a bat at it. In a million-to-one shot, the bat went through one of the small openings and landed in the aisle amidst the fans. Newk had turned away with a hand over his face as he saw the potential disaster unfolding, but his fear was alleviated when no one was hit. A fan picked up the bat and extended it to big Don, but Newcombe said, "Keep it," and walked away relieved. The Dodgers were relieved, too, after completing the two-game series in Cincinnati—relieved to be heading home to Brooklyn.

May 23: Brooklyn Dodgers vs. New York Yankees

The Yankees and Dodgers each had an open date on May 23, so they took the opportunity to play the annual Mayor's Trophy game for the benefit of sandlot baseball in the New York City metropolitan area. Started in 1946, the exhibition game featured the Yankees playing the Giants or Dodgers, but no game was held in 1956 due to scheduling conflicts. It was back on for 1957, however, although it would be only a brief reprieve as the fundraiser was cancelled for good once the Giants and Dodgers left for California. The game would be resurrected when the Mets were created in 1962, and it would be played into the early 1980s.

Exhibition or not, it was always a big deal when the Yankees and Dodgers met, and 30,000 fans packed Ebbets Field to see the game. First, the crowd was treated to a preliminary game featuring those for whom the extravaganza was staged to benefit—sandlotters. In that game, the Shore Parkway League All-Stars played to a six-inning, 2–2 tie against the Pee Wee Reese All-Stars, a team recruited from the sandlots of Brooklyn, Queens, and Nassau. Next, a home run hitting contest was played featuring four Dodgers against four Yankees. With each player getting five swings apiece, the Bums outslugged the Bombers, 5 to 3. The individual home run crown went to Roy Campanella who out-homered Duke Snider and Yankee Moose Skowron in a final "swing-off."

The main event featured lots of offense, including a mammoth upper-deck home run by Mickey Mantle, and when it was over the Yanks were 10–7 victors. While disappointed that their team didn't win bragging rights, Brooklyn fans were happy to see old favorite Carl Erskine back on the Ebbets Field mound. He'd yet to pitch in a regular season game in 1957 as he tried to nurse his sore shoulder into form, but he started the Mayor's Trophy game and pitched four solid innings, leaving the Flatbush crew hopeful that he'd soon be ready to join the Dodgers rotation.

A new face in the Dodgers lineup that day was that of 36-year-old Bob Kennedy, a longtime infielder/outfielder in the American League whom Brooklyn acquired from the White Sox a few days earlier for the bargain waiver price of $1. The Dodgers planned to use the right-swinging Kennedy as a pinch-hitter against lefties. Despite his long, fine record in the A.L., Kennedy hit like a $1, 36-year-old player that day, going 0-for-5. You can believe he wasn't worried about it, though, because Kennedy was a man that had been through the wars—baseball wars and "real" wars—so he wasn't likely to be concerned about a zero in an exhibition game. After breaking into the big leagues in 1939, Kennedy took three full years off to serve in World War II where he was a Marine fighter pilot. He was back in the game long enough to help the Cleveland Indians to a World Series championship in 1948, then he was recalled to active duty for part of 1952 during the Korean War. Kennedy had even served as Ted Williams' flight instructor, eventually flying several missions with the Splendid Splinter. Appearing in just 19 games for Brooklyn, Kennedy wouldn't see much action with the 1957 Dodgers, but he was ready and battle-tested should they call on him.

* * *

The sixth-place New York Giants filed into Ebbets Field for a three-game series on May 24 and opened the set by losing to the Dodgers, 6–0. Right-hander Don Newcombe went the distance, his sixth straight complete game, and pushed his record over the .500 mark to

1957

Brooklyn

DODGERS

DON NEWCOMBE
RIGHT-HAND PITCHER

11 **DON NEWCOMBE**   **Right-Hand Pitcher**
HEIGHT: 6'4"   WEIGHT: 220   BATS: LEFT   THROWS: RIGHT
BORN: JUNE 14, 1926   MADISON, NEW JERSEY

MAJOR LEAGUE PITCHING RECORD

	Games	IP	Won	Lost	Pct	Hits	Runs	ER	SO	Walks	ERA
YEAR: 1957	28	198.2	11	12	.478	199	86	77	90	33	3.49
CAREER: 10 YRS	344	2154.2	149	90	.623	2102	956	852	1129	490	3.56

5-24-57: Brooklyn opened a 3-game home series against New York with a 6-0 victory behind a complete game from big **DON NEWCOMBE**. Mixing his heater with a hard-breaking curveball, Newk fanned six Giants while registering his 2nd shutout of the season. His batterymate Roy Campanella was the hitting star, slugging two homers in the game. Newk had an up-and-down campaign in 1957, especially when compared to the career year he posted the previous season when he led the majors in victories with 27. Always dangerous with the lumber, Newk poled a solo homer while tossing a 5-hit shutout over the Reds on June 18, 1957.

GIDDYAP!

FOR THE 2ND TIME IN A WEEK, NEWK WAS EJECTED FOR BENCH JOCKEYING ON 8-21-57!

4-and-3. With the exception of 1952 and 1953 when he was in military service, Newcombe had been a pillar of the Brooklyn starting rotation since he joined the Dodgers in 1949. His 17-and-8 record was impressive enough to earn him the N.L. Rookie of the Year Award. A big man at 6-foot-4 and 235 pounds, Newcombe's bread and butter was his hard-breaking curve and intimidating fastball. The first big leaguer to face Newcombe was St. Louis Cardinals outfielder Chuck Diering on May 20, 1949. Diering struck out on three fastballs. Many subsequent batters also struck out against Big Newk's offerings, and by the time the 1957 season began Newcombe was a three-time 20-game winner with 112 victories under his belt.

Despite all his victories, Newcombe was unable to win with the pennant on the line in 1950 and '51, and he never bagged a World Series triumph in five starts. In the brutal New York press, he was branded a choker by sportswriters, and the characterization took hold with fans and even some teammates, according to Newcombe. It seemed an unfair label to hang on a player who had battled so long and hard for Brooklyn, but baseball is often not fair when it tries to apply a one-dimensional label to a three-dimensional person. But Newcombe didn't whine about it, and later stated the stark truth in saying, "Dick Young wrote a column stating I couldn't win the big games. The press ran me out of New York after the '56 World Series." Hampered by a sore arm, Newcombe would win just 11 games in 1957, and just 39 more by the time his big-league career ended in 1960. With Newcombe, though, there was simply too much good about being with the Dodgers—too much camaraderie and too much winning—to make him bitter in the long run. "I've loved the Dodgers from the day they signed me and Campy and Jackie," Newcombe would say, "and I will love the Dodgers as long as I live."

* * *

The Giants took game two of the series, defeating the Dodgers, 8–7, on May 25. Rookie right-hander Curt Barclay entered the game in the eighth inning amidst a Dodger uprising that tied the game, then the kid won it with an RBI-single in the ninth. Brooklyn came back to take the rubber match, downing New York by a score of 5–3 on May 26. Sandy Koufax and Clem Labine combined to hold the Giants in check, while Duke Snider delivered the Dodgers' only round-tripper—a long solo shot into the centerfield seats in the third inning. It was the 1,500th career hit for the Duke of Flatbush.

May 27: *The California Kid*

Don "Big D" Drysdale led the Dodgers to a 5–1 victory over the Phillies in Philadelphia on May 27. The six-foot-five right-hander from Van Nuys, California, limited the Phillies to just two hits in the ballgame while pushing his record to 4-and-1. It's a sure bet that the folks back in Van Nuys were pulling hard for the deal to bring the Dodgers to Los Angeles. Chavez Ravine, the proposed site for a *Los Angeles* Dodgers stadium, was just a 45-minute ride from Van Nuys, so there'd be plenty of opportunity for Drysdale's family, friends, and fans to see him pitch in person. One of Drysdale's Van Nuys acquaintances was none other than Robert Redford—also later known as Roy Hobbs of the film *The Natural*. Redford and Drysdale both graduated from Van Nuys High School in 1954, and while Redford did not play baseball on the high school team with Drysdale, it is believed they played some sandlot or American Legion ball together. When later asked about his movie star schoolmate, Drysdale would say, "Bobby—he was a pretty good ballplayer."

Drysdale had movie star good looks himself and would become a popular guest on TV shows after the Dodgers moved West—most memorably *Leave It to Beaver*, *The Rifleman*, *The Donna Reed Show*, and *The Brady Bunch*. But in 1957, it was on the pitcher's mound where Drysdale was establishing himself a star. In just his second full season in the big leagues, Drysdale posted numbers that would begin paving his road to the Hall of Fame: 17 wins and 9 losses; 2.69 ERA in 221 innings; 4 shutouts and 9 complete games; 148 strikeouts and just 61 walks. Drysdale was proving to be pretty good with the bat, too. He'd hit his first career home run in 1956, and he added two more in 1957—one off Reds right-hander Herm Wehmeier on June 16, and one off Braves right-hander Ernie Johnson on July 15. By the time he retired following the 1969 season, Drysdale had 29 circuit clouts to his credit. Big D was a long way from retirement in 1957—at age 20 he wasn't even old enough to vote! But by the end of the season he'd have the Dodgers' biggest rivals of 1957, the Milwaukee Braves, calling him the best right-hander in the league.

* * *

The Dodgers and the last-place Pirates opened a four-game series at Forbes Field on May 28. Brooklyn lost the opener, 3–2, in gut-wrenching fashion when Pee Wee Reese committed a rare critical error in the bottom of the 11th that allowed the winning run to cross. Johnny Podres

1957
Brooklyn
DODGERS

DON DRYSDALE
RIGHT-HAND PITCHER

DON DRYSDALE

12	HEIGHT: 6'5"	WEIGHT: 190			Right-Hand Pitcher					
	BORN: JULY 23, 1936			BATS: RIGHT	THROWS: RIGHT					
					VAN NUYS, CALIFORNIA					

	MAJOR LEAGUE PITCHING RECORD									
	Games	IP	Won	Lost	Pct	Hits	Runs	ER	SO	Walks	ERA
YEAR: 1957	34	221	17	9	.654	197	76	68	148	61	2.69
CAREER: 14 YRS	518	3432.1	209	166	.557	3084	1292	1124	2486	855	2.95

5-27-57: 20-year-old **DON DRYSDALE** ran his record to 4-and-1 after hurling a 2-hit victory over the Phillies at Connie Mack Stadium. Were it not for a Dodger error, big Don would have had a shutout. As it was, he would log four shutouts on the season — just two behind the league high mark of six set by teammate Johnny Podres. Don was smack dab in the middle of one of the most memorable incidents of Brooklyn's '57 season when he drilled the Braves' Johnny Logan with a pitch following a homer by Bill Bruton. A bench-clearing brawl ensued, but the only clean punch landed was a right from Don that opened a half-inch cut over the eye of Logan.

CLIMB ON MY BACK, BOYS -- I'M A WORKHORSE!

DON WON FOUR OF TEN GAMES THE DODGERS PLAYED FROM 8-20-57 THROUGH 8-30-57!

continued his excellent pitching the next day, May 29, and got the Dodgers back in the win column by crafting a three-hit shutout for a 1–0 victory. Next, playing just their second twin-bill of the season, Brooklyn worked a split on May 30, winning the opener, 4–3, then dropping the nightcap, 2–1. The Memorial Day double-header was attended by a crowd of 24,263. The Forbes Field fans decided not to hurl beer cans at Carl Furillo in right field this time as they'd inexplicably done on April 26 during the Dodgers' last trip to Pittsburgh. Maybe it was because they had sympathy for the old Dodger right fielder and his concern over the possible shift of his ballclub to Los Angeles. With obvious concern for his career and the future of his family, Furillo told the *New York Times*, "All I hope is I can keep going just a few more years. After that..." His voice trailed off.

Pirates general manager Joe L. Brown was asked about the proposed shift of the Giants and Dodgers to the West Coast. Without the concern heard in Furillo's reply to the same question, Brown said, "Since visiting clubs do not share in television or radio receipts, the expected increase in attendance these two clubs should pick up in California is certain to benefit the other six [National League] clubs." This, of course, was the last thing a Dodgers or Giants fan wanted to hear, but there it was in the *New York Times*. For Dodgers fans, it was a reminder to them that their feelings were really not a factor in the high-stakes game being played between Walter O'Malley, the borough of Brooklyn, and the city of Los Angeles. The game being played came down to one thing—the bottom line, and where it could be maximized. The fans were replaceable.

* * *

May 1957 for the Brooklyn Dodgers was officially in the history book following a 2–1 loss to the Phillies at Connie Mack Stadium on May 31. The loss put them at 15-and-12 for the month; 23-and-15 for the season; and in second place, two games in back of the Cincinnati Reds. Don Drysdale pitched well in defeat, but the Phils' Robin Roberts was a little bit better. It was only fair—Drysdale had bested Roberts just five days earlier when the two aces were last matched against each other. The only blemish to Roberts on this day was a seventh-inning home run he surrendered to Roy Campanella. It was Campanella's 236th career long-ball, which tied the National League record for homers by a catcher. Campy didn't want to talk about the record, though, for he, too, was concerned about the increasing likelihood that he'd have to relocate to Los Angeles. Originally from Philadelphia, Campanella had laid down roots in New York with his family. He had a big liquor store in Harlem. He had two yachts in Glen Cove, and he loved sailing them on the Long Island Sound. "Up to now, I never thought it could happen," said Campy, pensively. "But now, I dunno. It could."

FOUR

June

The month of June kicked off with the Dodgers playing game two of their four-game series against the Phillies on June 1. The month also started, as far as Brooklyn Dodgers fans were concerned, under the ever-present and ever-darkening cloud that the Dodgers were likely playing their last season in Flatbush. Brooklyn councilman Abe Stark's recent proposal that a new, bigger, better Ebbets Field be built on the ballpark's current site was laughed off by Walter O'Malley. Now, a $39,500,000 bond was overwhelmingly passed in Los Angeles, clearing the way for prepping the land for a stadium at Chavez Ravine.

Meanwhile, *New York Times* sportswriter John Drebinger wrote about the Dodgers' on-field malaise, attributing it to the franchise's pre-occupation with the Los Angeles deal. "The truth of the matter," wrote Drebinger,

> is the Dodger brass, overly busy with multi-million-dollar franchise projects that may or may not materialize, hasn't been keeping its customary tabs on what's happening on the ballfield. Leaving a manager with four able-bodied infielders, one on the disabled list, and another all taped up, isn't the way the Dodgers used to do it before all this California gold rush started to take over the headlines. Alston, who seems to be as much in the dark as the next one, was informed that Randy Jackson, eligible to come off the disabled list on Wednesday [June 5], will start working out when the Brooks return to Ebbets Field next Tuesday [June 4] night. At that time Alston is also to confer with Buzzie Bavasi, the vice president, on what's to be done about getting a little more manpower.

As if to validate Drebinger's supposition, the Dodgers produced a lackluster effort against the Phils on June 1, managing just two hits against right-hander Jack Sanford on their way to a 3–0 defeat. Philadelphia made it three wins in a row against Brooklyn the next day when they beat Don Newcombe, 5–3. The Philly crowd of 20,259 got a good laugh in the fourth inning following a disputed home run down the left field line. The Dodgers claimed it was foul and were arguing with

81

second base umpire Augie Donatelli when plate umpire Vic Delmore tossed a new ball to Newcombe. Newk, however, was still in full debate with Donatelli—and Delmore's lob bounced right off Newk's noggin. It seemed to perfectly sum up the Dodgers' current situation.

June 3: Chock Full o' Robbie

Brooklyn avoided a series sweep by downing the Phillies in the finale at Connie Mack Stadium, 4–0, on June 3. Johnny Podres played the role of stopper again, allowing just three hits while chalking up his league-leading fourth shutout. The long-dormant Dodger bats woke up in support of Podres, the big belts coming in the form of home runs by Gino Cimoli and Gil Hodges.

Among the 18,216 folks taking in the game was retired Dodger great Jackie Robinson. Now a full-time executive with New York coffee company Chock Full o' Nuts, Robinson had recently become eligible to return to the majors now that the required time had elapsed since he joined the voluntarily retired list back in January. It was then that Robinson had floated the idea that he could get in shape to play in June if he opted to come back. When asked if he was at the game to show his interest in joining the depleted Dodgers, Robinson playfully said, "Well, I'm available." The reality, however, was that Robinson was too deep into his post-baseball activities to ever play again. Later that week he was heading down to Howard University in Washington, D.C., to receive an honorary doctor of laws degree, then he would hustle back to New York to accept a position with the state Board of Parole. A truly busy man, there was certainly no grass growing under the feet of Jackie Robinson—be it at Ebbets Field or elsewhere.

* * *

Back at home on June 4, Brooklyn knocked off the Chicago Cubs, 7–5, in front of only 9,300 apathetic Ebbets Field customers. Sandy Koufax treated those in attendance to a 12-strikeout performance, but he also gave them fits by issuing five walks, a two-run homer in the sixth, and a three-run homer in the eighth. Clem Labine was brought in to settle things down—which he did, earning his tenth save of the season.

Koufax wasn't the only Brooklyn-born Dodger on the field on this day—batterymate Joe Pignatano, also born in Brooklyn, saw some rare playing time in this game. Roy Campanella left in the third inning

1957
Brooklyn
DODGERS

JACKIE ROBINSON
RETIRED

13	JACKIE ROBINSON			Retired
	HEIGHT: 5'11" WEIGHT: 195	BATTED: RIGHT		THREW: RIGHT
	BORN: JANUARY 31, 1919			CAIRO, GEORGIA

MAJOR LEAGUE BATTING RECORD													
	Games	At Bats	Hits	2B	3B	HR	HR%	R	RBI	BB	SO	SB	BA	SA
CAREER: 10 YRS	1382	4877	1518	273	54	137	2.8	947	734	740	291	197	.311	.474

6-3-57: Johnny Podres pitched a 3-hit shutout to break a 4-game losing skid as Brooklyn defeated Philadelphia 4-0 at Connie Mack Stadium. The win lifted the Dodgers to 3rd place. In the stands taking in the ballgame was Dodger icon JACKIE ROBINSON. Traded to the rival Giants following the 1956 season, Jackie retired rather than accept the deal. Instead, Jackie took an executive job with coffee company Chock Full o' Nuts while also stepping up his involvement in the growing civil rights movement. When asked if he was at the game to help his struggling teammates get back on track, Jackie smiled and said, "Well, I'm available."

SO LONG OLD PAL!

EBBETS FIELD

38-YEAR-OLD JACKIE BID FAREWELL TO THE DODGERS WHEN HE RETIRED ON 1-5-57!

after being drilled in the ribs by a Dick Drott fastball. Carl Erskine, still rehabbing his sore shoulder, pinch ran for Campy, then was replaced by Pignatano when the Dodgers went back out on defense. It was only Pignatano's second big league game, his first being a pinch-running appearance back on April 28. He made the most of it this time, singling to right field off Cubs right-hander Jim Brosnan in the fifth inning. Brosnan got the best of the rookie catcher the next time up, however, striking him out, but Pignatano was smiling broadly after the game after getting his first big league hit. It was even sweeter having come in a Dodgers win and in Brooklyn at Ebbets Field. The reward for Pignatano's big day: he did not play again before being sent down to Montreal ten days later.

Pignatano's journey to the Brooklyn Dodgers was a long one, even though he grew up in the shadow of Ebbets Field. A good athlete, the only sports Pignatano really played were baseball, softball, and stickball. In a fortuitous move, he became a catcher when nobody else wanted to do it. He was signed in 1948 after impressing Dodgers scouts at a tryout for fifty local players. Pignatano was ecstatic because, as he said, "Playing for the Dodgers was the pinnacle." Little did he know that he would have to wait ten years to take the field for the Dodgers and travel thousands of miles to minor league towns like Sheboygan, Cairo, Cambridge, Valdosta, Asheville, Elmira, Fort Worth, St. Paul and Montreal.

It was in those minor league towns that Pignatano got the experience he would need in the big leagues. He also got experiences that could only happen in the bushes. While at Asheville in 1953, Pignatano hit a grand slam off former Dodger Kirby Higbe—then belted a three-run shot off Higbe later in the same inning. Two innings later he added an inside-the-park homer. Then, at Ft. Worth in 1956, Pignatano again hit two homers in the same inning. Some even say it was done in the same at-bat! To wit: In his first trip to the plate that day against Shreveport, Pignatano slammed a round-tripper while batting in the number-7 spot in the lineup. He'd barely crossed home plate when he was informed that he had batted out of order—he was supposed to hit in the number-8 spot. The long-ball was nullified, instead recorded as an out. Joe immediately returned to the batter's box to hit in his proper number-8 spot. To the amazement of all in attendance, Joe clouted the first pitch he saw for another home run.

As ordered, Pignatano went down to Montreal in mid–June, but he'd return to the 1957 Dodgers when they expanded the rosters in September. In fitting fashion, the kid from Brooklyn would be behind the plate when the Dodgers closed the book on Ebbets Field on September

1957
Brooklyn
DODGERS

JOE PIGNATANO
CATCHER

14	JOE PIGNATANO						Catcher		
	HEIGHT: 5'10" WEIGHT: 180			BATS: RIGHT			THROWS: RIGHT		
	BORN: AUGUST 4, 1929						BROOKLYN, NEW YORK		

MAJOR LEAGUE BATTING RECORD

	Games	At Bats	Hits	2B	3B	HR	HR%	R	RBI	BB	SO	SB	BA	SA
YEAR: 1957	8	14	3	1	0	0	0.0	0		1	5	0	214	286
CAREER: 6 YRS	307	689	161	25	4	16	2.3	81	62	94	116	8	234	351

6-4-57: Brooklyn pushed their record to 25-and-17 after downing the Cubs 7-5 behind Sandy Koufax's 12-strikeout performance at Ebbets Field. A small subplot to the game was that it featured the first major league hit by home-grown rookie catcher **JOE PIGNATANO** – a 5th-inning single to right off Jim Brosnan. Joe had made his big league debut back on April 28, but had since been relegated to bullpen catching duties. Despite collecting his first hit, Joe was sent down to Montreal 10 days later, but was recalled in September. Joe knocked out two more hits in very limited playing time before the end of the 1957 season.

JOE SMOKED A DOUBLE OFF PHILLIES RIGHT-HANDER JACK SANFORD ON 9-21-57!

85

24. Joe went 0-for-1 in the game, striking out against right-hander Bennie Daniels in the 7th inning. In hindsight, playing in that game was one of the highlights of Pignatano's career. "I didn't realize we might move until the last week," Pignatano said. "Everyone in Brooklyn blamed O'Malley then, but it was really [city planning official Robert] Moses. He thought O'Malley was bluffing and wouldn't arrange for him to purchase land at the site [in Brooklyn where] he wanted to build a new stadium." Fifty years later, Pignatano, with his old batterymate Danny McDevitt, returned to Brooklyn to reenact the last pitch at Ebbets Field. The event took place before a game by Class-A Mets affiliate the Brooklyn Cyclones at Key Span Park on June 24, 2007, just 7½ miles from the former site of Ebbets Field.

* * *

Game two of the Dodgers–Cubs series was played at Roosevelt Stadium on June 5. As if it wasn't hard enough for Cubs hitters to catch up to Don Drysdale's 90 mile-per-hour fastball, there was a thick fog in the air that significantly reduced visibility. All Chicago could muster was five hits off Big D who picked up his first big league shutout, 4–0. Gil Hodges seemed immune to the fog and lifted his average to .359 with a 3-for-4 performance at the dish. The Dodgers and Cubs were back at Ebbets Field the next day for the series finale, but the fog was back, too. Hindsight being 20–20, except when fog gets in the way, the game should have never been started. So dense was the cloud that an accurate head-count seems to have been impossible. As best as could be seen, it is believed that approximately 5,000 fans attended the game.

The Cubbies failed to score on Don Newcombe in the top of the first inning, but Chicago right-hander Moe Drabowsky wasn't so lucky in the bottom half of the frame and was touched for a run. Play on the field took on a circus atmosphere in the top of the second as the fog thickened—silliness that might even make frowning Dodger clown Emmett Kelly crack a smile. Using a sixth sense, Don Zimmer made a last-second lunging catch of a normally routine pop fly to short center. No other Dodger had any idea where the ball was. Cubs outfielder Bob Speake wasn't so lucky in the bottom of the second when he was nearly hit on the head by a typically easy fly ball to left.

"Call time!" Cubs second baseman Bobby Morgan hollered at umpire Tom Gorman. "It's impossible out here. This inning will never end if they keep hitting the ball in the air." The umpires conferred for a few minutes, then ordered the game be delayed. Ebbets Field announcer

Tex Rickards informed the crowd, "The game will be delayed pending the results of this fog. So please be patient while Gladys Goodding entertains you." Goodding, the Ebbets Field organist, thereupon ran through her entire repertoire during what amounted to a one hour and 26 minute delay.

In a not-so-subtle message, Goodding opened her set with "California Here I Come." Finally, at 9:57 p.m., the game was called on account of "failing light."

June 7: Red Menace

An unexpected challenger for the National League pennant had arisen in 1957—the Cincinnati Redlegs. With Senator Joseph McCarthy's communist witch hunts at a fever pitch in 1953, Cincinnati officially changed their name from "Reds" to "Redlegs" in 1956. Most folks still called them the "Reds," however, and by 1961 they'd officially switch back to "Reds." Still, for those caught up in McCarthyism, it must have seemed downright un–American to have the "Reds" leading the National League!

McCarthyism aside, the pace-setting Reds arrived in Brooklyn on June 7 to play a four-game series against the second-place Dodgers, with first place on the line. Brooklyn moved to within three percentage points of the Reds after taking the first game, 6–3, behind a three-hit complete game from Roger Craig. It was Johnny Podres on the hill the next day, June 8, as the Dodgers won again, 9–2. Podres was brilliant, going the distance and lowering his ERA to 2.03. The victory moved the Dodgers into first place in the senior loop, a half-game ahead of the pack.

The Dodger hitters laid the lumber to the Reds pitching in the two games, compiling 24 hits and three home runs. Homering once in each game was Dodgers backup catcher Rube Walker, a surprise addition to the lineup after a split nail knocked Roy Campanella out of action. Walker wasn't a power hitter by any stretch of the imagination—he would hit just 35 long-balls in his 11-year big league career—but Dodgers fans knew he could hit the occasional big fly after he blasted a two-run shot onto the Polo Grounds roof in game two of the 1951 playoff series against the Giants.

Walker, a backup to Roy Campanella, was only in game two of that series because a pulled thigh muscle forced Campy to the bench.

Campanella still couldn't go in Game Three, so Walker was behind the plate when Bobby Thomson hit his Shot Heard Round the World. "When Branca came in to the mound," Walker told Peter Golenbock in *Bums*, "we talked about how if we got ahead of Thomson, we'd waste a pitch inside and move him back. The first pitch was a fastball down the middle. Thomson took it. The next fastball was supposed to be inside, but it wasn't inside enough, and he hit it."

Walker came to the majors in 1948 with the Chicago Cubs, and he may have developed into their full-time catcher had he not been dealt to the Dodgers in 1951. But with Campanella starring behind the plate for Brooklyn, Walker's destiny as a backup was sealed. He took it well, though, and was one of the best-liked players on the Dodgers. Roscoe McGowen of the *New York Times* summed Walker up by saying,

> He can do everything but run. Rube is a highly competent catcher, who can throw with the best and is no palooka with a bat. He has all the agility, receiving, and throwing skill any catcher needs. There are mighty few foul balls within any catcher's range that Rube doesn't get. And even the better base thieves are cut down by Rube if his pitcher gives him a chance. He just can't run. He never could.

Walker's slow-footedness was known throughout the league. During pre-game batting practice back on May 15, Walker bet Mays five dollars that he could beat him in a foot race. The catch—Mays would run backwards. Don Zimmer claimed Walker's slow-footedness had cost him money prior to the 1957 season. "I got my contract from Bavasi around Christmas time," Zimmer told a group of sportswriters:

> I looked at it and said, "Oh-oh, must be some mistake." I called up Bavasi and told him, "Look, you said if I expected to make money, I couldn't be a .240 hitter. Well, I hit .300 last season—6-for-20." He told me I didn't drive in enough runs. You know, he had me there. Two stinking ribbies, that's all I had. I was robbed, though. I should have had another, but Rube Walker got thrown out at the plate.

As if that wasn't bad enough, there was a joke going around the clubhouse about Walker's lack of speed: "Hey, they made a movie about you—*Around the Bases in 80 Days*." It wasn't just Walker's lack of speed they made fun of—his lack of hair was also the object of ridicule. One day he came into the Dodger washroom at Ebbets Field to find a toothless comb bearing a label that read "Rube Walker." Rube took it all with a smile, though, and was great for clubhouse morale. He even joined in on the joking, saying, "I'd hit .500 if they'd move the second baseman out of there!"

1957

Brooklyn

DODGERS

RUBE WALKER

CATCHER

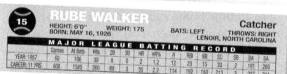

RUBE WALKER

15

HEIGHT: 6'0" WEIGHT: 175 BATS: LEFT THROWS: RIGHT
BORN: MAY 16, 1926 LENOIR, NORTH CAROLINA

Catcher

MAJOR LEAGUE BATTING RECORD

	Games	At Bats	Hits	2B	3B	HR	HR%	R	RBI	BB	SO	SB	BA	SA
YEAR: 1957	60	166	30	8	0	2	1.2	12	23	15	33	2	.181	.265
CAREER: 11 YRS	608	1585	360	69	3	35	2.2	114	192	150	213	3	.227	.341

6-8-57: Continuing his mini-rampage, Brooklyn catcher **RUBE WALKER** belted a 3-run homer off Hersh Freeman as the Dodgers trounced the Reds 9-2 at Ebbets Field. Rube also had a single and a double in the game – and this following his solo blast off Johnny Klippstein the day before. These two homers constituted Rube's entire 1957 home run output as he had the unfortunate situation of playing behind a future Hall-of-Famer in Roy Campanella. Legendarily slow of foot, Rube shocked everyone when he stole a base on August 9, then swiped another bag the next day. Rube totaled just three steals in his entire 11-year career.

YOU WANNA HEAD START, TOO, RUBE?!

SO SLOW WAS RUBE THAT WILLIE MAYS AGREED TO RACE HIM -- BACKWARDS -- ON 5-15-57!

* * *

Rube Walker was still the starting catcher for Brooklyn as the Dodgers and Reds concluded their series with a Sunday twin-bill on June 9. Walker stayed hot with the bat, too, collecting three hits in the opener, but the Dodgers lost anyway, 3–1. Walter Alston had planned to return Roy Campanella to the lineup in the nightcap, but he couldn't bring himself to bench the hot-hitting Walker—so he gave Rube another start. Walker's bat went cold, though, and he went hitless, as did most of the rest of the Dodgers as they lost again, 3–0. A huge Ebbets Field crowd of 33,850 turned out with hopes of seeing their first-place Dodgers put some space between them and the Reds, but they instead went home with their Bums in second, 1½ games back.

* * *

Milwaukee came to town for a four-game series with Brooklyn, beginning with a game at Roosevelt Stadium on June 10. Gil Hodges continued to pound the ball, going 3-for-4 to raise his league-leading average to .371, but it wasn't enough as the Dodgers lost, 3–1. The series moved to Ebbets Field the next day, but the result was the same as Brooklyn went down to defeat, 7–2. Roger Craig was deadlocked in a 1–1 pitcher's duel with Braves right-hander Ray Crone until the fifth inning when Bobby Thomson unloaded a grand slam to break open the ballgame. Dodgers fans had little to cheer as their team lost its fourth straight, but they were able to applaud Roy Campanella in the seventh inning as he uncorked a solo homer. The clout was the 237th of his career, moving him past Gabby Hartnett for sole possession of the National League lifetime home run record for catchers.

The Dodgers snapped their losing streak by winning an 11–9 slugfest on June 12. Charlie Neal led the Dodgers attack with a home run, a triple, and four RBIs, but Brooklyn still needed an emergency ninth-inning appearance from relief ace Clem Labine as the Braves rallied for three runs in the final frame behind long-balls by Hank Aaron and Eddie Mathews. Labine put out the fire, though, retiring the only three batters he faced to end the game and earn his 11th save.

June 13: Milwaukee Melee

The Dodgers–Braves series concluded on June 13 with Milwaukee defeating Brooklyn, 8–5. Six thousand Ebbets Field knothole gang kids were on hand for the game, and the adults on the field did not fail to make quite an impression on the youngsters. Don Drysdale, angered by issuing first- and second-inning home runs to Braves outfielder Bill Bruton, took out his frustration the old-fashioned way—with a "duster." Bruton had barely taken his seat on the bench following his second home run, a "mighty two-run blow that cleared the protruding wing of the centerfield upper deck," when Drysdale drilled second baseman Johnny Logan in the back with a 0–1 fastball.

Logan was a tough little guy with a reputation as a fighter. "I'll get you when you come into second base," Logan said fearlessly to the 6-foot-5-inch Drysdale.

Handsome Don, while not looking the part of a scrapper, actually had a reputation back home in Van Nuys for his willingness to mix it up. Ron Lachman, the shortstop on Drysdale's Van Nuys High School baseball team, said, "Don had that attitude in high school. He was a good guy, but on the field a tough kid. He would do anything to win." Jim Heffer, a pitcher on the Van Nuys team, said he once fought with Drysdale over a silly prank. "I cut his face, and he left me with a scar over my left eye," Heffer laughed. "He swung that vicious right of his. I'm reminded every time I comb my hair."

Like Heffer, Logan would soon sport a half-inch cut over his left eye, courtesy of Drysdale's vicious right. "If you've got a beef, come on and get it over with now," Don said matter-of-factly in reply to Logan's threat. Johnny took Big D up on his offer and lit off for the mound, running square into Drysdale's fist. A huge melee ensued. Gil Hodges chased Logan but was tackled by Braves first base coach John Riddle. Walter Alston grabbed Logan, who was swinging ineffectually against Drysdale. Braves third baseman Eddie Mathews sucker-punched Drysdale from the side as Don was engaged with Logan. More combatants joined as the fight devolved into a group wrestling match on the ground. Soon, peacemakers got a foothold and the brawl was broken up.

Afterward, in the Dodger clubhouse, Drysdale said, "I'm sorry it happened. I was mad about the homer, but I didn't throw at Logan. It was just a close pitch, and my fastball runs in on a right-handed batter."

Logan, over in the Braves clubhouse, wasn't buying Drysdale's narrative, and was convinced that Big D had thrown a duster at him. More than anything, however, Logan, always the tough guy, seemed hell-bent to ensure that nobody thought Drysdale had landed a punch on him. "That's an old cut, from my last fight [with Hal Jeffcoat of Cincinnati on May 27]," Logan said with a grin. Small fines were subsequently levied on Drysdale and Logan by National League president Warren Giles, but there were no suspensions. What was left, though, was a deepening of the rivalry now simmering between the two ballclubs.

*   *   *

The fifth-place St. Louis Cardinals came to Ebbets Field on June 14 for a three-game series against Brooklyn. The Dodgers took the opener, 2–1, in a classic pitcher's duel. Don Newcombe, celebrating his 30th birthday, squared off against 21-year-old Cards right-hander Lindy McDaniel. Both men pitched the full game—ten innings—and each allowed just eight hits, but it was Newcombe who emerged victorious when Jim Gilliam stole home with the winning run with two out and the bases loaded in the bottom of the tenth. It was a daring bit of strategy and, as *New York Times* sportswriter Joseph M. Sheehan put it, "It was Gilliam's tenth and most important steal of the season."

Prior to the game, the Dodgers sold left-handed pitcher Ken Lehman to the Baltimore Orioles for the waiver price of $10,000. To date, Lehman had appeared in just three games for the 1957 Dodgers, but most recently he had pitched 5⅓ scoreless innings against the Braves in relief of Don Drysdale after the big brawl against the Braves. In fact, Lehman had been un-scored upon in his previous two appearances of '57, too. Signed by the Dodgers out of Seattle, Washington, in 1946, Lehman was poised to break into the majors with Brooklyn late in the 1950 season when he enlisted in the Army and served in the Korean War. After a year-and-a-half in the service, Lehman was back in baseball in 1952 and up with the Dodgers in September. He made his big-league debut on September 5 of that season with a solid start against the Braves, and soon found himself pitching in the 1952 World Series, where he tossed two scoreless innings of mop-up relief in game two.

Despite some excellent seasons in the minors, Lehman never quite made the grade with Brooklyn. Still, he was respected by his teammates, like fellow left-hander Tommy Lasorda: "Ken was a tremendous guy that knew how to pitch in the big leagues. A typical Dodger player—hardnosed. And when he was on that mound, he was tough. An outstanding guy." The Orioles would find themselves agreeing with Lasorda's assessment of Lehman. After joining Baltimore, Lehman appeared in 30 games for them in '57, mostly out of the pen, winning eight against just three losses, while pitching to a 2.78 ERA.

*   *   *

1957

Brooklyn

DODGERS

KEN LEHMAN
LEFT-HAND PITCHER

16	**KEN LEHMAN**						**Left-Hand Pitcher**				
	HEIGHT: 6'0" WEIGHT: 170						BATS: LEFT THROWS: LEFT				
	BORN: JUNE 10, 1928						SEATTLE, WASHINGTON				

	MAJOR LEAGUE PITCHING RECORD										
	Games	IP	Won	Lost	Pct	Hits	Runs	ER	SO	Walks	ERA
YEAR: 1957*	3	7.1	0	0	.000	7	0	0	3	1	0.00
CAREER: 5 YRS	134	265	14	10	.583	273	125	115	134	95	3.91

6-13-57: In a game marked by a wild 2nd-inning melee, the Dodgers lost to the 1st-place Braves 8-5 at Ebbets Field. Dodger left-hander **KEN LEHMAN**, in relief of the ejected Don Drysdale, pitched a scoreless 5-1/3 innings until being pulled for a pinch hitter in the 7th with the score tied 4-4. This was only Ken's third appearance of the year for Brooklyn, but he'd been perfect in those games, too – a scoreless inning against the Reds on May 7 and again on June 9. "Perfect" wasn't anything new for Ken as he threw a perfect game with Montreal in 1955.

* Only statistics from the 1957 Brooklyn Dodgers are displayed. Ken played in an additional 30 games with the 1957 Baltimore Orioles.

I HOPE YOU LIKE CRABCAKES, HON!

THE DAY AFTER PITCHING FIVE PERFECT INNINGS, KEN WAS SOLD TO THE O's ON 6-14-57!

Farewell to Flatbush

Perhaps the Dodgers had second thoughts about selling Ken Lehman the day after they sent him off to the Orioles, for things didn't go so well as the Cards evened the series at one game apiece after topping Brooklyn, 6–5, on June 15. Flatbush favorite Carl Erskine finally made his 1957 mound debut after spending the first two months of the season trying to get his chronically bad pitching shoulder in shape. Carl entered the game in relief of Roger Craig in the third inning, and looked good for a while, but was eventually dinged for a two-run homer by Wally Moon in the sixth. But Oisk seemed to be on his way back—and he chipped in a single at the plate for good measure.

Also in uniform for the game that day was a new Dodger coach—Greg Mulleavy. He joined coaches Jake Pitler, Joe Becker, and Billy Herman, rounding out a respected staff. Mulleavy began the '57 season as manager of the Dodgers' Triple-A affiliate Montreal Royals, but resigned earlier in the week as the club languished in last place in the International League. The downturn in Montreal was a new thing for Mulleavy, who had led the club to a pennant in 1955 and a first-division finish in 1956. But his new misfortune in Montreal turned out to be a blessing in disguise as he was now back in the big leagues. He was first in the big show as a shortstop with the 1930 Chicago White Sox, where he played in 77 games and hit .263 after joining the Sox in the first week of July. Despite his decent showing with the bat, Mulleavy was a bit error-prone in the field, prompting *Chicago Tribune* sportswriter Irving Vaughn to write, "Mulleavy has failed to impress Manager Bush. The lad is a long way from a finished product." Mulleavy was returned to the minors where he would play another 16 years, with just two brief trips back to the majors—one game with the 1932 White Sox and one game with the 1933 Red Sox.

Mulleavy would learn every aspect of the game during his many years of minor league experience, and he proved to be very good at communicating that knowledge to the players he played with and coached—including Hall of Famer Lou Boudreau. One day after Mulleavy joined the Dodgers, Boudreau, then a broadcaster for the Cubs, saw his old Buffalo Bisons teammate and said to all within earshot,

> There's the man who taught me how to play shortstop. I had just come out of the University of Illinois when the Indians sent me to Buffalo. I had been a third baseman and catcher in college, but the Indians wanted to use me at shortstop because a fellow named Ken Keltner was at third. Greg was the Bisons' regular shortstop, and although he knew I was to take his place, he was wonderful with his advice.

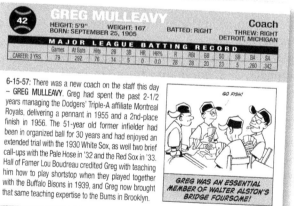

42	GREG MULLEAVY											Coach	
	HEIGHT: 5'9" WEIGHT: 167 BATTED: RIGHT THREW: RIGHT												
	BORN: SEPTEMBER 25, 1905								DETROIT, MICHIGAN				

	MAJOR LEAGUE BATTING RECORD												
	Games	At Bats	Hits	2B	3B	HR	HR%	R	RBI	BB	SO	SB	BA	SA
CAREER: 3 YRS	79	292	76	14	5	0	0.0	28	28	20	23	5	.260	.342

6-15-57: There was a new coach on the staff this day – GREG MULLEAVY. Greg had spent the past 2-1/2 years managing the Dodgers' Triple-A affiliate Montreal Royals, delivering a pennant in 1955 and a 2nd-place finish in 1956. The 51-year old former infielder had been in organized ball for 30 years and had enjoyed an extended trial with the 1930 White Sox, as well two brief call-ups with the Pale Hose in '32 and the Red Sox in '33. Hall of Famer Lou Boudreau credited Greg with teaching him how to play shortstop when they played together with the Buffalo Bisons in 1939, and Greg now brought that same teaching expertise to the Bums in Brooklyn.

GREG WAS AN ESSENTIAL MEMBER OF WALTER ALSTON'S BRIDGE FOURSOME!

The Dodger brass liked Mulleavy, and he would stay with the club after it moved to Los Angeles. Being in Los Angeles turned out to be a good thing for the Mulleavy family. Greg's son, Greg Jr., was a promising baseball player in his own right, but he was also a promising young actor, and the proximity to Hollywood after the Dodgers moved to Los Angeles helped young Greg embark on a successful acting career. His most notable role was that of Tom Hartman in the TV show *Mary Hartman, Mary Hartman,* but he also appeared in countless shows like *The Rockford Files, All in the Family, Bonanza, The Virginian,* and *Hawaii Five-O,* to name a few. But Dad was a true-blue Dodger and would remain with the franchise for his entire life in various capacities.

June 16: Alston Gets the Thumb

The long homestand that started so promising with four straight wins early in the month ended with a thud as the Dodgers were swept by the Cardinals in a double-header on June 16. Clem Labine, who had pitched lights out all season, was now suffering shoulder soreness, and it was impacting his effectiveness. He entered the opener in the seventh with the score tied, 6–6 and immediately gave up a lead-off home run to Cards third baseman Ken Boyer. That turned out to be the difference-maker as St. Louis won, 7–6. The loss was the Dodgers' seventh in their last nine games, and frustration was showing as manager Walter Alston was ejected for arguing balls and strikes with plate umpire Frank Secory. Pee Wee Reese was also tossed for good measure.

Things got worse in the nightcap as Brooklyn fell, 8–4, making it eight losses in their last ten and dropping them to fifth place. It was a tight ballgame through five innings, but the Cards led Johnny Podres and the Dodgers, 3–2, going into the sixth. It was then that St. Louis routed Podres, however, with a four-run inning highlighted by a play in which first baseman John Roseboro collided violently with second baseman Jim Gilliam as both pursued a ground ball by Cardinals catcher Hal Smith. Roseboro, a catcher, had been pressed into service at first base because Gil Hodges was still suffering from sore ribs incurred during a collision with Braves second baseman Bob Malkmus on June 12. The list of Brooklyn's walking wounded was rising as their place in the standings was falling, and Alston was left to ponder what to do.

Although Alston was a .295 hitter with 176 home runs in 13 minor league seasons, his big-league career consisted of just one at-bat—a strikeout while playing with the St. Louis Cardinals in September of 1936. Still, he eventually earned the respect of the Dodgers players because he had done what no other Dodgers manager had been able to do—win the World Series. Dodgers managers like Wilbert Robinson, Leo Durocher, Burt Shotton, and Charlie Dressen had all lost in the Series, but Alston had won it in just his second year at the helm in 1955. When the hiring of Alston was announced on November 24, 1953, one of the typically gruff New York papers ran a headline saying, "Alston (Who's He?) New Dodger Manager." The article went on to say, "The Dodgers do not need a manager, and that is why they got Alston." The insinuation was that any manager could win with the strong line-ups Brooklyn produced, but their World Series failures proved they *did* need a manager—just the right one. And Alston, once he settled into the best way to utilize his players, proved to be the right man for the job, delivering four World Series championships in his first 12 years as Dodgers manager.

The son of farmers from Ohio, Alston became known for his quiet managerial style, but it didn't start out that way as he cast about looking for a way to gain the respect of his players. A big man at six-foot-two, Alston wasn't averse to using his size to intimidate players early in his managerial tenure with the Dodgers, and on more than one occasion he challenged players to a fight. Nobody ever took him up on his challenge, although Jackie Robinson was ready and willing in the spring of 1955—but Roy Campanella stepped in and told both men to grow up, diffusing the situation. But by 1957, Alston had settled into his style. He didn't over-manage, usually just writing in the lineup and letting the players play while conferring with his coaches when strategy was needed. He became somewhat mellow on the field, which worked for him in the long run but annoyed some players because they felt he wasn't fighting for them—especially in the case of battling with umpires. Alston simply was not an umpire baiter, which was why it was so surprising that umpire Frank Secory was so quick to thumb Walter from the June 16 ballgame. Even more surprising was how hard N.L. president Warren Giles came down on Alston the next day, fining him $75 and suspending him for three games. It was the first time Alston had been suspended in his 18 years in baseball, and it came as quite a jolt to him. "I can't imagine what I was supposed to have said to Secory," said the mild-mannered Alston, who never had a reputation for using profanity. "Furthermore, it can't be said that I wasted any time."

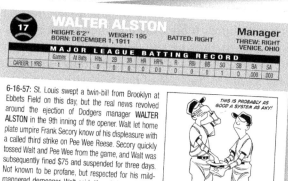

6-16-57: St. Louis swept a twin-bill from Brooklyn at Ebbets Field on this day, but the real news revolved around the ejection of Dodgers manager **WALTER ALSTON** in the 9th inning of the opener. Walt let home plate umpire Frank Secory know of his displeasure with a called third strike on Pee Wee Reese. Secory quickly tossed Walt and Pee Wee from the game, and Walt was subsequently fined $75 and suspended for three days. Not known to be profane, but respected for his mild-mannered demeanor, Walt said, "I can't imagine what I was supposed to have said to Secory. Furthermore, it can't be said that I wasted any time."

Four. June

*   *   *

Dodger coach Billy Herman was the manager of record as Walter Alston began his suspension on June 17, and Billy skippered Brooklyn to a 7–2 triumph over the Reds at Crosley Field in Cincinnati. It was a rookie left-hander making his big-league debut that made Herman look like a managerial genius. Danny McDevitt, 24 years old, was called up from St. Paul the day before, and 24 hours later he pitched a seven-hit complete game victory. He even executed a perfect squeeze bunt to aid his cause. Maybe the cynical New York sportswriters were right—maybe the Dodgers didn't need a manager after all. The next day it was Don Newcombe's turn to make Herman look like a genius as Newk pitched a five-hit shutout to defeat the Reds, 7–0. Big Don was in a groove at the plate, too, going 3-for-3 with a home run and a double.

Herman had a chance to manage the Dodgers to their third win in a row on June 19 as Alston sat out the final game of his suspension, but Billy's luck ran out as the Reds tripped the Dodgers, 4–3, in front of a Crosley Field gathering of 18,800. Don Drysdale had a tough act to follow in matching the efforts of McDevitt and Newcombe, and in the end he just couldn't quite measure up, going 6⅓ and giving up two runs before being relieved by Clem Labine who quickly dished up a loss-clinching two-run clout to former Dodger Don Hoak. After the game a sportswriter asked catcher Roy Campanella if he'd called for the wrong pitch in the crucial Labine-Hoak showdown. "Sure, I called for the wrong pitch," said Campy with a touch of cynicism. "The catcher always calls for the wrong pitch when the ball winds up in the stands."

Billy Herman was a great second baseman with the Cubs from 1931 to 1940, and his fine play helped Chicago win three pennants. Larry MacPhail brought Herman to the Dodgers in early 1941 with hopes that Billy would help the up-and-coming Dodgers win the pennant—and that's exactly what happened. Leo Durocher, the Dodgers manager in '41, would later say Herman was "the classic number-two hitter in baseball, an absolute master at hitting behind the runner. A smart player who would be able to give Pee Wee Reese just the kind of help he needed. The deal for Billy Herman won the pennant for us."

It's amazing that Durocher would have anything nice to say about Herman after what Billy did to Leo in 1943. Herman, hitting around .330 at the time, was given the take sign twice in the same at-bat with one out and the bases loaded against the Giants. Herman finally lined into a double-play to kill the rally but was furious at Durocher for taking

		Games	At Bats	Hits	2B	3B	HR	HR%	R	RBI	BB	SO	SB	BA	SA
CAREER: 15 YRS		1922	7707	2545	486	82	47	0.6	1163	839	737	428	67	.304	.407

6-17-57: Behind a 7-hitter from left-handed rookie Danny McDevitt, the Dodgers defeated the Reds 7-2 at Crosley Field. Thanks to a 3-day suspension being served by Brooklyn skipper Walter Alston, it was Dodger coach BILLY HERMAN who managed the ballcub to victory on this day. Continuing his temporary assignment, Billy managed the team to a split in the next two games. Billy was one of the game's best during his playing days. He got his first shot as a big league manager with the 1947 Pirates, but was replaced by Billy Meyer in '48. Herman joined the Dodgers coaching staff in 1952, but jumped to the Braves when the Dodgers headed to Los Angeles.

GET IN THE HOLE!

BILLY WON THE ALL-STAR HOLIDAY GOLF TOURNAMENT FOR BIG LEAGUERS ON 7-9-57!

the bat out of his hands during good hitter's counts early in the at-bat. Herman was still fuming as Dolph Camilli rolled warm-up grounders to him prior to the next inning. The sight of Durocher sitting in the dug-out looking down with his chin in his hand was too much for Herman. Claiming he became "temporarily mad," Herman fired his return throw, not to Camilli, but right at Durocher. The ball skipped off the grass in front of the dugout and hit Durocher right between the eyes. "Down he went, headfirst, onto the floor of the dugout," recalled Herman in Peter Golenbock's *Bums.* "I tell you, I made one hell of a throw!" Herman fig-ured he was in for a serious fine, but Durocher never said a word to him about it.

Durocher knew Herman had intentionally hit him, but he valued what Herman brought to the club too much to discipline him. And, as Durocher had predicted, the knowledge Herman had been imparting to Reese was invaluable to the Dodgers' long-term success. And it was that ability to coach that brought Herman back to the Dodgers as a coach in 1952 under Charlie Dressen. The Dodgers let go of Herman after the 1957 season, but he would stick around as a coach and manager in the big leagues for many years to come.

* * *

Duke Snider hit his 12th homer of the season on June 20, but it was all the offense the Dodgers could generate as they lost to Cincin-nati, 6–1. The win earned the Reds a split of the four-game series, bump-ing them up to third place in the N.L. standings while the Dodgers were mired in 5th place. Walter Alston's return to the bench this day was on track to be a happy occasion as Brooklyn was leading, 1–0, through 3½ frames, but Cincinnati right-fielder Wally Post blew the game open with a grand slam off Dodgers right-hander Ed Roebuck in the bottom of the fourth.

June 21: McDueling Rookies

An 18-year-old Cardinals rookie right-hander, just a few short weeks after delivering his valedictorian address at Arnett High School in Hollis, Oklahoma, hurled a brilliant two-hit shutout to beat the Dodg-ers, 2–0, at Busch Stadium in St. Louis on June 21. Von McDaniel was his name, and he was the younger brother of Lindy McDaniel, St. Louis' 21-year-old right-hander. Plucked right out of high school and signed for a $50,000 bonus, Von made his debut with a scoreless four-inning relief appearance in Philadelphia on June 13. His second appearance came two days later when he pitched the final four frames at Ebbets Field, allowing no runs again and earning his first big league win. Now, McDaniel was handed the ball for his first start, and he dazzled the crowd of 27,972 by completely shutting down the Dodgers attack. The unfortunate opposing pitcher that day was Danny McDevitt, making just his second big league appearance. McDevitt was excellent again, as he'd been in his complete game debut four days earlier, but it was McDaniel's day, and McDevitt took the tough loss.

* * *

Don Newcombe was not at his best on this day, but back-to-back run-scoring triples in the top of the ninth by Pee Wee Reese and Duke Snider broke a 4–4 tie and lifted Newk to a 6–4 victory, knotting the Dodgers–Cardinals series at one game apiece on June 22. Much of the Dodgers' scoring came early in the game when Gil Hodges clubbed a three-run homer in the third off right-hander Willard Schmidt. It was Hodges' ninth long-ball of the season, and the win was Newcombe's seventh. The loss was just the fourth in the last 16 games for the upstart Cardinals, but they bounced back on June 23 to defeat Don Drysdale and the Dodgers, 4–3. Cardinals outfielder Wally Moon was the key antagonist for the Dodgers that day. Moon hit a two-run triple in the fourth, then scored what turned out to be the winning run by stealing home. Drysdale was so surprised by Moon's surprise dash for home that Big D rushed his delivery and sailed the pitch beyond the reach of Roy Campanella.

Hitting on all cylinders for a change, Brooklyn pitched, hit, and fielded their way to a 10–3 win over St. Louis on June 24, earning a split in the four-game series with the first-place Redbirds. One-time staff ace Carl Erskine got his first start of the season for Brooklyn, and responded by tossing six solid innings, which turned out to be plenty to gain his first win of 1957. There's no doubt that Erskine did it while enduring the same shoulder pain he'd dealt with his entire career, but he seemed to have regained his "stuff," which was crucial to his success. The Dodgers needed him, too, because their list of ailing pitchers was growing: Johnny Podres—elbow; Sal Maglie—thumb; Sandy Koufax—elbow. Brooklyn's 12-hit attack was highlighted by Duke Snider's 13th and 14th home runs of the season. Carl Furillo chipped in some heavy hitting, too. Benched before the game due to a prolonged slump that saw him get just two hits in his last 52 at-bats, Furillo came up with a pinch-hit two-run double in the seventh, then a solo homer in the ninth.

* * *

The Brooklyn Dodgers road show rolled on to Milwaukee for a three-game series with the Braves at County Stadium. The Braves finished second to the Dodgers for the National League pennant in both 1955 and 1956, but the power seemed to be shifting between the two clubs in 1957 as Milwaukee looked like a team on the rise while Brooklyn looked somewhat tired and old. In the meantime, the rest of the N.L. hadn't seemed to resolve themselves to the idea that the '57 pennant race was a two-team battle to be waged between Brooklyn and Milwaukee. At the moment, the N.L. was a muddled mess, with the St. Louis Cardinals in first place and the next four teams (Cincinnati, Milwaukee, Philadelphia, Brooklyn) all within 2½ games.

The Braves led the season series against the Dodgers five games to three as the teams took the field for the series opener on June 25, and when the day was over the Dodgers edged closer with a 2–0 triumph. Danny McDevitt, in just his third big league start, continued to be masterful, stifling the Braves' powerful attack by limiting them to just four singles. The Dodgers' attack wasn't much better against Lew Burdette and his spitter, but a first-inning Duke Snider home run and a ninth-inning insurance run was enough for McDevitt on this day.

June 26: Everything's Jake

Trailing 9–7 in the bottom of the eighth inning on June 26, the Braves pounded reliever Clem Labine for six runs as Milwaukee rolled to a 13–9 win. Don Newcombe started the game but was routed in the fifth when he served up back-to-back-to-back round trippers to Hank Aaron, Eddie Mathews and Wes Covington. Duke Snider was ejected by umpire Stan Landes in the seventh after Landes ruled Snider was out at second while trying to stretch a single into a double. Jumping into the argument between Snider and Landes was first base coach Jake Pitler, who was also quickly thumbed from the ballgame. Pitler had been the only first base coach Snider had ever known since he'd come up to the Dodgers back in 1947, so the two were almost joined at the hip. In fact, Pitler had been integral in developing a young, raw Snider during Duke's first year

in professional ball in 1944 when he played for the Pitler-managed Newport News Dodgers of the Piedmont League.

Pitler came to the Brooklyn Dodgers in 1946 following 33 years in
organized ball. He'd broken in as a player with Class-D Jackson in 1913,
then made it to the majors by 1917 where he played second base for the
Pittsburg Pirates. To his left in the infield played the great Honus Wagner, then a 43-year-old first baseman. Pitler was back in the minors for
good by 1919, playing and managing in many places until finally arriving
in Brooklyn in '46. Since then he'd become one of the favorites among
the fans and players at Ebbets Field. He was a savvy baseball man who
was a fine instructor of the game's fundamentals, and he was especially
adept at stealing opposition signs from his coaching spot at first base.
When the fans in the stands looked at Pitler in his coach's box, they saw
a very spirited and animated character—a buoyant cheerleader. The
players saw Pitler as a helpful teacher of the game, a psychologist and a
father figure. They also saw a fellow who was a world-class joker; a man
responsible for keeping their spirits high through salty, playful insults
directed at them. They gave it back to him, too, and he enjoyed every
minute of it.

In 1956 Pitler told sportswriters of a time when Pee Wee Reese had
pranked him real good. "Pee Wee was on first base in a game against the
Cubs," recalled Pitler:

> Dixie Walker's bat flew from his hands when he took a cut. The bat rolled
> nearly all the way to first base, so Pee Wee walked over, picked it up, and
> threw it back to Dixie. When Pee Wee went back to first, the Cub first base-
> man said, "Look what I have," and tagged him out. We were way ahead, so I
> couldn't help laughing. Pee Wee fixed me, though. He charged me and went
> through all the motions of giving me the dickens for letting him get caught,
> while the crowd booed. All the time he was really saying, "Was that movie
> any good last night, Jake? I'm thinking of seeing it myself."

Pitler's ejection from the June 26 game was a rare occurrence for
him. It had been five years since the last time he was given the heave-ho,
so it wasn't something he took lightly. To make matters worse, the
next morning Pitler received a telegram from National League president Warren Giles informing Jake that he had been suspended for three
games. Pitler was stunned. The incident for which he was banished
seemed trivial, so much so that umpire Landes didn't even file a report
with the league office. Pitler lit out on a quest to correct the unjust suspension. After sweating it out for a day, he finally discovered the truth—
he'd been pranked again. It was Walter Alston who'd sent the telegram,

1957

Brooklyn

DODGERS

JAKE PITLER
1st BASE COACH

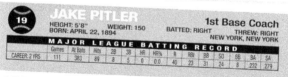

		JAKE PITLER										1st Base Coach		
19	HEIGHT: 5'8" WEIGHT: 150 BATTED: RIGHT THREW: RIGHT														
	BORN: APRIL 22, 1894									NEW YORK, NEW YORK					
MAJOR LEAGUE BATTING RECORD															
	Games	At Bats	Hits	2B	3B	HR	HR%	R	RBI	BB	SO	SB	BA	SA
CAREER: 2 YRS	111	383	89	8	5	0	0.0	40	23	31	24	8	.232	.279

6-26-57: The defending National League champion Brooklyn Dodgers continued to languish on this day, remaining in 5th place after falling to the Braves 13-9 at Milwaukee's County Stadium. The Dodger frustration boiled over in the 7th inning when Duke Snider tried to stretch a single into a double and was called out by umpire Stan Landes. Duke kicked up a rumpus with Landes and was soon joined by Dodger 1st base coach **JAKE PITLER**. Both were quickly ejected. Jake joined the Dodger coaching staff in 1947 after eight years of managing in Brooklyn's minor league system. Jake was a true favorite of Dodger players and fans alike.

OY VEY! I'M TOO OLD FOR THIS!

BALLPARK

JAKE ACCEPTED A NEW POSITION AS A DODGER SCOUT ON 10-29-57!

105

not Giles. Once again, everyone had a good-natured laugh at old Jake's expense.

The affection felt by all for Pitler was on full display on September 18, 1956, when the club held "Jake Pitler Night" before a game against the St. Louis Cardinals. Fans in attendance (13,784) cheered the 62-year-old coach that evening, as well as showering him with a horde of gifts including a brand new Cadillac sedan. They'd given him a "night" two years earlier where $3,000 was raised—all of which Pitler donated to Beth-El Hospital, his favorite charity. Pitler loved visiting the ill children there, and the hospital honored him with a plaque marking the Jake Pitler Pediatric Playroom. But the gifts raised in 1956 all went to Jake, and, for a change, he struggled to find the words to express himself as he stood behind the microphone at home plate. "It's difficult for me to say how happy your kindness has made me," said Jake. "From the bottom of my heart, I want to thank each and every one of you."

* * *

Don Drysdale and Braves crack right-hander Bob Buhl waged a hard-fought pitcher's duel during the rubber match of the Brooklyn–Milwaukee three-game series on June 27, but in the end it was the big bat of Hank Aaron that was the decider, leading the Braves to a 2–1 win. For 7½ innings Drysdale and Buhl had put nothing but zeros on the County Stadium scoreboard, but a walk and an infield error by Charlie Neal gave an opportunity to Aaron, and Hammerin' Hank capitalized on it by booming a two-run triple. Brooklyn wrecked Buhl's shutout with a run in the ninth, but hopes of a come-from-behind win died as pinch-hitter Sandy Amoros struck out to end the game.

June 29: Erskine Wins Again

With the help of a long two-run homer by Roy Campanella, Carl Erskine pitched the Dodgers to a 2–1 triumph over the Cubs at Wrigley Field on June 29. It was just Erskine's second start of 1957, and it was an unexpected one at that. Sal "The Barber" Maglie was slated to start the game but was scratched at the last minute when he felt pain in his shoulder, so Walter Alston ordered Erskine to warm up quick. Ignoring the ever-present pain in his own shoulder, Erskine took the ball and turned in a gutsy six-inning performance to earn the victory. Clem Labine pitched the final three innings to collect his 10th save of the season.

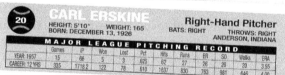

		Games	IP	Won	Lost	Pct	Hits	Runs	ER	SO	Walks	ERA
YEAR: 1957		15	66	5	3	.625	62	27	26	26	20	3.55
CAREER: 12 YRS		335	1718.2	122	78	.610	1637	830	763	981	646	4.00

6-29-57: Looking like the **CARL ERSKINE** of no-hitter and World Series fame, "Oisk" set down the Cubs 2-1 in just his second start of the season. Shoulder miseries limited Carl through the first half of 1957, and this was just his second start and fourth appearance overall. But Carl showed why he was a winner, relying on wit and grit to limit Chicago to just one run in six innings on the road at Wrigley Field. Clem Labine pitched the 7th and 8th to earn the save with the two Dodger runs coming on a 5th-inning homer by Roy Campanella. The shoulder would continue to plague Carl for the rest of the year, limiting him to just 11 more appearances in '57.

THIS "W" IS FOR ALL THE FLATBUSH FAITHFUL!

CARL GOT HIS LAST WIN AS A "BROOKLYN" DODGER, A 4-HIT MASTERPIECE, ON 9-14-57!

Farewell to Flatbush

Erskine had been a warrior for the Dodgers for a decade by 1957. He'd worked hard to get to a point where he could return to the mound that June, but he knew that there were only so many innings left in his damaged right shoulder. At 30 years of age, Erskine was still a young man in the real world, but it was becoming clear that Carl was nearing the end as a player in the baseball world—he just hoped to hold on a little longer. And if anybody could hold on, it was Erskine. Tom Sheehan, the New York Giants' big, burly, brash-talking chief scout, had found that out the hard way back on May 12, 1956, when he told the New York papers that Erskine was washed up. "The Dodgers are over the hill," said Sheehan. "Jackie's too old. Campy's too old. And Erskine—he can't win with the garbage he's been throwing up there."

Erskine and Robinson both saw Sheehan's comments in the papers that morning. "I read that article that Saturday morning, and it hurt because I was having severe arm problems but was scheduled to pitch that afternoon at Ebbets Field against the Giants," Erskine wrote in his book *Tales from the Dodger Dugout*. "My spirits were low, and I literally had nothing going for me but a prayer." Continuing the story, Erskine wrote,

> The game started and the opposing pitcher was Al Worthington. I got through one inning, then two, three, and four. In the fifth, Willie Mays hit a shot to Jackie's left at third base. Jackie made a marvelous clean pickup of the smash on one hop and threw Willie out easily. Through six innings, no score. Finally, we scored three runs in the seventh. I breezed through the eighth, and when Alvin Dark hit a one-hopper back to me with two out in the ninth, I had miraculously pitched a no-hit, no-run game—thanks to Jackie.

A smiling, jubilant Robinson rushed to the mound to congratulate Erskine, then turned and raced towards the Giants dugout where Sheehan was seated. Robinson reached into the back pocket of his uniform pants, pulled out the newspaper clipping, waved it at Sheehan and shouted, "How do you like that garbage?!" A former pitcher himself, Sheehan was right about Erskine's diminishing capabilities on the mound, but hopefully he learned a lesson about Carl's ability to overcome his physical ailments through sheer determination. Dodger fans knew about Oisk's grit, and after two nice starts in June of '57, they were hoping he still had some magic left in his old soupbone.

* * *

The Dodgers and Cubs concluded their three-game series with a double-header split at Wrigley Field on June 30. Don Newcombe held the Cubs scoreless through eight innings in the opener but left in the ninth with men on first and third and a slim 2–1 lead. Clem Labine came in to put out the fire, but the tying run scored on a double-play and the game went into extra innings. Cubs shortstop Ernie Banks capped the drama in the 11th with a game-ending RBI double. Danny McDevitt got the Dodgers back in the win column with a 5–1 triumph in the night-cap. McDevitt's glittering performance continued his sensational story by gaining his third complete-game victory in just four starts since coming up from St. Paul. Despite McDevitt's excellence, Brooklyn was fortunate to earn a split in the twin-bill because the Dodgers were not swinging the bats very well. In fact, they struck out 27 times in the double-header—a new major league record for futility.

FIVE

July

The sign on the outside edifice of the Polo Grounds read: NIGHT GAME: N.Y. GIANTS VS. BROOKLYN; MON. JULY 1. It seemed mundane enough, for the Giants and Dodgers had waged their rivalry there at the Polo Grounds, and at Ebbets Field, for decades. But, as history now knows, the Giants and Dodgers would play just eight more times at the Polo Grounds and eight more times at Ebbets Field—then never again. The fans of both teams were still not convinced that this could possibly happen, and the same could be said of veterans of the game—like the great Rogers Hornsby. When asked a few days earlier about the possible shift of the Dodgers and Giants to California, the blunt and outspoken Hornsby told the *New York Times*, "I would consider it a disgrace if the National League gave up New York."

As for the Dodgers and Giants ballclubs, their seasons were playing out in quite different manners as July of 1957 got under way. The Dodgers seemed to be treading water; floating in the middle of the pack in the National League. At the start of play on July 1, Brooklyn was in fourth place with a 37-and-32 record, and they had won an unimpressive nine games in their last 20. The Giants, on the other hand, were surging. After a poor start, they had crept back into the mix and, after winning 15 of their last 20, were now within two games of the Dodgers. That was enough to get Tom Sheehan shooting off his mouth again—just as he'd done the year before when he'd predicted the premature demise of Carl Erskine. Asked how much longer he thought the Giants' surge could last, the chief scout said, "Listen, did you ever stop to recall that every time the Braves made a deal with us we finished on top?" Sheehan was referring to a trade two weeks earlier when the Giants sent Red Schoendienst to the Milwaukee Braves in exchange for Ray Crone, Danny O'Connell, and Bobby Thomson. It was after that deal that the Giants fortunes had turned and their surge began. "Alvin Dark and Eddie Stanky won us the pennant in '51,"

Sheehan continued. "Johnny Antonelli won it in '54. And now... well, I ain't sayin' nuthin,' but it could happen again."

Maybe Sheehan jinxed them just as he'd done prior to Erskine's no-hitter in '56, but the Giants were unable to generate anything against Don Drysdale on July 1, losing to the Dodgers by a score of 3–0. The shutout was Drysdale's second of the season and the league-leading tenth for the Dodger staff as a whole. The Sheehan jinx extended to the next day, too, as Sal Maglie tossed another Dodger shutout, downing the Giants, 6–0. The Giants slowly slipped back to mediocrity after the two-game series against Brooklyn, then sub-mediocrity by the end of the campaign, when they lost 15 of their final 18 games. They would finish their last season in New York in sixth place with a humbling 69-and-85 record.

* * *

The Dodgers began a long homestand with a fourth of July double-header against the Pirates at Ebbets Field. From the way the twin-bill went—a split—July already looked a lot like June for Brooklyn. Bob Friend continued his mastery of the Dodgers in the opener, pitching the Bucs to a 5–1 win. Friend beat the Dodgers four times in 1956, and his victory on this day was his second triumph over Brooklyn for 1957. Carl Erskine drew the unfortunate assignment to oppose Friend, so Carl's two-game comeback win streak came to a sudden end. With Friend out of the picture for the nightcap, the Dodger bats came to life and powered Brooklyn to an 8–2 win. Don Newcombe went the distance for the Dodgers to earn his eighth win of the season, and Duke Snider was heartily cheered when he smashed a lofty solo homer over the right field wall in the seventh inning. It was Snider's 16th long-ball of the season.

Danny McDevitt's race to the Hall of Fame was stalled on July 5 when the Phillies reached him for four runs and knocked him out of the game in the seventh inning. Roy Campanella got McDevitt off the hook for the loss, however, when the good-natured catcher crushed a three-run homer off Robin Roberts in the eighth, helping Brooklyn to a 6–5 victory. Philadelphia turned the tables on Brooklyn by taking the next three games from them, leaving the Dodgers reeling as they went into the All-Star break. The three-game losing streak began with a 9–4 loss to right-hander Jack Sanford on July 6. Walter Alston, the 1957 N.L. All-Star manager, had recently named Sanford as his starter for the upcoming All-Star game, and Sanford seemed to validate Alston's choice by tossing a complete-game win against Walter's crew. Sanford even adding a single and an RBI to drive the point, and the run, home. July 7 saw the Dodgers lose both ends of a double-header, 2–1 and 5–3. Notable in the first game was the sound booing Duke Snider received from the Ebbets Field crowd—those same folks who had cheered Snider's 16th home run just days earlier. It was a fluke play that drew their ire. The *New York Times'* Gordon S. White described it this way:

> With Charlie Neal on third, Gilliam on second, and no one out, Snider slammed a hot one-hopper to Hamner at second. Hamner scooped the ball out of the dirt and threw home to get Neal. Snider thought the ball was a line drive that Hamner caught in the air, so he let up on his run to first and headed toward the dugout. Lonnett, the Phils' catcher, threw to first for a twin-killing after tagging Neal.

Not hustling was one thing Brooklyn fans wouldn't put up with—even from stars like The Duke. They had to bust their humps every day to make ends meet at all manner of mundane jobs in and around Brooklyn, so the least they expected from their ballplayers—men playing a kids game—was all-out hustle on every play. They let Snider know their disappointment loud and clear, adding another chapter to the complicated love-hate relationship between The Duke and the Flatbush fans.

It was an old friend that sent the Dodgers to defeat in the nightcap—Chico Fernandez. Traded to the Phillies the day before the '57 season opened, Fernandez broke up a 2–2 tie with a bases-loaded double to right off Clem Labine in the sixth inning. With that loss, the Dodgers headed into the All-Star break in fifth place, five games behind the pace-setting St. Louis Cardinals. But there was hope. The previous season the Dodgers were two games off the pace as they entered the 1956 All-Star break, yet they came back to win the pennant. It would be tougher this season, but Dodger fans were hoping for a repeat performance—and they were hoping that it would not be the last pennant race *in Brooklyn* for the Dodgers.

July 9: All-Star Finale

Cincinnati fans stuffed All-Star ballot boxes at an all-time high in 1957, the result being that Reds players were voted in as starters at every position for the National League squad. Baseball commissioner Ford Frick stepped in, however, and scratched three Reds from the starting lineup, then added Stan Musial, Hank Aaron, and Willie Mays—pretty good players in their own right. No Dodgers were voted to the team, but there would still be a Brooklyn stamp on the game—for the last time ever. By virtue of managing the previous year's pennant winners, Walter Alston was the skipper of the '57 N.L. All-Stars. A few days before the game he added Clem Labine, Gino Cimoli, and Gil Hodges to the team, and promised to use them in the action if possible. And use them he did, albeit it in a losing effort, as the American League won, 6–5, before a crowd of 30,693 at Busch Stadium in St. Louis on July 9.

The first of the Dodgers to see action was Gino Cimoli. Trailing the Americans, 3–2, Alston sent Cimoli in to lead off the 8th as a pinch-hitter for Cardinals pitcher Larry Jackson. White Sox left-hander Billy Pierce fooled Gino, ringing him up on a called strike three. The Nationals failed to score and still trailed by one as they headed into the top of the ninth. Alston dispatched Labine to the mound, inserting him into Cimoli's slot in the lineup. Hits, errors and good execution by the Americans came down on Labine, and when he finally retired the side on a grounder by Moose Skowron, the Americans led, 6–2. The Nationals rallied in the ninth, however, and were trailing, 6–5, with two out and Cubs shortstop Ernie Banks on second with the tying run. Alston sent Hodges in to pinch hit against Indians left-hander Don Mossi. Casey Stengel, manager of the Americans, countered by sending Yankee right-hander Bob Grim to the slab. It would be the last time a New York Yankee player would face off against a Brooklyn Dodger player, and, as was so often the case, the Yankee came out on top, getting Hodges on a liner to left to end the game.

Conversation about the Dodgers and Giants leaving New York buzzed throughout baseball during the All-Star break. People still found it hard to believe that the National League would abandon New York and leave the entire city and its dollars to the American League and the Yankees. Playing upon this theme, *New York Times* sportswriter John Drebinger opened his game-day article by noting the irony of the All-Star game being played in St. Louis—a city abandoned by the American League when the St. Louis Browns left for Baltimore after the 1953 season. While people supposedly in the know—people like Rogers Hornsby—refused to believe the National League would leave New York, other insiders believed it was a real possibility. Referring to the Boston Braves' move to Milwaukee in 1953, N.L. president Warren Giles cavalierly told sportswriters, "The National League left New England, and how's that working out?" No one could argue that it was working out great—for now—but not so much by 1966 when the Braves bolted from Milwaukee to Atlanta.

And while Dodger fans would love to hear their players being outspoken about wanting the club to remain in Brooklyn, the players were often noncommittal about the whole thing. That should be expected, though. While fans often remained in one place for their lifetime, players are an itinerant lot, moving often from team to team and place to place, sometimes hampering their ability to empathize with the fans' situation. Then there's the love-hate relationship between fans and players that can sometimes taint a player's compassion for the fans. Case in point—Don Newcombe.

Newk was a man that pitched his heart out for Brooklyn. He won a lot of games, but he lost some big ones, too—and was even considered a choker in the minds of many fans and sportswriters. He'd had a career year in 1956, winning 27 games while nabbing the Cy Young and M.V.P. Awards—yet he was being booed by Brooklyn fans in 1957. Being human, these factors negatively influenced Newcombe when he was asked how he felt about the possible move to Los Angeles, and he bitterly said, "Go ahead and boo me. You won't have nuthin' to boo next year." While Newk's statement may have angered Dodger fans, they had to admit that he might be right.

July 11: New Fighting Spirit

The three-day All-Star lay-off seemed to reinvigorate the Dodgers with a new fighting spirit. They won their first game of the second half, 5–4, over the Reds at Ebbets Field on July 11, then went on to win 18 of their next 26 games to get themselves back into the thick of the pennant race. This new fighting spirit was not just figurative—it was literal—as Jim Gilliam squared off with a number of Reds players during this game in a wild seventh-inning brawl. According to Carl Erskine, the trouble actually started back on June 18 when Reds rookie right-hander Raul Sanchez intentionally drilled Charlie Neal in the ribs in the eighth inning of a Dodger rout of Cincinnati at Crosley Field. Neal peacefully took his base, but Sanchez's purpose-pitch enraged Gilliam, and Jim vowed to get even when the next opportunity presented itself. Erskine described Sanchez as a "middle reliever, by today's terminology. He'd be called into the game in about the sixth inning to hold the opposing team and try to keep the Reds in the game. However, he quickly established a reputation for hitting two or three guys in the inning in which he was due to be lifted for a pinch-hitter."

Gilliam's choice to lay low until he got a chance to get even with Sanchez was, according to Erskine, reminiscent of Jackie Robinson, and it was a spark the 1957 team badly needed now that the fiery Robinson was no longer there to provide it. Erskine called Gilliam's vengeance on Sanchez the "one big team moment" of 1957. He said it

> defined the year that ironically had us break hearts. It reminded us of the tenacity of Jackie Robinson, even though he was no longer in uniform. His soul was echoed through Jackie's protégé, Jim Gilliam. Jim told me that nothing needed to be said. He remembered Jackie's philosophy about keeping your mouth shut and letting your playing speak for you. Jackie's credo lived on while his uniform number 42 lay folded away in the Dodgers' clubhouse. The Reds were due back in town in just a few weeks. Jim said he'd be ready.

The Dodgers game against the Reds on July 11 was the first time Sanchez pitched against Brooklyn since he'd hit Neal back in June. Cincinnati manager Birdie Tebbetts sent Sanchez in to relieve in the fourth with the Reds trailing, 3–1. Sanchez put out the fire by retiring Roy Campanella, Don Zimmer, and Danny McDevitt in order, but new trouble began brewing in the fifth. Neal led off the inning and was retired on a come-backer. That brought up Gilliam—and he was still bent on exacting revenge on Sanchez. In an age-old bit of baseball payback strategy, Gilliam dropped a bunt down the first base line with the intent of running into Sanchez when he came over to field the ball. It worked to perfection as Sanchez scooped up the roller but dropped the ball when Gilliam plowed into him at the first base bag. Gilliam was safe and the old score was settled—at least in the mind of Gilliam. Sanchez, however, was oblivious to the vendetta Gilliam had been carrying, so this new incident only served to anger Raul.

Sanchez upped the ante when Gilliam batted in the seventh, knocking Jim down with a fastball aimed at his head. After dusting himself off and stepping back in the batter's box, Gilliam redeployed his bunting strategy, only this time he did it with the force of an F-5 tornado as opposed to the thunder-storm-level run-in of the fifth inning. Erskine described it this way: "Jim dragged a bunt down the first base line with the precision of an artist painting a rolling ball on a piece of canvas. Sanchez came over to field the ball and Jim hit him like an 18-wheeler roaring down I-95! Once Sanchez was on the ground, Jim pounded the living daylights out of him."

The *New York Times* described the ensuing fracas this way:

The next moment they were squared away punching, then went down as players rushed from both dugouts. Roy Campanella was one of the first arrivals but seemed intent on pulling somebody out of the fight. Gil Hodges, as usual, used his great strength to separate combatants. But the melee persisted for 15 minutes, with the crowd, meanwhile, in an uproar.

The story arc of this brawl may give the impression that Charlie Neal needed Jim Gilliam to fight his battles for him. Nothing, actually, could be further from the truth—and Reds third baseman Don Hoak found that out the hard way. Erskine recalled that in the middle of the free-for-all he saw

Hoak coming toward Jim, like a madman. Don's nickname was "Tiger." He was a former Marine, and proud of it in every way. Charlie Neal, who stood about two inches shorter than Hoak, saw Hoak's eyes affixed on Jim. Neal raced toward Hoak. At the very moment when Hoak attempted to land a haymaker, Charlie Neal connected on Hoak's chin with a punch that would have devastated any heavyweight boxing champion. I have never seen, in all my years watching boxing matches, a punch landed with such force, and so uncontested because of the element of surprise. Hoak was sent reeling backward, causing him to fall flat over the pitcher's mound. And Charlie Neal was the new heavyweight champ. Gilliam had made his point—Jackie Robinson must have been proud.

Dazed and lying on his back, Hoak was not thinking about Gilliam's point or Jackie Robinson's pride. The rhubarb had been somewhat settled by the time the cobwebs cleared from Hoak's head as he lay across the mound. Then, according to the *Times*, "Hoak set things off again by racing toward the Dodger dugout in search of Neal. He was stopped by Hodges, who held Don easily. Finally, the umpires got everyone reasonably quiet and before the game was resumed four players had been banished." Hoak had been a promising young Dodger in 1954 and '55, but he fell on hard times with the Cubs after being dealt to them in 1956. He landed in Cincy for the 1957 season and was enjoying a nice bounce-back season, much of it at the expense of the Dodgers who had difficulty getting him out that year. That said, there might have been a little extra intensity between the Dodgers and Hoak due to their past, and Don wasn't ready to let the incident go in the clubhouse after the game. When asked by a sportswriter if he'd be calmed down by game-time tomorrow, Hoak adamantly declared, "I will not. I'm going to get him [Neal] either inside or outside the ballpark. I actually went in there to stop the fight and out of a clear sky I was hit."

Upon hearing Hoak's threat, National League president Warren Giles sent a telegram warning against retaliation and issuing fines to the four ejected players. "Such actions are not part of the game," wrote Giles, "are not helpful to what the game stands for, and are not to be engaged in. Any revival of the affair or repetition will be dealt with more severely." While the donnybrook may not have been helpful to what the game stands for, in Giles' opinion, it seems to have been helpful in getting the Dodgers off to a roaring start in the second half of the 1957 season.

*   *   *

The Dodgers–Reds series moved to Roosevelt Stadium for game two on July 12. Hostilities among the players remained in check—possibly aided by the fact that Don Hoak was on the bench with a hand injured during the big fight. Hostilities among the Jersey City fans were there as usual, however, with many Dodgers players being booed vociferously. Don Newcombe was the main target of the jeers, but he shut up the hecklers by pitching one of his best games of the season, going the distance and gaining a 3–1 victory. A two-run triple by Gino Cimoli in the eighth was the blow that ultimately did in the Reds, sending them to their seventh consecutive defeat. The series finale on June 13 was washed out when the skies opened up in the second inning with Brooklyn leading, 2–0, so the Reds left town reeling while the Dodgers prepared to open a series against the second-place Braves.

The Dodgers stayed hot as they took game one from Milwaukee on June 14 when Gil Hodges hit a game-ending home run in the ninth inning to win, 3–2. While fan enthusiasm for the Dodgers seemed to be waning under the weight of the feared move to Los Angeles and the team's lackluster play, the club's recent reversal of fortunes on the field seemed to infect the fans with a new dose of pennant fever. Roscoe McGowen of the *New York Times* described the excitement when he wrote, "Not often has a more full-throated roar greeted a game-winning blow than that which swelled from the throats of the 20,871 paying customers." The players, too, were caught up in their team's surge. "And it has been quite a while," continued McGowen, "since such a welcoming delegation has rushed to home plate in Ebbets Field to hammer its congratulations into the back of the conquering hero."

July 15: Blasting the Braves

Five Milwaukee Braves pitchers were battered by the Brooklyn Dodgers as the Bums stormed to a 20–4 triumph on July 15. The worst of the beating was absorbed by Braves left-hander Taylor Phillips upon whom the Dodgers scored nine times in the eighth inning. Home runs were flying out of Ebbets Field on this day—five off Dodger bats and two by the Braves. But only one player hit for the circuit twice in the game—Dodgers' shortstop Charlie Neal. The 26-year-old right-handed hitter from Longview, Texas, led off the game with an opposite field drive over the barrier in right field, then homered into the lower left-centerfield stands in the fourth. Neal was not considered to be one of the Dodgers' heavy hitters, but, as he exhibited on this day, he had some pop in his bat. His pair of round-trippers were his fifth and sixth of 1957 on his way to a total of 12 for the season. He'd bash a career-high 22 long-balls in 1958, but finish with a modest total of 87 when he retired from the game after the 1963 season.

One of a number of candidates being groomed as an heir apparent to the aging Pee Wee Reese at shortstop, the speedy Neal signed in 1950 and joined the Class-D Hornell Dodgers of the PONY League. Actually, Neal had got his first taste of pro ball in the fading Negro Leagues with the Atlanta Black Crackers. Teammate Maurice Peatros recalled the club picking up a baby-faced Neal while passing through Longview, Texas. "His mother didn't want him to go," said Peatros,

> she said he was too young. She said if we would sign a thing saying we would be protective of Charlie, she would let him play. However—we had to take his brother, too. His brother was an outfielder. Charlie was playing second base and I was playing first, and that gave us a brick wall on the right side of the infield. The Atlanta players wanted to give a prize to anyone that could hit a ball between me and Charlie Neal!

By 1954, Neal was starring for Brooklyn's Triple-A affiliate in St. Paul, Minnesota, but the stacked Dodgers were a tough lineup to crack and Charlie remained in the minors for another season. Controversial sportswriter Dick Young believed that the Brooklyn Dodgers, after spearheading the integration of big league baseball, now held back some of their black prospects too long for fear of allowing their lineup to become "too black," something the Dodgers brass feared could possibly alienate white fans in Brooklyn. The ultimate alienation of white fans in Brooklyn took place later, however, when the franchise moved to Los Angeles, and it was in L.A. where Neal thrived—especially in 1959 when Charlie had a career year that culminated with him batting .370 with two doubles, two homers, and six runs batted in as the Dodgers beat the Chicago White Sox in the World Series. Despite the move to Los Angeles, Neal was not done making his mark on big league baseball in New York. On April 11, 1962, Charlie Neal was the starting second baseman

1957
Brooklyn
DODGERS

CHARLIE NEAL
INFIELDER

CHARLIE NEAL

21
HEIGHT: 5'10"   WEIGHT: 165
BORN: JANUARY 30, 1931

BATS: RIGHT

Infielder
THROWS: RIGHT
LONGVIEW, TEXAS

MAJOR LEAGUE BATTING RECORD

	Games	At Bats	Hits	2B	3B	HR	HR%	R	RBI	BB	SO	SB	BA	SA
YEAR: 1957	126	448	121	13	7	12	2.7	62	62	53	83	11	.270	.411
CAREER: 8 YRS	970	3316	858	113	36	87	2.6	461	391	337	557	48	.259	.394

7-15-57: The Dodgers exploded for nine runs in the 8th inning as they trounced the Braves 20-4 at Ebbets Field. Although not known as a pure power hitter, Brooklyn shortstop and lead-off man **CHARLIE NEAL** muscled up to blast two round-trippers. Charlie's first circuit clout was a drive over the rightfield barrier off Bob Trowbridge in the 1st inning. His second was another solo shot, this time into the lower left-centerfield stands off Ernie Johnson in the 4th. Charlie broke in with the Dodgers in 1956 but was almost the property of the Red Sox in '54 when they offered to purchase him from Brooklyn for $125,000... an offer the Dodgers wisely refused.

WHO TURNED OUT THE LIGHTS?!

CHARLIE DECKED DON HOAK WITH ONE PUNCH IN A BRAWL WITH THE REDS ON 7-11-57!

for the expansion New York Mets in the first game of their now-storied history. Neal went 3-for-4 that day and drove in the new franchise's first RBI, and it seemed perfectly appropriate that it would be a former Brooklyn Dodger who would help usher in a new era of National League baseball in New York—four long years after the Dodgers and Giants vacated the city.

* * *

Brooklyn won their fifth in a row since the All-Star break with a 7–5 victory over St. Louis at Ebbets Field on July 16. The Dodgers were still in fourth place following the triumph, but they were just one game out of first place. It was fool's gold, though, for the Dodgers would never again occupy first place during their remaining time in Brooklyn. As it turned out, June 8 was the last day they ever sat atop the National League, a lofty position they had become accustomed to residing in for so much of the last decade. Mound sensation Danny McDevitt had cooled a bit since his fast start and was knocked out of this game after just one inning. Carl Erskine was rushed into emergency service and pitched well, earning his third win of the season. The Dodgers' win streak was broken on July 17 when the Cardinals took game two of the three-game set, 7–3. Don Newcombe took the loss—a rare thing for him as far as the Cardinals were concerned. Newk had not lost to the Redbirds since 1951 and owned a 12-game winning streak over them until his loss on this day. It wasn't enough for many of the Flatbush fans, however, and they serenaded Newcombe with boos as he trudged off the mound in the fourth inning.

July 18: Hodges Is Grand

Gil Hodges homered on July 18—a grand slam—to help Brooklyn take the rubber match of their series against St. Louis, 10–9. Hodges had now homered in three of the Dodgers' last five games, and Brooklyn had won all three of those contests. The game was on the line when Hodges hit his grand slam on this day. Trailing 9–5 with one out in the ninth and the bases loaded, Hodges unloaded on a 1-and-1 fastball from Cards left-hander Vinegar Bend Mizell. The drive landed amongst the Ebbets Field fans in the lower left-centerfield seats, and it forced the game into extra innings. The Dodgers ended it in the 11th when Duke Snider scored the winning tally following an error by Cardinals third baseman Eddie Kasko. The grand slam was the 12th of Hodges' career, and it tied him with Rogers Hornsby and Ralph Kiner for the National League's all-time lead. Hodges had 14 grand slams by the time he retired as a player during the 1963 season. That was good enough for sole possession of the N.L. lead in that category, and it remained the high-water mark until 1974.

So Hodges was swinging a hot home run bat when the Cubs came to Ebbets Field for a Friday night double-header on July 19, an evening that had, coincidentally, been promoted for weeks in advance to be "Gil Hodges Night." The Dodgers swept their first double-header of the season that evening, winning 6–3 in the opener and 5–3 in the nightcap. Hodges picked up a hit in each game, but he picked up a lot more in a between-games ceremony where he was bestowed an impressive array of gifts to thank him for his dedicated service to the Dodgers since he debuted with them in 1943. Organized by Joann Duffy, president of the Gil Hodges Fan Club, the 45-minute ceremony was held at home plate where Gil was surrounded by his family. There he was regaled by emcee Happy Felton, host of WOR-TV's pregame Dodgers show featuring Felton's Knot-Hole Gang, and presented with nearly 80 gifts.

Among the presents were two heartfelt items from Gil's teammates and colleagues with the Brooklyn Dodgers: a beautiful silver tray engraved with 30 names, and a large "Players Popularity Award" plaque featuring 33 photos and signatures. The text of the plaque did a great job in summing up how Gil's teammates, colleagues, and opponents felt about him:

> For having won the respect and admiration of all who have played with or against him through many years of distinguished competition.... For his outstanding ability, genuine talents, and sincere and unending devotion to our national pastime.... For his character, generous understanding of his fellow man, on and off the baseball diamond, and for his complete sportsmanship in the best tradition of a true gentleman.

Also presented to Gil that evening were gifts ranging from a new Dodge convertible to a lifetime supply of dill pickles.

President Dwight D. Eisenhower was an avid baseball fan, and when he heard that Gil Hodges was being honored, the President immediately wired a telegram. Addressed to Al Bonnie, chairman of the Hodges committee, the President's telegram read:

> Through Congressman Dorn I have learned of the tribute to be given Gil Hodges by his friends in baseball and it is a pleasure to join in this occasion.

1957
Brooklyn
DODGERS

GIL HODGES
1st BASEMAN

22	**GIL HODGES**									1st Baseman				
	HEIGHT: 6'1"		WEIGHT: 200				BATS: RIGHT			THROWS: RIGHT				
	BORN: APRIL 4, 1924									PRINCETON, INDIANA				

	Games	At Bats	Hits	2B	3B	HR	HR%	R	RBI	BB	SO	SB	BA	SA
YEAR: 1957	150	579	173	28	7	27	4.7	94	98	63	91	5	.299	.511
CAREER: 18 YRS	2071	7030	1921	295	48	370	5.3	1105	1274	943	1137	63	.273	.487

7-18-57: With the Dodgers trailing the Cards 9-5 in the bottom of the 9th at Ebbets Field, GIL HODGES stroked a grand slam off Vinegar Bend Mizell to send the game into extra innings. Brooklyn won 10-9 in the 11th when Duke Snider scored on a sac bunt by Gino Cimoli. The granny by Gil was the 12th of his career and it tied Rogers Hornsby and Ralph Kiner for most in the N.L. Gil claimed sole possession of the record two weeks later when he poled another slam, this one against the Cubs in a 12-3 win at Wrigley. Always beloved by the Brooklyn fans, Gil was given a "night" on July 19, 1957, where he recieved a new Dodge in addition to many other gifts.

AIN'T NO TOOTHACHE GONNA STOP THIS MARINE!

GIL WENT 3-FOR-5 AFTER HAVING A TOOTH PULLED PRIOR TO THE GAME ON 7-26-57!

Five. July

As a distinguished player and as an outstanding gentleman, Gil Hodges makes a splendid contribution to the game. His quality of sportsmanship is an example to the youth of the land. Please give my congratulations to Gil Hodges and my best wishes to all gathered in his honor.

Anyone that knew about President Eisenhower knew that his well wishes were not just ceremony—they were sincere. He loved baseball and made it a point to throw out the ceremonial first pitch at Washington Senators opening days whenever possible. Despite all of his amazing achievements—Supreme Commander of the Allied Forces in Europe, Army Chief of Staff under President Harry S. Truman, Supreme Commander of NATO, President of Columbia University, President of the United States—Eisenhower was a frustrated baseball player. "When I was a small boy in Kansas, a friend of mine and I went fishing," Eisenhower reportedly said. "As we sat there in the warmth of the summer afternoon on a riverbank, we talked about what we wanted to do when we grew up. I told him that I wanted to be a real major league baseball player, a genuine professional like Honus Wagner. My friend said that he'd like to be President of the United States. Neither of us got our wish." So, when Eisenhower wrote his telegram to Gil, his admiration for Hodges was genuine.

As for the 28,724 fans at Ebbets Field that night, their warm feelings for Gil were genuine, too. In fact, the warm feelings they felt for him were so strong that for a few hours they were able to set aside their bitter feelings for the Brooklyn franchise and their proposed move to California and simply cheer Hodges, one of their most beloved Bums ever. "Thank you very much," Gil told the crowd when he finally stepped up to the microphone. "To all you friends, I thank you from the bottom of my heart for making this wonderful evening for me and my family. May God bless you." When all the gifts were removed and the nightcap ready to begin, Gil's dad, Charles, walked out to the mound to throw out the first pitch. With Gil squatting behind the plate, Charles threw his son a perfect strike.

* * *

Brooklyn took their third in a row from Chicago with a 7–5 victory at Ebbets Field in July 20. Don Drysdale earned his eighth win of the season, but his young batterymate, catcher John Roseboro, was knocked out of the game in the fourth inning when a Bobby Morgan foul ball fractured the index finger of John's bare hand. This came a day after Roseboro had experienced a true high—clouting his first big league homer. This was no ordinary homer, though. It was a bottom-of-the-10th, game-ending, three-run bomb in the opener of that day's twin bill. Now, 24 hours later, he was injured. Roseboro, a recent convert to catching, was quickly finding out just how physically punishing the position could be. This was just the fifth game he appeared in behind the plate for the '57 Dodgers, and he was already needing to be relieved by the man he was in there to spell—Roy Campanella. Roseboro would recover quickly and catch hundreds of games over the next decade, but he might have had second thoughts on this day about his decision to strap on the tools of ignorance. Despite Roseboro's injury on this day, it was his durability that would be one of the hallmarks of his career. Following Campanella's career-ending car accident, the starting catcher's job was handed to Rube Walker who'd long paid his dues as Campy's backup. But Walker failed to hit, and the starting job was soon offered to Roseboro. Not only did Roseboro hit—he made the '58 All-Star team. From then on, Roseboro had a lock on the position and would go on to catch more than 100 games in 11 of 12 seasons.

Gabby, as he was ironically nicknamed due to his quiet personality, was behind the plate for the Dodgers through 1967, a period of time in which the club won four pennants and three World Series titles. "Roseboro was a fierce competitor, and he was tough—a former football player," Duke Snider said. "He was great at handling pitchers, and he threw very well. Very accurately. And very intelligently. He knew how to play baseball. In 1959, when we won the World Series in L.A., Roseboro was one of the big reasons for the win." With the season on the line in the last game of the 1959 campaign, Roseboro hit an eighth-inning, go-ahead, two-run homer to beat the Cubs and force a season-ending tie with the Milwaukee Braves. Then in game one of a best-of-three playoff, Roseboro's sixth-inning solo homer turned out to be the game-winner in the Dodgers' 3–2 victory.

Reflection on Roseboro's fine career is often overshadowed by the infamous brawl in 1965 in which Giants pitcher Juan Marichal clubbed Roseboro over the head with a bat. "I think he was scared and he flipped the panic button," Roseboro said the day after the fight. Later he'd say, "The thing I'm remembered for is the Juan Marichal incident. It's too bad, because a ballplayer would like to be remembered for something better." The incident overshadowed Marichal's career, too, possibly even preventing him from election to the Hall of Fame in his first two years of eligibility. Fearing this, Marichal called Roseboro. The two had barely spoken since that dark day 17 years earlier. Marichal then asked Roseboro for an amazing favor—to publicly forgive him, something Juan

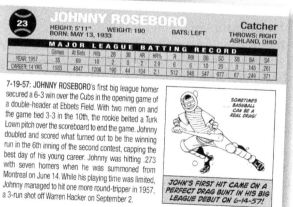

1957

Brooklyn

DODGERS

JOHNNY ROSEBORO
CATCHER

23	JOHNNY ROSEBORO									Catcher			
HEIGHT: 5'11"	WEIGHT: 190					BATS: LEFT				THROWS: RIGHT			
BORN: MAY 13, 1933										ASHLAND, OHIO			

MAJOR LEAGUE BATTING RECORD

	Games	At Bats	Hits	2B	3B	HR	HR%	R	RBI	BB	SO	SB	BA	SA
YEAR: 1957	35	69	10	2	0	2	2.9	6	6	10	20	0	.145	.261
CAREER: 14 YRS	1585	4847	1206	190	44	104	2.1	512	548	547	677	67	.249	.371

7-19-57: JOHNNY ROSEBORO's first big league homer secured a 6-3 win over the Cubs in the opening game of a double-header at Ebbets Field. With two men on and the game tied 3-3 in the 10th, the rookie belted a Turk Lown pitch over the scoreboard to end the game. Johnny doubled and scored what turned out to be the winning run in the 6th inning of the second contest, capping the best day of his young career. Johnny was hitting .273 with seven homers when he was summoned from Montreal on June 14. While his playing time was limited, Johnny managed to hit one more round-tripper in 1957, a 3-run shot off Warren Hacker on September 2.

SOMETIMES BASEBALL CAN BE A REAL DRAG!

JOHN'S FIRST HIT CAME ON A PERFECT DRAG BUNT IN HIS BIG LEAGUE DEBUT ON 6-14-57!

hoped would facilitate his election to the Hall. Incredibly, Roseboro agreed, saying, "Hey, over the years you learn to forget things." Several months later, Marichal joined the roster at Cooperstown—and Roseboro joined the roster of incredible humanitarians.

* * *

Also memorable in Brooklyn's July 20 victory—Duke Snider smashed his 300th career home run, a drive that sailed over the scoreboard in right, then bounced from Bedford Avenue to the roof of a garage before settling into a parking lot. The victim of Snider's blast was Cubs right-hander Dick Drott, who'd also dished up Duke's 286th homer a month-and-a-half earlier. The year 1957 was to be the last big power year for Snider—his fifth straight 40-plus homer season, and he joined Babe Ruth and Ralph Kiner as the only men ever to achieve the feat. With his sweet-swinging, pull-hitting style, Snider deposited a lot of baseballs on Bedford Avenue during his 11 years as a Brooklyn Dodger, including the last home run hit at Ebbets Field—a two-run, seventh-inning shot off Robin Roberts on September 22, 1957.

Born and raised in Los Angeles, one might have thought Snider would be rooting for the Dodgers to move to L.A., but that wasn't the case. He'd put down roots in Brooklyn and was hoping the Dodgers would remain there, but Snider began to believe the move was inevitable when the franchise bought his childhood team, the Pacific Coast League Los Angeles Angels, just weeks prior to the opening of the 1957 season. "Suddenly, all of us—fans, players, reporters, and everyone else—began waiting for the second shoe to drop," Snider wrote in his book *The Duke of Flatbush*.

The aforementioned game of September 22, 1957, was the second-to-the-last game ever played at Ebbets Field. Snider belted two home runs in that contest, the second of which, as mentioned, landed on Bedford Avenue. With the news of the Dodgers move to Los Angeles having already been announced by then, Snider wanted his Bedford Avenue round-tripper from that game to stand as his last memory of playing at Ebbets Field. He recalled in his book:

> After the game, I told Walt Alston I didn't want to play the next game against Pittsburgh, the last major league game that would be played in Brooklyn. I'd hit the home run onto Bedford Avenue, not knowing it would be the last by anyone, and I wanted to remember that as my last Ebbets Field experience. I was being torn away from my baseball home, and I wanted to remember her that way. Walt understood.

1957

Brooklyn

DODGERS

DUKE SNIDER

CENTERFIELDER

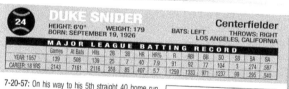

24 **DUKE SNIDER** Centerfielder
HEIGHT: 6'0"   WEIGHT: 179
BORN: SEPTEMBER 19, 1926   BATS: LEFT   THROWS: RIGHT
LOS ANGELES, CALIFORNIA

MAJOR LEAGUE BATTING RECORD

	Games	At Bats	Hits	2B	3B	HR	HR%	R	RBI	BB	SO	SB	BA	SA
YEAR: 1957	139	508	139	25	7	40	7.9	91	92	77	104	3	.274	.587
CAREER: 18 YRS	2143	7161	2116	358	85	407	5.7	1259	1333	971	1237	99	.295	.540

7-20-57: On his way to his 5th straight 40 home run season, DUKE SNIDER walloped career long ball number 300 as the Dodgers beat the Cubs 7-5 at Ebbets Field. The milestone blow, a solo shot in the 8th inning, cleared the rightfield screen, bounced from Bedford Avenue atop a garage, and then into a parking lot. It was Duke's 24th round-tripper of the season and his 8th in ten games. Despite being slowed by a troublesome left knee in '57, Duke still managed to put together the last great power season of his career. Duke would hit 407 lifetime homers, but his last in a Brooklyn uniform came on September 22, 1957, when he belted two at Ebbets Field.

HUH?!

A FAN WHO WAS HIT BY A DUKE SNIDER FOUL BALL SERVED HIM PAPERS ON 6-18-57!

A few years later, when they sent the wrecker's iron ball crashing into Ebbets Field, one of our friends, Barney Stein, a photographer in New York, sent Bev and me pictures. I saw the wall I used to aim at, the wall which Skoonj and I stood in front of and leapt against, with the familiar signs of Gem Razor Blades and Esquire Boot Polish. And I saw the clock I cleared for my first World Series home run in 1952, the one that said "Bulova—official timepiece of the Brooklyn Dodgers." Only the wall wasn't standing. In each picture, and in the ones of the grandstand and bleachers, Ebbets Field was tumbling down under the impact of that big iron ball. The good people of Brooklyn had lost their team. Now they had lost their last link to their Dodgers and to our past. At home in California, 3,000 miles away from what used to be Ebbets Field, Bev and I looked at those pictures from Barney Stein and cried.

Two years after Snider and his wife, Bev, cried while looking at the photos of Ebbets Field being demolished, Duke returned to New York to play a big-league game. As promised when the Dodgers and Giants had left the city, National League baseball had returned to New York in the form of the 1962 expansion New York Mets. It had been more than four years since New Yorkers had seen Snider play, and they were hoping to get their chance to see him again on May 30 when the Los Angeles Dodgers came to town to face the Mets at the Polo Grounds. Snider, it turned out, had a jammed wrist and would not play in the series, but that did not stop the fans from chanting, "We want Duke!", as the players prepared to take the field for pregame workouts. A roar erupted from the crowd when Snider emerged from the dressing room onto the field. "The fans were on their feet and really letting me hear them," Snider later recalled.

I talked to some of the Met outfielders, and the standing ovation continued. When I took batting practice, the fans were hollering for me to hit one out, just like old times. Carl Berringer was pitching, the best BP pitcher I ever saw because he threw nothing but strikes—except then. He couldn't get a ball over the plate to save his soul. They started to boo him, but he was finally able to throw a strike and I hit it out. The place went nuts all over again. It was the longest ovation of my career, even greater than the one I would receive the following April when I came back to New York as a Met.

July 21: Miracle Wrists Stops Time

A Sunday double-header against the visiting Cubs on July 21 saw the Dodgers lose the opener, 5–4, then bounce back in the nightcap with a 7–2 win. Big flies were limited to just two on the afternoon: Charlie

Neal homered in the first game and Cubs first baseman Bob Speake went deep in the second game. Those long-balls were not the topic of discussion, however, as they were overshadowed by a batting practice clout by Dodger leftfielder Sandy Amoros. "Amoros stopped the clock over the scoreboard with a batting practice drive at 1:23 P.M.," wrote Roscoe McGowen of the *New York Times*. "Later the timepiece was started again."

At five-foot-seven and 170 lbs., Amoros was not a feared slugger, but he could muscle up on occasion, and did so in 1956 when he hit a career-high 16 round-trippers. One man who wasn't surprised by Amoros' power was the scout who signed him back in 1952, Al Campanis, who'd nicknamed the little Cuban "Miracle Wrists." Amoros had come to Campanis' attention thanks to a tip from Billy Herman who managed the Cienfuegos team in the Cuban League in the winter of 1951–52. Amoros batted .333 for Havana that season and was named a league All-Star. It was in Havana that Edmundo Amoros got his nickname "Sandy." Teammate Bert Haas thought Amoros resembled featherweight boxer Sandy Saddler, tagged Amoros with the moniker, and over time it stuck. Based on Herman's tip, Campanis moved in and signed Amoros to the Dodgers for a $1,000 bonus.

Amoros began his career with the Dodgers with an assignment to their Triple-A St. Paul affiliate in the American Association. By August Amoros was hitting .337 with 19 home runs for the Saints, prompting Dodgers' chief scout Andy High to comment that Amoros had been worthy of a $150,000 bonus. Worthy as he may have been, Amoros was not, of course, given an extra $149,000. He was, however, called up to the big club on August 21, 1952, to help the Dodgers in their drive for the pennant—and help them he did the next day in his debut appearance. Enjoying a big lead over the Pirates in the first game of a double-header at Forbes Field, Dodger manager Charlie Dressen sent Amoros in to pinch hit in the ninth with one out and Gil Hodges on second. Amoros connected for a single off Pittsburgh right-hander Woody Main, then came all the way around to score when the ball got through the legs of Bucs centerfielder Brandy Davis. Amoros' speed, and Hodges' lack of it, was quite apparent from the sight of Gil crossing the plate with Sandy right on his heels.

Amoros played sparingly through the rest of the '52 season, hitting just .250 in 44 at-bats. "Change-ups fooled Miracle Wrists," wrote Roger Kahn, and Amoros was back in the minors for the entire '53 season. Amoros had a big year at Montreal in 1953—.353 with 23 home runs

	Games	At Bats	Hits	2B	3B	HR	HR%	R	RBI	BB	SO	SB	BA	SA
YEAR: 1957	106	238	66	7	1	7	2.9	40	26	46	42	3	.277	.403
CAREER: 7 YRS	517	1311	334	55	23	43	3.3	215	180	211	189	18	.255	.430

7-21-57: The Dodgers and Cubs split a double-header at Ebbets Field, leaving Brooklyn in 2nd place in the crowded battle for the National League pennant. The Chicago pitchers kept the fireworks to a minimum with the only Dodger home run of the day coming off the bat of Charlie Neal. However, one of the more momorable Brooklyn homers of the year came before the start of the twin bill. With former Dodger hero Joe Black pitching batting practice, **SANDY AMOROS** drove a ball off the famous Bulova clock over the rightfield scoreboard, stopping the timepiece at 1:23 PM sharp. Technicians got the clock restarted later that afternoon.

THIS REMINDS ME OF THE 1955 WORLD SERIES!

SANDY MADE A GAME-SAVING CIRCUS CATCH IN THE LEFTFIELD CORNER ON 9-5-57!

and 100 RBIs, yet he was not called up to Brooklyn. There was specu-
lation that, again, the Dodgers were reluctant to overload their lineup
with black players, and that resulted in Amoros remaining in Montreal.
He was back with Brooklyn when the 1954 season opened, however,
sent down in May, then brought back up for the remainder of the season in July. In 1955 Amoros finally become the primary leftfielder for the
Dodgers. He hit just .247 in 119 games, but cemented himself as an eternal hero for Brooklyn fans when he made his now-famous game-saving
catch in game seven of the '55 World Series. For the true Flatbush
Faithful, Amoros' Series heroics went back to game five when his
second-inning, two-run homer gave Brooklyn a lead they never relin-
quished—but it was "The Catch" for which he is forever remembered.

Now, in the ESPN era of non-stop 24-hour sports highlights, Amoros' catch does not have the visual sex appeal of the athletic circus
catches shown daily on the network. Amoros' catch probably wouldn't
even make ESPN's nightly Top Ten highlights. Shading way toward center against Yogi Berra, a lefty-swinging pull-hitter, Amoros had to run
full speed for approximately 100 feet in order to catch Berra's slicing
drive. Amoros hauled it in just shy of the leftfield foul line with only a
few short feet between himself and the unpadded wall, then fired the
ball to Pee Wee Reese who was able to double Gil McDougald off first. It
was the timing of Amoros' clutch play, and the losing legacy of Brooklyn's past, that combined to elevate the play to mythic status. Better
catches have been made, but none more important to the story arc of
a fabled franchise. Sportswriters' words, not ESPN highlights, determined the narrative in those times, and the sportswriters knew that the
play they had witnessed Amoros make was one of the all-time greats.
They wrote it that way, and their conclusion still holds up today.

"I dunno. I run like hell," was how Amoros, who spoke only broken English, described his catch after the game. "It really too good to
describe." *Bohemia Magazine*, the most popular news-weekly of its day
in Cuba, did its best to describe it for its readers with a caption below a
photo of a smiling Amoros. "His performance in the World Series has
produced intense joy in our nation ... a triumph and corroboration for
the quality of our sports ... and assure him a place of honor in the history of the pastime of Cuba." Brooklyn couldn't have agreed more.

* * *

The second-place Dodgers took to the road for a six-city road
trip beginning with a 1–0 win in St. Louis on July 23. Johnny Podres

went the distance to gain the shutout, his league-leading fifth white-washing. Brooklyn collected just three hits off Cardinals right-hander Toothpick Sam Jones, but a timely run-scoring single by Rube Walker in the second inning was just enough to get a win. Brooklyn again totaled just three hits the next day, July 24, but this time it wasn't enough as the Cards got their retribution in a 3–0 victory. Sal Maglie pitched well in the loss after a shaky start in which he surrendered a run in the first and another in the third. Known for his tendency to pitch inside, The Barber kiddingly hinted that Alvin Dark might need to be on his toes at the plate after an earlier incident where he knocked Maglie down, but nothing came of the threat. St. Louis won the series by capturing the finale, 3–2, on July 25. The Dodgers' bats continued to be anemic, mustering just six hits against Redbirds right-hander Herm Wehmeier. Brooklyn totaled just 12 hits for the three-game set. Like a lot of Dodgers, Roy Campanella's bat had been stone cold as of late, so he sat out the game. He did, however, smoke a scorching line drive during batting practice, scoring a direct hit on Don Zimmer's ankle. "That's the first hard ball Campy's hit in a month," cracked Zip, "and look where I am!"

The Dodgers' road-trip moved to Crosley Field in Cincinnati on July 26. Brooklyn's bats came to life in an 11 hits attack, but they couldn't keep up with the Reds' 14 hits and fell, 6–5. The game was a long, three-hour, 11-inning affair. Brooklyn attempted to grab the lead in the top of the 11th when Randy Jackson lined a single to right field with Gil Hodges on second base. It was deja vu for Hodges who scored in the first when Jackson singled him home, so Gil once again tried to score. This time, however, he was cut down at the plate by a perfect peg from Reds right fielder Wally Post. Cincinnati made Brooklyn pay in the bottom of the inning when Reds reliever Hersh Freeman whacked a two-bagger off the scoreboard, then crossed with the game-winner following a single by Johnny Temple.

July 27: Handsome Ransom Goes Down Again

Two-run homers by Gil Hodges and Carl Furillo had Danny McDevitt on his way to a 5–0 shutout as he toed the rubber to start the ninth inning in Cincinnati on July 27. By the time the inning ended, however, Clem Labine had to be called in to douse a fire and secure a 5–3 triumph for the Dodgers. A nightmare season for Dodgers third baseman Randy

Jackson continued in this game when his knee buckled while fielding a foul dribbler off the bat of Johnny Temple in the third inning. It was something Handsome Ransom had done very well throughout his seven years in the big leagues—coming in and fielding slow rollers with his bare hand, then gunning out baserunners at first. But nothing was easy anymore since Jackson's knee was injured back on April 26 in a collision at first base with the Pirates' Frank Thomas. "I stepped on first base," said Jackson in his easy-going, matter-of-fact Arkansas drawl, "and Thomas came down on top of me and bent my knee the wrong way." Jackson missed 2½ months after his run-in with Thomas, and he'd been back in the lineup for just two weeks before his knee gave out on this day. Randy gutted it out for two more innings before finally giving way to Pee Wee Reese in the fifth.

Fragility wasn't the reason Jackson got injured in the collision with Thomas. It was always a potentially dangerous situation when runner and first baseman arrived at the bag at the same instant. Throw in the fact that the six-foot-three, 200-lb. Thomas was new at first base and you have a formula for disaster—particularly for Jackson who gave up two inches and twenty pounds to Thomas. Jackson was tough and had survived the rough-and-tumble rigors of big-time college football without serious injury, yet he was no match for the lumbering Thomas that unfortunate day in April. Through the U.S. Navy's officer training program during World War II, Jackson was sent to Texas Christian University for a year-and-a-half where he played baseball and football. He was then transferred to the University of Texas for another year-and-a-half where he also played baseball and football. As it turned out, Jackson, who played halfback and defensive back, played in the 1945 Cotton Bowl for TCU and then the 1946 Cotton Bowl with UT. Future Dallas Cowboys head coach Tom Landry was a teammate of Jackson on the Texas football team, as was future football Hall of Famer Bobby Layne who was also a star on the baseball team. "In the two years I played baseball with Bobby at Texas," recalled Jackson, "he was 28-and-0 as a pitcher, which isn't too bad."

Jackson had been a fine player with the Cubs for six seasons before the Dodgers traded for him in December of 1955. He'd been Chicago's regular third baseman from 1951 to 1955, averaging 20 homers per season and earning a spot on the N.L. All-Star team in '54 and '55. Brooklyn acquired Jackson with the plan of platooning him at third base in 1956 with the aging Jackie Robinson, then eventually handing the full-time job to Randy when Robinson retired. Robinson wasn't too keen on the platooning idea and it caused some friction between him and Walter Alston, but it worked well for the ballclub. Jackson appeared in 101 games (80 at third base) for the '56 Dodgers and hit .274 with eight homers and 53 RBIs; Robinson appeared in 117 games (72 at third base) and batted .275 with 10 home runs and 43 RBIs. The friction between Robinson and Alston over platooning did not extend to Jackie and Randy. In fact, Randy admired Robinson as one of the best. "Jackie Robinson could do everything," said Jackson. "He was the best all-around player I ever played with or against. He was a great hitter. He stole a lot of bases. And he was a great defensive player. He just really knew baseball."

Everything continued according to plan in 1957. Robinson retired and Jackson was the opening day starter, but it all went south for Randy when he wrecked his knee in the collision with Frank Thomas. Jackson played in just 26 more games for the '57 Dodgers after he re-injured his knee on July 27, many of those appearances as a pinch-hitter. He went with the team to Los Angeles in 1958, but appeared in only 17 games for them before being sold to the Cleveland Indians on August 4. There is no doubt, Jackson's knee injury robbed him of some potentially good years with the Dodgers, and he was out of baseball by 1960 at the age of 34.

Despite it being the place where he suffered his career-shortening injury, Jackson loved playing for Brooklyn. It was quite a contrast to playing for the Cubs who struggled to win during Jackson's years with them. He recalled:

> With the Cubs, when you come to Ebbets Field you're about two runs behind before you even walk to the plate—because of the crowd and the intimidation of playing there, and the teams they had. The Dodgers had fantastic players. When you switch and come over there, it's like old home week. Everybody loves you and you love everybody, and you feel like you're the one that's intimidating the other teams when they come in because of the closeness of the fans, and the fact that most of them had about 48 cards in their deck. They were a little short on cards. And they had that band. It was about the only place that had something like that. It was a really fun place to play, especially if you were winning. And I wasn't used to winning with the Cubs, so this was quite a change.

In the grand scheme of things, Jackson's impact on the Brooklyn Dodgers was limited by the brevity of his time there and his knee injury. Still, he was there long enough to do something that would ensure that his name is forever linked to Dem Bums—he hit the last home run in franchise history. No one from the Dodgers homered in the last game of

1957

Brooklyn

DODGERS

RANDY JACKSON
3rd BASEMAN

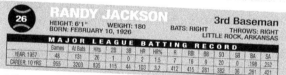

26	RANDY JACKSON									3rd Baseman			
HEIGHT: 6'1" WEIGHT: 180								BATS: RIGHT THROWS: RIGHT					
BORN: FEBRUARY 10, 1926								LITTLE ROCK, ARKANSAS					

MAJOR LEAGUE BATTING RECORD

	Games	At Bats	Hits	2B	3B	HR	HR%	R	RBI	BB	SO	SB	BA	SA
YEAR: 1957	48	131	26	1	0	2	1.5	7	16	9	20	0	.198	.252
CAREER: 10 YRS	955	3203	835	115	44	103	3.2	412	415	281	382	36	.261	.421

7-27-57: Carl Furillo and Gil Hodges were feeling great as each contributed 2-run homers in the Dodgers' 5-3 victory over the Reds at Crosley Field. Not feeling so great was Brooklyn 3rd baseman **RANDY JACKSON**. While fielding a foul roller from Johnny Temple, "Handsome Ransom" reinjured his left knee and was forced to leave the game. Randy originally injured the knee in a violent collision with Frank Thomas at 1st base against the Pirates on April 26. The damaged knee reduced Randy's effectiveness while limiting him to just 48 games in 1957, and sadly hastened the former All-Star's exit from the game following the 1959 season.

IT'S THE END OF AN ERA!

RANDY HIT THE LAST BROOKLYN DODGER HOMER ON 9-28-57!

the season, so Jackson's three-run shot in the previous game, September 28, turned out to be the final long-ball ever hit by a Brooklyn Dodger. There was no fanfare made over it at the time, and for decades Jackson didn't even know it. "I was the last Brooklyn Dodger to hit a home run," Jackson revealed in the early-2000s.

> I found that out several years ago. I hit it off Don Cardwell. My son called me from down south Georgia and said, "Dad, did you watch *Good Morning America*?" I said, "No I didn't—I was shaving." He said, "Well, your name was mentioned." I said, "Why would I be on *Good Morning America*?" It was a trivia question: "Who was the last Brooklyn Dodger to hit a home run?" He said, "I just happened to be listening to it and your name came up." I said, "That's news to me!"

It's old news to Jackson now, and he has since signed countless ball and photos this way: "Ransom Jackson, last Brooklyn Dodger to hit a home run 9/28/57."

* * *

"Balls that cross the plate on the first bounce don't count as strikes!" hollered Don Newcombe from the dugout to plate umpire Stan Landes after the heavy-set ump called a strike on the first pitch thrown to Jim Gilliam by Reds right-hander Brooks Lawrence in the first inning. In a flash, a shouting match erupted between Newcombe and Landes with Walter Alston quickly jumping in. The incident appeared over, but reignited after the inning, prompting Alston and Newcombe to be ejected. It mattered not for Brooklyn as they went on the win the series finale against Cincinnati, 7–2, behind a complete game from Johnny Podres and a grand slam by Carl Furillo on July 28. It was Podres' ninth victory of the season and Furillo's eighth career slam—four of which he'd hit at Crosley Field.

After an off-day on Monday, the Dodgers opened a five-game series against the Chicago Cubs at Wrigley Field with a double-header on July 30. Brooklyn had been charging hard at the first-place Milwaukee Braves, pulling to within 1½ games by winning 15 of their last 18, but the best the Dodgers could do against the cellar-dwelling Cubs on this day was a split. Sal Maglie and Clem Labine combined to produce a 1–0 shutout in the opener despite the fact that Moe Drabowsky struck out 11 Dodgers. The quirky Cubs hurler had whiffed 33 Dodgers in 30½ innings so far in 1957, but all he had to show for it was a 1-and-3 record against Brooklyn. Newcombe started the nightcap but wasn't sharp and lasted just six innings before being relieved by Sandy Koufax. Charlie

Neal and Sandy Amoros homered for the Brooks, but it wasn't enough as the Cubs came out on top, 4–3.

July 31: Roebuck Sears Cubs

Chicago and Brooklyn squared off for their second twin-bill in two days on July 31 at Wrigley Field, and when the day was done Dodger right-hander Ed Roebuck emerged with the win in both games. Roebuck entered the opener in the seventh inning with the Dodgers trailing, 2–1. He tossed two scoreless innings, and by the time he gave way to closer Clem Labine in the ninth, Brooklyn was leading, 3–2. Labine closed the door to earn his 14th save. Roebuck was later called upon in the eighth inning of the nightcap with Brooklyn again trailing by a run. Ed again held the Cubs scoreless and was again the recipient of a two-run Dodgers rally. He once again gave way to Labine who pitched the ninth to earn the save as the Dodgers triumphed, 2–1. The final tally on Roebuck's big day: 3 innings, 3 hits, 1 strikeout, 0 walks, 0 runs, 2 wins.

Roebuck had been in the Dodgers organization since 1949 when he was signed out of Brownsville High School in southwestern Pennsylvania. He fully came into his own while with Triple-A Montreal from 1952 to 1954, culminating with an 18-win, 3.07-ERA season in 1954. "I went from trying to overpower hitters to making the ball move," Roebuck said of his time in the minors. "I started to understand that I should be able to pitch to both sides of the plate and that I had a natural sinker when I reduced speed for a bigger break."

When he followed his fine 1954 season with a solid spring training in 1955, Dodgers general manager Buzzie Bavasie decided it was time to bring Roebuck up to Brooklyn. "Buzzie called me into the office when we got to Brooklyn after spring training to tell me I made the team and have me sign a contract for the minimum, which was about $5,500 then," Roebuck said. "We also agreed at that point that if I stuck for 30 days I would get a $250 bonus." With an eye on the $250 bonus, Roebuck bore down. Pitching strictly out of the bullpen, he worked a heavy load of 34 games by the All-Star break, tallying a 5-and-5 record and an impressive 2.43 ERA.

Right before the All-Star break I went to see Buzzie to remind him that I had lasted longer than 30 days and was due my bonus. Buzzie then told me that they didn't give those bonuses anymore because they had given one to Clyde

King and he didn't win a game the rest of the season. So in my case, they didn't give me a bonus—and I didn't win a game the rest of the season.

As Roebuck indicated, he struggled in the second half after his meeting with Bavasi, appearing in just 14 games and watching his ERA rise to 4.17 by season's end. Despite his second-half swoon, Roebuck ended the season on a high note as the Dodgers defeated the Yankees in the World Series. Ed made one appearance in the Series, tossing two scoreless innings in game six.

The 1956 season was very similar to '55 for Roebuck—a strong first half and a bit of a fade in the second half. The conclusion was different this year, however, as the Dodgers again reached the World Series—but this time they would not earn a high school–like championship ring, instead falling to the Yankees four games to three. Roebuck pitched well in the Series, though, retiring 13 of 14 batters he faced in three games. The one batter to reach was Mickey Mantle, who walloped a 440-foot solo homer in game four at Yankee Stadium.

The year 1957 turned out to be Roebuck's best season with Brooklyn. Appearing in 44 games, he compiled an 8-and-2 record with a 2.71 ERA in 96⅓ innings pitched. And instead of fading in the second half, Roebuck got stronger in the dog days of '57—and was perhaps the Dodgers' best pitcher for the final three months of the season, with a 1.39 ERA in that span. The year of 1957 also featured a few special moments that Roebuck would not experience in any other year of his big-league career: starting a game and homering in a game. Roebuck appeared in more than 450 games during his 11-year big league career, but only once did he start—on June 9, 1957. Walter Alston gave Roebuck a surprise spot start that day in the second game of a Monday double-header. Ed pitched well enough to win, surrendering just two runs in five innings while striking out six Cincinnati Reds, but he was bested by right-hander Hal Jeffcoat—a converted outfielder who that day tossed the only shut-out of his career. Roebuck took the tough luck, 3–0 loss.

Roebuck belted just two home runs in his career, and both came in 1957. The first was a solo shot off Cincy's Raul Sanchez in the opening game of a twin-bill at Ebbets Field on August 20. Eleven days later Roebuck homered again at Ebbets; the victim this time was Giants right-hander Stu Miller. While Roebuck homered just these two times in 137 major league at-bats, he was considered a good-hitting pitcher. In fact, when Roebuck suffered serious arm trouble in 1958 and '59, Buzzie Bavasi, in an effort to take advantage of Ed's bat, sent Roebuck

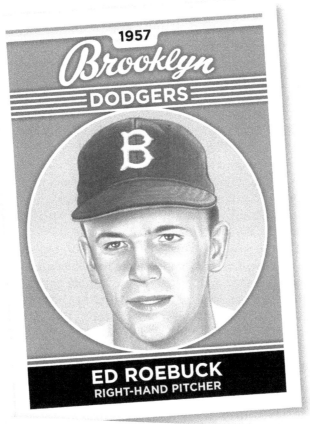

1957
Brooklyn
DODGERS

ED ROEBUCK
RIGHT-HAND PITCHER

ED ROEBUCK

27

	Right-Hand Pitcher
HEIGHT: 6'2" WEIGHT: 185	BATS: RIGHT THROWS: RIGHT
BORN: JULY 3, 1931	EAST MILLSBORO, PENNSYLVANIA

MAJOR LEAGUE PITCHING RECORD

	Games	IP	Won	Lost	Pct	Hits	Runs	ER	SO	Walks	ERA
YEAR: 1957	44	96.1	8	2	.800	70	37	29	73	46	2.71
CAREER: 11 YRS	460	791	52	31	.627	753	374	294	477	302	3.35

7-31-57: Brooklyn closed out the month of August with a double-header sweep of the Cubs at Wrigley Field. Picking up the win in both games was Dodgers relief ace **ED ROEBUCK**. Ed pitched just three innings total, but he allowed no runs and upped his record to 3-and-1. Dodger manager Walter Alston had leaned heavily on Ed since his rookie season of 1955 when his 12 saves and two scoreless innings in the World Series helped Brooklyn win their one and only championship. 1957 saw more of the same as Alston summoned Ed from the pen 43 times, as well as giving him a spot start in the second half of a twin bill against Cincinnati on June 9.

ED EARNED A VICTORY AND ALSO HIT HIS FIRST MAJOR LEAGUE HOMER ON 8-20-57!

to Triple-A St. Paul where he was to try and reinvent himself as a first baseman. As it turned out, Roebuck's arm miseries were cured when the painful adhesions in his shoulder broke loose following a snap throw he made while playing at first.

There were many ups and downs on the ballfield for Roebuck after the 1957 season. He remained with the Dodger franchise into the 1963 season before moving on to pitch for the Senators and Phillies, then embarked on a long career as a scout in 1968. Looking back, though, Roebuck fondly recalls his days with the Dodgers as some of his best in baseball—and he considers the 1955 championship experience the high-light of his days in Brooklyn. "It looks like a high school graduation ring," Roebuck said of his '55 World Series ring. "I'm afraid to wear it because the blue part is crumbling." He earned another World Series ring for his work scouting with the 2004 Boston Red Sox, and that ring, remarked Roebuck, looked like it was made by Tiffany.

Based on the colorful history that preceded Brooklyn's long-awaited 1955 title, it seems perfectly appropriate that the cherished ring from that special ballclub would have a quirky, humble quality about it. "I've been offered huge amounts of money for it," explained Roebuck, "but not because of how it's made or what it looks like. The value in my Dodger ring is that it's the *first* and *only* Brooklyn championship ring." Arm trouble, season-ending failures, and other circumstances may have cost Roebuck as many as four more championship rings, but he never let the failures steal the joy from the successes like the 1955 championship. "I have no complaints," he said. "I had a good time."

Six

August

"Dodgers Disclaim Firm Moving Plan," wrote the *New York Times* as July gave way to August. With four months of the 1957 season in the rearview mirror, the people of Brooklyn were no more clear on the future of their Dodgers than they were when the season opened. Two immovable forces were still being unmoved by the other. Immovable force number one, Dodgers owner Walter O'Malley, wanted a new stadium at Atlantic and Flatbush avenues in Brooklyn. He was willing to put $5,000,000 toward the construction, then pay a "reasonable rent" for the use of the arena. Immovable force number two, Park Commissioner Robert Moses, rejected the Atlantic and Flatbush site, instead offering a location in Flushing Meadows in Queens. Moses also believed that O'Malley's offer of $5,000,000 toward construction was not a "fair share" of what the Dodgers should pay for an arena that was estimated to cost at least five times that amount.

The battle between the two men also appeared to have become personal, something that seemed not in the best interest of Brooklyn fans. "For years, Walter and his chums have kept us dizzy and confused," Moses told the *Times*. "He has memorized a speech indicating that he would die for old Brooklyn. I have heard this speech over and over again ad nauseam. From time to time Walter has embroidered it with shamrocks, harps, and wolfhounds, and has added the bouquet of liqueur and Irish whiskey." Moses solidified his doubt that O'Malley cared about Brooklyn by saying that he believed the Dodgers were "already on their way to the West Coast."

"Mr. Moses is speaking only for Moses," O'Malley said. He claimed that city officials, which included Moses, had twice "sabotaged" his efforts to keep the team in Brooklyn, and warned that "time was running out" as Los Angeles was coming up with "constructive" proposals to bring the Dodgers there. However, O'Malley said his mind was still "open" to ways to keep the Dodgers in Brooklyn, but he said that the city officials behind the recent effort to hold the Dodgers at home had better "show something" more concrete than previous actions.

Meanwhile, the Brooklyn Dodgers played on, opening the new month with a 12–3 rout of the Cubs at Wrigley Field on Thursday, August 1. With the win the Dodgers remained just 1½ games behind the first-place Braves, but it was the last time in franchise history that the *Brooklyn* Dodgers would ever be that close to the National League lead, as their slow descent away would begin the next day. But on August 1 Brooklyn fans still had hopes for another Dodger pennant run as a Gil Hodges grand slam and a Sandy Koufax four-hitter powered the Bums to victory. It was just Koufax's fifth win of the season, and only his ninth win since he joined the Dodgers in 1955. No-hitters, a perfect game, ERA crowns, 20-win seasons, strikeout titles, Cy Young Awards, and an MVP Award—they were all in the future for Koufax, but those successes were still unfathomable for Sandy in 1957 as he struggled to simply get the ball over the plate. It was a vicious circle—he wasn't going to conquer his wildness unless he pitched often, but Walter Alston was reluctant to pitch Koufax with regularity because of the bases on balls.

The reality was that Koufax had pitched very little in his entire life. He'd played some sandlot ball and didn't even play baseball in high school until his senior year at Brooklyn's Lafayette High in 1953. Even then he had to be urged by friends to try out for the team, and mostly he played first base. Actually, basketball was the sport in which the six-foot-two-inch, muscular Koufax excelled at in high school. He was a strong rebounder with great jumping ability. "Sandy was an incredible athlete," said Burt Abramowitz, a childhood friend. "When he was 14, he had these muscles. He didn't lift weights. No one did back then. And he could jump like a kangaroo. I'd play on the second team and we'd guard each other, and he said, 'If I could shoot like you, I'd be in the NBA.' I'd say: 'Give me your legs, I'd start in the NBA.'"

The 1953 Lafayette High School Yearbook said that Koufax "has been scouted and will most likely be a professional basketball player." He ended up going to the University of Cincinnati where he did well on the Bearcats' freshman basketball team. Coach Ed Jucker felt that Koufax had the ability to make it as a pro basketball player, but Jucker was also the baseball coach at Cincinnati and was impressed with the pitching he'd seen Koufax do on the fall baseball squad. Martin Stolzenberg, Koufax's former basketball teammate at Lafayette, ran into Koufax back in Brooklyn during Christmas break and was surprised at what they discussed.

"I saw him on 86th Street in Bensonhurst," Stolzenberg said, "and I asked him, "How are you doing at school, Sandy?" and he said, "I've been playing fall baseball, and Cincinnati, the Dodgers, and Pittsburgh are interested in me." I nodded my head, said, "Uh-huh," and I went around the neighborhood saying, "Sandy is out of his mind; he thinks he's going to be a baseball player.""

Koufax returned to the University of Cincinnati after Christmas break, determined to make good on the baseball team. While he suffered the same control problems that would plague him for years, he showed flashes of greatness that could not be ignored. He threw a four-hitter and struck out 16 against Wayne. He set a school record by striking out 18 against Louisville. He ended the season with a 3-and-1 record with 51 strikeouts in 31 innings. It was a small sample size, but it was enough to draw serious interest from major league scouts. Trying to capitalize on the fact that Koufax was Jewish, the Yankees dispatched a Jewish scout. This, in addition to their offer of only $4,000, offended the Koufax family, so they passed on the Yanks. Next there was a failed tryout with the Giants at the Polo Grounds. Koufax did not bring his glove and had to borrow one from Giants pitcher Johnny Antonelli. Koufax was uptight and wild, and the Giants did not make an offer.

Following a tip from Jimmy Murphy, a *Brooklyn Eagle* reporter who covered school sports, Dodgers scout Al Campanis arranged for Koufax to work out at Ebbets Field in front of general manager Buzzie Bavasi and Alston. They liked what they saw. On December 14, 1954—almost exactly a year after Koufax told Stolzenberg about his interest in playing big league baseball—Sandy signed with the Dodgers for a $14,000 bonus and a $6,000 salary. And that's when the vicious circle began. Alston favored experience over youth, and the fact that the Dodgers were in the hunt for the pennant in 1955 meant that Walter felt he had little opportunity to work on developing Koufax. It was June 24, 1955, before Koufax made his big-league debut in a relief appearance at Milwaukee. By the time the 1957 season rolled around, Koufax had appeared in only 28 games over the course of the 1955–56 seasons, starting just 15 times while compiling a mere 100⅓ innings.

The Dodgers seemed determined to pitch Koufax more in 1957, so they sent him to Caguas Criollos of the Puerto Rican winter league to work on his control following the 1956 season. Tim Thompson caught Koufax while there, and his theory was that Sandy's control problems were not always because he couldn't throw strikes, but often it was his reputation for wildness that caused issues with umpires. "The reputation followed him, and the umps went along," said Thompson. "He could throw the ball close to the plate and they'd call it a ball because the umpire expected him to throw balls. I think they squeezed him." Because of roster regulations regarding foreign players, Koufax did not play a full season at Caguas. His record was an unspectacular 3-and-6, but Sandy, as usual, showed flashes of greatness, including a one-hit shutout and a two-hit shutout.

When Koufax showed up at spring training a few weeks later, he looked to be in the best shape of his brief career. "His physical condition is better with his weight down," wrote Roscoe McGowen of the *New York Times*. "He looks much trimmer and seems to have a much better all-around coordination. Maybe until this year he had the awkwardness of an overgrown kid. Anyway, here he is, and here he will probably stay." That was a reference to the fact that Koufax would be eligible to be sent down to the minors when his Bonus Rule restriction expired on May 15. But McGowen, like almost any who saw Koufax pitch, recognized the southpaw's brilliant talent and felt like he had the stuff to remain with the big club. And he did for the entire 1957 season—and the rest of his career, in fact, for Koufax would never spend a day in the minor leagues. But after showing legitimate signs of improvement in '57, especially after his high-profile victory back on May 16, Koufax developed forearm soreness and pitched very little in June and July.

The year 1957 saw another small step forward in the progression of Koufax. He finished with a 5-and-4 record in 104⅓ innings pitched—and an eye-popping 122 strikeouts. He would struggle for a few more years to put it all together, but when he finally figured it out, he was spectacular. Unfortunately for Brooklyn fans, they did not get to witness Koufax's greatness—that privilege would be enjoyed by fans in Los Angeles. And while Koufax's era of true greatness would come in L.A., he would always have fond memories of Ebbets Field. "My first memory of Ebbets Field was in high school," said Koufax. His parents would take him and his step-sister "to one game a year. It would start at eleven in the morning. You'd see the game, then get on the subway and go home. Of course, I grew up in Brooklyn, so it was special for me to play in the stadium where I watched Hodges and Snider and Jackie and Pee Wee and Newk. Those were guys I saw playing when I was a kid." It seemed only fitting that Sandy Koufax would turn out to be the last man to throw a pitch in a Brooklyn Dodgers uniform. That happened on September 29, 1957, when the Brooklyn-born lefty struck out the Phillies' Willie Jones on three pitches in the last game in Brooklyn Dodgers history.

1957
Brooklyn
DODGERS

SANDY KOUFAX
LEFT-HAND PITCHER

28 **SANDY KOUFAX** Left-Hand Pitcher
HEIGHT: 6'2" WEIGHT: 210 BATS: RIGHT THROWS: LEFT
BORN: DECEMBER 30, 1935 BROOKLYN, NEW YORK

MAJOR LEAGUE PITCHING RECORD

	Games	IP	Won	Lost	Pct	Hits	Runs	ER	SO	Walks	ERA
YEAR: 1957	34	104.1	5	4	.556	83	49	45	122	51	3.88
CAREER: 12 YRS	397	2324.1	165	87	.655	1754	806	713	2396	817	2.76

8-1-57: Continuing the process of learning to master his rocket-like pitching arm, 21-year-old bonus baby **SANDY KOUFAX** turned in one of his best outings of the year as he struck out 11 Cubs in a 4-hit win at Wrigley Field. The 11 K's lifted Sandy's 1957 total to a major league best 94 in just 76-2/3 innings pitched. A sore arm slowed the southpaw in June, but he rebounded to pitch well in 21 appearances from July 4 through September 29. Sandy's name finally came off the bonus baby list on May 16, meaning the Dodgers could now send him down to the minors if they chose, but he was in the bigs to stay – and he whiffed 13 Cubs that day to prove it.

ALRIGHT, TIME TO END IT!

SANDY GOT A WIN IN RELIEF BY PITCHING A PERFECT 14TH INNING AT MIDNIGHT ON 5-6-57!

* * *

Brooklyn won six of eight games from July 27–August 1, but something happened on August 2 to cool them off—they departed Chicago and arrived in Milwaukee. Four of their six previous wins had been at the expense of the last-place Cubs, but now the Dodgers would be facing the second-place Braves—and they lost the series opener, 1–0. A fine performance by Johnny Podres was wasted as the Dodger hitters failed to solve Braves six-foot-eight-inch right-hander Gene Conley. Conley, who also doubled as a forward in the NBA, was the hitting hero, too, driving in the only run with a line single in the fifth inning. The Dodgers pitching staff delivered another crackerjack performance the next day when Danny McDevitt and Ed Roebuck combined to hold the Braves to one run. This time Brooklyn won, however, when the bats finally awoke with four runs in the eighth and two more in the ninth to run the final score to 7–1.

The Braves took the series by defeating the Dodgers in the finale, 9–7, on August 4. Milwaukee exploded for four home runs in the game, but Brooklyn still had a chance to take the lead in the ninth when Jim Gilliam was rung up with the bat on his shoulder and the bases loaded to end the game. It was not your standard punch-out, though, and the way it went down caused the home plate ump to be swarmed by protesting Dodgers. Wrote the *New York Times*:

> The game ended in a dispute, with all the Dodgers, including manager Walter Alston, storming around Eddie Sudol, the plate umpire. With a one-ball two-strike count on Jim Gilliam, Sudol made no gesture on the next pitch by Warren Spahn, until Del Rice, the catcher, triumphantly waved the ball and started for the dugout. Then Sudol's arm went up in an emphatic strike call. In their anger the Dodgers apparently were charging that Rice had usurped the umpire's powers.

In reality, it was simply that after years of finishing second to pennant-winning Brooklyn teams, the Braves had finally usurped the Dodgers' powers, surpassing them as the team to beat in the National League. And by the time the powers shifted back to the Dodgers, the team would belong to Los Angeles.

August 5: Chop Top Saves the Night ... Again

With the Ebbets Field clock atop the right field scoreboard reading approximately 10:35 p.m., Walter Alston signaled to the bullpen for ace fireman Clem Labine. It was only August 5, yet it was the 47th time Alston had gone to Labine for relief. Leading 5–2 with two out in the bottom of the ninth, the Dodgers were in a tight spot. Don Drysdale had battled for 8⅔ innings, but now Willie Mays was striding to the plate with Giants runners on first and second. Alston didn't want to put the tying run on first base by intentionally walking Mays, but he also didn't want to see Drysdale pitch to Willie again. Mays already had four hits off Big D, including a home run in the third. Drysdale had to "low bridge" Mays in the seventh to keep Willie from digging too deep a toe-hold, but all that did was hold Mays to a single. So, Drysdale gave the ball to Alston who then handed it to Labine, and the crafty 30-year-old right-hander (Labine would turn 31 the next day) went to work on Mays. Carefully locating his fastball to set up his curve and sinker, Labine ran the count full to Mays. Clem curved Willie on the pay-off pitch, and Mays hit a routine grounder to shortstop Charlie Neal who threw Willie out easily at first base. Labine had done it again, and the save was his 16th of the season.

Labine was in his fifth full year with the Dodgers by the 1957 season, and he was at the peak of his effectiveness in spite of some mid-season shoulder soreness that hampered him for a few weeks. In fact, Labine had been one of the game's best relievers for a few years. Toting a heavy load for skipper Walter Alston, Labine had led the National League with 60 appearances in 1955. He topped that by pitching in 62 games in 1956 and leading the circuit in saves. He would again lead the league in saves in 1957. Labine earned well-deserved All-Star selections in '56 and '57, the only two All-Star appearances in his 13-year big league career.

Sporting a friendly smile and a distinctive crew cut that earned him the nickname "Chop-Top," Labine was an important man on four Brooklyn pennant winners—1952, 1953, 1955, and 1956—yet he landed with the Dodgers through pure luck. Gus Sabaria, Labine's Woonsocket High School baseball coach, knew a scout for the Boston Braves, so a tryout for Labine was scheduled at Braves Field on a day the Dodgers happened to be in town in 1944. Recalled Labine:

> My coach and I went to old Braves Field, but we couldn't get into the dressing room—it was locked. I don't know why. Maybe they just didn't know I was coming. My coach went to look for someone to let us in and all of a sudden Charlie Dressen comes by. Charlie was then a Dodger coach under Leo "The Lip" Durocher. Charlie asked me what I was waiting for, and when I told him a tryout with the Braves, he said, "Come on, let's go." So instead of a tryout with the Braves, I got one with the Dodgers. I wasn't signed on the spot, but

Dressen told me I had the best slider he ever saw. I never threw a slider—not a single one! But if he said I had one, that was okay with me. What he saw was that my ball sunk a little bit, even in those early days. After the team went back to Brooklyn I got a call from Branch Rickey, Jr., asking me if I wanted to play for the Dodgers. They wanted me and my father to come to Brooklyn. They gave us a contract to take home and it included a $500 bonus.

Labine and his father signed the contract and Clem finished high school. After graduation he was assigned to the Newport News Dodgers of the Class-B Piedmont League where he appeared in 12 games. Upon turning 18 later that summer, Labine enlisted in the Army and was out of organized ball until his discharge in 1946. He returned to Newport News late in the '46 season to resume his journey through the Dodger chain until he made his big-league debut in 1950. He'd done well in spring training that year and made the big club, then soon found himself pitching in his first big league game. "They gave me a one-game cup of coffee early in the 1950 season (April 18)," Labine said. "Back then they could keep some extra players until the end of April. They had three options on you then, so they could bounce you up and down and play with your salary as they did it." Labine pitched the final two frames of a 9–1 loss to the Phillies that day, allowing one run on a single by Eddie Waitkus. Shortly thereafter Labine returned to St. Paul where he'd spent the entire 1949 season.

In 1951 Labine was up and down between Brooklyn and St. Paul. He had yet to be turned into a full-time reliever, so he was still starting and working out of the bullpen for the Dodgers. He appeared in only 14 games for Brooklyn in '51, but the games in which he pitched were memorable, as were the ones in which he didn't pitch—most notably game three of the 1951 playoff against the New York Giants. With the Dodgers collapsing and the Giants surging late in the '51 season, Labine got himself benched by Dressen for insubordination. Dressen was no longer a coach as he'd been when he discovered Clem over five years earlier—Charlie was now the Dodgers' manager. Labine started a game against the Phillies at Ebbets Field on September 21 but got into fast trouble in the first inning when he loaded the bases. When Dressen saw Labine go to the stretch to pitch to Phillies slugger Willie "Puddin' Head" Jones, Dressen called time out, went to the mound, and told Labine to pitch from a full windup. Labine said he hadn't been able to throw his curveball for strikes from the windup that day. Dressen stuck to his guns and told Labine to use the windup anyway, then returned to the dugout. Labine, also self-admittedly stubborn, rolled the dice and pitched to Jones from the stretch—and Puddin' Head belted a grand slam.

Dressen let Labine pitch into the second inning, but quickly pulled the plug when Clem continued to struggle. "Charlie didn't talk to me," Labine said. "He came out and got the ball. He never talked to me. Not one day, two days, three days, four days. Never talked to me. Never said one lousy word to me. This is the type of man he was—he bit off his nose to spite his face." Dressen punished Labine by pitching him just twice over the last two weeks of the season—and this at a time when the Brooklyn staff was fatigued and could use Clem's help hold off the charging Giants. Desperate after losing game one of the 1951 playoff against the Giants, Dressen finally gave the ball to Labine in game two— and Clem responded by pitching a shutout win. Labine had made Bobby Thomson look bad striking out in that game, but Dressen chose not to bring Labine in from the pen the next day when Thomson came to bat as the winning run in the ninth inning. "And," said Labine, "everyone knows what happened after that."

The year 1952 was mixed bag for Labine—up and down from St. Paul and Brooklyn, and up and down results on the mound. A sore shoulder was part of the reason for his struggles, but he'd worked through them by September and was feeling good. Still, Dressen wouldn't use Labine in the World Series against the Yankees. "He said he didn't want to risk hurting my arm," Labine recalled. "You can't imagine anything that breaks your heart more than watching a World Series, feeling you could contribute, and being held out." That sentiment shows what a fierce competitor Labine was, and by 1953 he was settling into a role that would feed his desire to compete more regularly than a starting pitcher, and, quite often, in more pressure-packed situations: the role of reliever.

"I liked it," Labine said. "You know, if you really love the game of baseball, you've got to enjoy doing it more than once every four or five days. I always liked to walk into a ballgame knowing what I was going to do would have a lot to do with the outcome, if not everything." That dynamic was magnified for Labine as he settled into the role of late-inning fireman, or "closer" in modern terminology. "If you had a lead, there was this thing where about the 7th or 8th inning, where he'd get up, sort of a ritual, and walk down to the bullpen," Roger Craig told Bob Cairns in the book *Pen Men*. "Clem was kind of a cocky, arrogant type, which was good. I liked it. He'd fold his glove up and put it in his pocket. I can see him now, strutting down to the bullpen and the fans cheering."

1957

Brooklyn

DODGERS

CLEM LABINE
RIGHT-HAND PITCHER

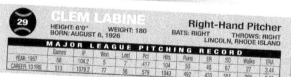

CLEM LABINE

29

HEIGHT: 6'0"   WEIGHT: 180
BORN: AUGUST 6, 1926

Right-Hand Pitcher

BATS: RIGHT   THROWS: RIGHT
LINCOLN, RHODE ISLAND

MAJOR LEAGUE PITCHING RECORD

	Games	IP	Won	Lost	Pct	Hits	Runs	ER	SO	Walks	ERA
YEAR: 1957	58	104.2	5	7	.417	104	50	40	67	27	3.44
CAREER, 13 YRS	513	1079.2	77	56	.579	1043	492	435	551	396	3.63

8-5-57: With Brooklyn fighting to stay in the pennant race, the Dodgers downed the Giants 5-3 at Ebbets Field. The Flatbush faithful were on the edge of their seats when Willie Mays strode to the plate as the tying run with two on and two out in the 9th. Willie already had four hits including a home run in the game. But their fear was for naught as skipper Walt Alston signaled for his ace out of the pen – **CLEM LABINE**. After running the count full, Clem got Willie to ground meekly to shortstop to end the game. It was Clem's 16th save of the year on his way to 17. It would be Clem's second year leading the league in saves after posting an N.L. high mark of 19 in 1956.

MAXIMUM EFFICIENCY... THAT'S ME!

①②③

CLEM THREW JUST THREE PITCHES FOR A 3-UP-3-DOWN 9TH INNING ON 4-24-57!

It took some time, however, for Labine to acclimate himself to his new role of fireman, but the sometimes-inflammatory sportswriter Dick Young wasn't cutting Clem any breaks for his early failures. After one early blown save, Young wrote, "This young fireman's sole equipment to put out a fire seems to be gasoline." Labine laughed at it, praising it as good writing. But when Young later wrote that he didn't think Labine had the fortitude to be a fireman—that sent Clem into a rage. It was one thing to question his baseball ability, but it was another thing to question his guts. Labine was a former paratrooper, so he knew all about guts. "I could hardly wait to get to the clubhouse the next day," Labine told author Peter Golenbock in 1984. "I wanted to hit him so badly, but I wanted it to be fair." Labine had the trainer tape one hand behind his back, then Clem confronted Young when he came in the clubhouse. "He ran out of the clubhouse," said Labine. "I ran out after him. But from that day on, we were never friendly again."

But Clem was friendly with the Brooklyn fans, and those fans got used to the scene Roger Craig described—Labine strutting to the bullpen to get warm. He was a trailblazer for the coming age of relievers, but he was still asked to start occasionally—especially when everything was on the line. There was the playoff game in '51, then there was game six of the 1956 World Series. After going down three games to two following Don Larsen's perfecto in game five, Alston gave the ball to Labine for game six at Ebbets Field. All Clem did was pitch a 10-inning, complete-game, 1–0 win to extend the Series to seven games. "Clem Labine had the heart of a lion and the intelligence of a wily fox," said Dodgers announcer Vin Scully, "and he was a nice guy, too."

Labine was a favorite of the Flatbush faithful, and he was unhappy about leaving them when the Dodgers headed West after the 1957 season. "While it didn't take us by surprise, we didn't like it," Labine recalled in 1990. "We were all comfortable in Brooklyn. It had been our home, and while it was a large borough, in some ways it was very small. And, of course, the Dodgers could do no wrong."

* * *

After winning game one of their four-game series against the Giants on August 5, the Dodgers' fading pennant hopes became dimmer as New York took the next three games starting with a 5–0 win on August 6 at Ebbets Field. They pounded Dodger pitching for an 8–5 victory the next day at Roosevelt Stadium, then wrapped up the series back at Ebbets with a 12–3 blow-out triumph on August 8. The Giants piled up nine runs in the first two innings of the finale. "Almost before Walter O'Malley could spell out 'Chavez Ravine,' his stalwarts were too deep in a rut to help themselves," wrote Louis Effrat of the *New York Times*. By the time the Dodgers hurried to catch a train to Pittsburgh, they had fallen to five games behind the pace-setting Braves.

Following a week on the bench due to his ailing knee, Duke Snider returned to action in the opener of the series against the Pirates at Forbes Field on August 9 and helped the Dodgers break their three-game losing skid by clouting his 27th home run. While he told reporters that his knee was not healed, Snider said, "It's easier to play than to sit and watch." Danny McDevitt was happy to see Snider back in the lineup as the little lefty was the beneficiary of the Duke's go-ahead, eighth-inning solo shot. The win was McDevitt's fifth of the '57 campaign. Snider's bat was booming the next day, too, as he homered again, this one a 400-foot, bases-empty bomb off Bucs right-hander Bob Purkey in the fourth to break a 0–0 tie. The run turned out to be all Don Drysdale would need as he shut out the Pirates, but the Dodgers added two insurance tallies to run the final score to 3–0. The series at Pittsburgh ended on a sour note, however, as the Dodgers lost both ends of a double-header on August 11. The opener was lost, 4–3, when Gene Freese scored the game-winner on a bloop single by Bill Mazeroski in the 10th inning. Snider stayed hot, though, homering in his third straight ballgame, but his round-tripper streak was stopped in the 6–2 nightcap defeat.

The Dodgers returned to New York following their series in Pittsburgh and opened a three-game series against the Giants at the Polo Grounds on August 13. Brooklyn now sat 7½ games behind the first-place Braves, and things got even more bleak as Giants right-hander Ruben Gomez pitched a four-hitter to defeat the Dodgers, 4–2, in the opener. Sal Maglie was knocked out of the box after surrendering two runs in the third inning and Ed Roebuck took over for the remainder of the game. Roebuck saw his 13-inning scoreless streak come to an end when he was reached for two more tallies in the fifth, but Ed started a new scoreless streak by hanging zeroes on the Giants in the sixth, seventh, and eighth frames.

August 14: A Valiant Effort

Brooklyn notched a must-win in game two of their series against the Giants at the Polo Grounds, 7–6, on August 14. Danny McDevitt,

Clem Labine, and Ed Roebuck combined to get the job done, but the victory was really earned on the strength of three home runs hit by the Dodgers. Gil Hodges blasted his 17th of the season in the first inning—a two-run shot off Giants right-hander Ray Crone. Up to that point the Giants were the only club against whom Hodges had not homered in 1957, but they now completed Gil's long-ball hit list. Dodger left-fielder Elmer Valo unloaded on Crone in the 6th, his third round-tripper in just 96 at-bats to date in '57. Don Zimmer capped the big-fly parade with another circuit job in the seventh, a lead-off wallop against the beleaguered Crone.

Never known as a power hitter, the home run by Valo that day was just the 54th of his 16-year career. Thirteen of those years were spent with the American League Philadelphia Athletics where he became a favorite of the fans there for his humble personality, plentiful line drives, and fearless play in the outfield—courage that earned him the nickname "Elmer Valiant." Injuries (mostly from colliding with unpadded outfield walls) and World War II military service (1944–45) usually prevented Valo from playing full seasons during his time with the Athletics, and only once did he amass more than 500 at-bats. But when he was healthy, he played all-out in the field and was usually near or above the .300-mark with the stick. Specifically, it was Valo's left-handed bat the Dodgers were most interested in as they prepared to open the 1957 season. So the Phillies, whom Elmer had been with in 1956, sent Valo to Brooklyn along with four other players plus cash in exchange for the Dodgers' promising young shortstop Chico Fernandez. The date of the transaction was April 5, 1957—Valo's 36th birthday. It was quite a fine birthday present for him, too, as he would be joining the defending National League champions who were certainly favored by many experts to win yet another pennant. Being on a winner was something foreign to Valo as almost all of his seasons in the majors had been spent on bad, second division ballclubs.

Earlier in his career Valo had been a fine right fielder. By his own admission, however, he was not a natural athlete—but he was gifted with sprinter's speed and excellent leaping ability which helped make up for deficiencies of instinct and grace in the outfield. But at 36 years of age, Brooklyn was not looking for Elmer to bolster their defense. "I think Valo will help us as a pinch-hitter," manager Walter Alston told the press after the trade. Apparently unafraid of Valo's history of running into walls, Alston added that Elmer would see some time in the outfield. One of Valo's first serious run-ins with an outfield wall came early in the 1946 season when he robbed Ted Williams of a home run, but he paid dearly and had to be carried from the field. He made news two years later when he took on the Yankee Stadium wall to steal a home run from Yogi Berra. Valo lay in a heap at the base of the wall after the play, unmoving, with no one sure as to whether or not he made the catch. It was still a mystery until A's second baseman Pete Suder rushed over, pulled the ball from Valo's glove, and held it up for all to see—then 69,419 Yankee fans cheered wildly for Valo's reckless abandon. The *New York Times'* James P. Dawson called the catch a "glittering effort." Another *Times* writer referred to it as "pulse pounding," while a third scribe described Valo as "the American League's version of Pete Reiser."

As glorious as the Yankee Stadium catch was, it was costly to Valo. He broke three ribs when he landed on the armrest of one of the right field seats. He taped himself up and played through the pain for two weeks, but finally had to shut it down to heal for a couple weeks. When asked later in life how many times he hit the wall in his career, Valo said, "I don't know. I hit a few—maybe twice a year. You know, you hit 'em and nothing happens. But I got hurt about four or five times. I only challenged when it meant the ballgame. I practiced going back to the fences, so I had good knowledge in my head."

The years brought more fine hitting—and more outfield crashes, but Valo's days of slamming into walls had slowed considerably by the time he joined Brooklyn. Early in the '57 season, however, Valo showed his new ballclub that he didn't, in fact, need the game to be on the line to challenge an outfield fence—he could do the trick in pregame warm-ups. Prior to the game against the Braves at County Stadium on May 15, Valo ran into the chain link fence while chasing a fly ball during outfield practice. He suffered cuts on his forehead, under his left eye, and on his lip, requiring a couple stitches. Asked why he would risk injury chasing a fungo, Valo said, "Sometimes you do strange things for no good reason at all."

Fortunately for Brooklyn, Valo played outfield in just 36 games in 1957—the rest of his 81 appearances came as a pinch-hitter, lessening his likelihood of slamming into outfield walls. All told, Valo delivered exactly what the Dodgers wanted when they traded for him—he hit .273 and was 8-for-34 in tough pinch-hitting duty. Sadly for Valo, though, the '57 Dodgers didn't deliver the pennant that had always eluded him. He remained with the club during their first year in Los Angeles, but they again failed to return to the World Series. Valo was released following the '58 season, and, as luck would have it, the Dodgers won it

1957

Brooklyn

DODGERS

ELMER VALO
OUTFIELDER

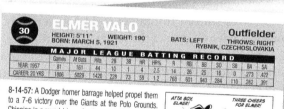

30

ELMER VALO

HEIGHT: 5'11"   WEIGHT: 190
BORN: MARCH 5, 1921

BATS: LEFT   **Outfielder**
THROWS: RIGHT
RYBNIK, CZECHOSLOVAKIA

MAJOR LEAGUE BATTING RECORD													
	Games	At Bats	Hits	2B	3B	HR	HR%	R	RBI	BB	SO	SB	BA	SA
YEAR: 1957	81	161	44	10	1	4	2.5	14	26	25	16	0	273	422
CAREER: 20 YRS	1806	5029	1420	228	73	58	1.2	768	601	943	284	110	282	391

8-14-57: A Dodger homer barrage helped propel them to a 7-6 victory over the Giants at the Polo Grounds. Chipping in a round-tripper for the Brooks was 36-year-old Czechoslovakian-born **ELMER VALO**. Acquired a few days before the '57 season opened, Dodger execs hoped Elmer would strengthen their bench, especially as a pinch hitter. Elmer did not disappoint, chipping in eight clutch pinch hits while also playing some fine defense in the outfield. Elmer had always been an excellent flychaser with a reputation of fearlessness when it came to crashing into outfield walls – behavior that had earned him the nickname Elmer "Valiant."

ATTA BOY, ELMER!   THREE CHEERS FOR ELMER!

ELMER CRACKED A 14TH-INNING GAME-WINNING PINCH HIT TO DEFEAT THE CUBS ON 8-28-57!

all in 1959 without him. Still, in two short years with the Dodgers Valo made a positive impact on his teammates, the fans, and the press. Famed sportswriter Red Smith captured the essence of Valo when he wrote, "Hundreds of kids have come up to the major leagues and played out their time and departed. None was ever more sincere than Elmer Valo, none ever tried harder, none was quicker to blame himself for a mistake, none more stubbornly unwilling to offer or accept an excuse for error."

August 17: Campy's Still Got It

The Dodgers concluded their series against the Giants with a 9–4 loss at the Polo Grounds on August 15. Talk of the Giants moving to California had reached fever pitch and only 7,587 spectators turned out to see the ballgame. The *New York Times'* Joseph M. Sheehan wrote that it was "the smallest Giant-Dodger crowd in recent memory." Those who came saw catcher Valmy Thomas, an emergency call-up from Minneapolis, wreck the Dodgers with a two-run triple and a two-run homer. Don Drysdale took the defeat, his first loss to the Giants in six starts against them so far in 1957.

Brooklyn cruised to a 4–1 win against the Pirates in Jersey City on August 16. Despite the Dodgers' win, the Roosevelt Stadium experiment was flaming out in glorious fashion as only 9,592 cash customers were present—and most of them spent their energy booing the Brooklyn players. Johnny Podres gained the victory, his 10th of the season, while also displacing Milwaukee's Gene Conley as the N.L. earned run leader. The four-game series shifted to Ebbets Field the next day. While the Flatbush crowd was friendlier than the Jersey City gathering, it was even more sparse—just 8,665. Koufax got the start and was not sharp, lasting just 4⅔ innings and taking the loss, 7–3. It was a forgettable game except for the fact that it turned out to be the last great offensive game in the career of Roy Campanella. Certainly no one in the crowd was thinking that at the time. While many surely feared that they were no longer going to see their beloved Campy play if the team moved to Los Angeles, few probably imagined that 1957 would be his last season. And, according to Campanella, '57 wouldn't have been his final season had not his fate been tragically altered by the winter automobile crash that confined him to a wheelchair.

"The only Dodger who gave the hard-throwing Pittsburgh right-hander [Ron Kline] any real trouble was Roy Campanella," wrote the *New York Times*. "Brooklyn's roly-poly catcher had a perfect day at bat with four hits, including a two-run homer. In the second, after Elmer Valo had walked, Campanella drilled the first pitch into the left-centerfield seats for his first homer since July 5." It was also the last homer of Campanella's decorated career as he failed to go deep in the 17 games he appeared in for the duration of the 1957 campaign. Campanella was 35 years old when the '57 season began—but, physically, he was an old 35. He was still the smiling, happy-go-lucky, eternal optimist he'd always been, but his body was wearing out. While 1957 was just Campanella's 10th season in the majors, he'd spent the prior decade catching countless games in the Negro, Mexican, and minor leagues. The cumulative effect of 20 years behind the plate had eroded the skills that had made Campanella, at his peak, the best catcher in the game and a three-time winner of the N.L. M.V.P. award.

The year 1955 was Campanella's last great season, and it was followed by a 1956 campaign that saw Roy hit just .219 and 20 homers. Pain in his battered hands was what hampered him in '56. The catcher's mitts of Campanella's time were not engineered like those of subsequent generations that allow receivers to protect their throwing hand by catching one-handed. The old-style mitts had no hinge, so catchers had to catch two-handed, which meant their bare hand was exposed and vulnerable. This resulted in repeated injuries to Campanella's bare hand from foul balls and back swings. He'd had his left hand operated on in 1954, then the right one was operated on following the 1956 season. The surgery had Campanella hoping for a bounce-back season in 1957. He wrote in his 1959 book:

> One big reason why I was looking to a good year was because the pain had left my hands. The numbness was still there but the pain was gone, and I could grip a bat again and had been strengthening my hands by swinging a loaded bat in the cellar of my store. And finally, this was the odd year. This was '57, and I had won the National League's Most Valuable Player award three times, all in odd years—1951, 1953 and 1955. If ballplayers are superstitious, this at least was a happy hunch.

Campanella's longtime teammate, Jackie Robinson, did not share Roy's happy hunch that he could make a comeback. Robinson, himself retired by March of 1957, irked Campanella by telling sportswriters he thought Campy was through. "You can't hit a man over the head and make him believe the way you do," Campanella told reporters in spring training in response to Robinson's prediction of Roy's demise. The relationship between Robinson and Campanella was complex. After a successful rookie season in 1947 in which he steadfastly stuck to Branch Rickey's directive NOT to fight back against the racism he faced that year, Robinson became increasingly more outspoken about civil rights each successive year. Campanella joined the Dodgers in 1948 and became a star soon thereafter. Robinson wanted Campanella to follow his lead and use his celebrity platform to be more vocal about civil rights issues, but Roy resisted. In the wake of Robinson's comments about Campanella being finished, Sportswriter Dick Young wrote about an old incident that served to remind readers about the occasional friction between Jackie and Roy in this realm.

> Contrary to general belief, Robinson was not closest to the other Negro players. There were times when Roy Campanella and Don Newcombe resented his dictation. One such incident involved living quarters on the road. St. Louis had been the last outpost of segregation in the N.L. The colored players stayed at The Adams, a Negro hotel; the others at The Chase, which is perhaps the most pleasant hostelry in the league. A few seasons back, The Chase informed the Dodger management that it would accept the Negro players. Robinson leapt at the opportunity of breaking this last barrier. Newk and Campy said, "No, thanks, we'll stay at The Adams." They contended that the manager of the Negro hotel had been good to them for years, and that they should not chuck him just because The Chase changed its mind. Robinson argued that it was their duty in the fight against segregation to change over to The Chase. A lively argument ensued in the clubhouse—Robby against Newk and Campy. "I'm no crusader," snapped Campy. "I'm a ballplayer. And I'm happy right where I am."

Much has been written about the contrast between Robinson and Campanella and their individual ways of dealing with the struggles of being a black player in the newly integrated major leagues. Campanella, as he so succinctly stated, saw himself as simply a ballplayer. To Robinson, however, being an activist for racial progress was just as important as being a ballplayer, so he was somewhat intolerant of Campanella staying out of the fight for civil rights. "There's a little 'Uncle Tom' in Roy," Robinson once derisively said, and Jackie's negative characterization of Campanella took root with many black players and fans. Despite their differences, the always-gracious Campy praised Robinson, saying, "Jackie made things easy for us. [Because of him] I'm just another guy playing baseball."

In 1958 while Campanella was still in the hospital recuperating from his crippling injury, Frank Gibbons of the *Cleveland Press* wrote a piece that offers additional insight into the "Uncle Tom" slur Robinson hung on Campy. It is worth noting that Gibbons' thoughts were written in 1957, just ten years into the integration of the majors. For that reason, his terminology and sentiments are much closer to those of the populace of the time and can sometimes be misconstrued as unenlightened by people of the 21st century who have had, at the time of the writing of this book, 70 years to ponder the desegregation of baseball. Wrote Gibbons:

> I didn't know Campanella very well, but the few times I interviewed him during World Series play he made a deep impression. He was my notion of a very strong man off the field. He was among the Negroes who came early to the big leagues, and he came without fear, without suspicion, and without a plan. I don't mean by that he was an "Uncle Tom" type, which was the way he was tagged in a kidding spirit by younger and less tolerant Negro players. What I liked about Campy was the way he handled the "situation" before it practically disappeared from the face of the baseball earth. I always felt that Campanella trusted me and I felt honored by that trust. I have known some Negro players, who were my friends, who interpreted opinion as prejudice, and who made me uncomfortable in my effort to do an honest job. There were times when I felt they were more intolerant than I was, although I never blame them long because their problem was so much more acute. Campanella never made me feel that way. There was no wall to be broken down, no chasm to throw a bridge across. We talked baseball as friends, and in doing so I believe we accomplished a great deal in other ways. I'm sure that Campanella endured his share of slurs early in his career and I'm equally sure that there would have come a time when he would have fought. When to endure and when to fight is one of the great artistic maneuvers of life, and in this regard he was an artist in my book.

As the product of a biracial marriage (Campanella's father was white and his mother was black), Roy certainly possessed a racial insight not encoded into black players from non-mixed marriages. Perhaps that insight was at the root of his reluctance to be a civil rights activist. Perhaps it simply wasn't in his DNA to lead in that realm. Whatever the reason, Campanella's lack of activism has garnered a great deal of attention from historians that have written about his career and life. Campy simply wished to be seen as a ballplayer, but he played in a time of complicated race relations—a time that denied him his simple wish. People will always debate who was right—Robinson or Campanella— when it came to determining the role Campy should have played in the civil rights movement. Roy's close friend and batterymate, Carl Erskine, summed up the Campanella-Robinson dynamic best when he wrote, "There weren't any divisions between the two. They loved and respected one another. They just understood where each man differed. Both were right. Both were entitled to their own beliefs."

One thing that should never be debated, however, is what kind of ballplayer Campanella was. Without a doubt, the man was one of the greatest catchers of all time. For validation of that assertion look no further than the words of Ty Cobb who said, "Campanella will be remembered longer than any catcher in baseball history." Defensively, Campanella was a slick and nimble catcher and a brilliant handler of pitchers. At five-foot-nine-inches and 210 to 220 pounds, he had a perfect catcher's body that was stout with a low center of gravity. Often described by sportswriters as "roly-poly," Roy's shape belied the rock-hard musculature he possessed. And he could run, too, although he certainly lost a step or two later in his career. Offensively, Campanella was a prolific power-hitting catcher who batted .276 with 1,161 hits, 242 home runs, and 856 RBIs in his 10-year career. His statistics certainly would have been even more gaudy were his career not shortened by baseball's color barrier and his career-ending automobile accident.

Catching has always been and will always be the most physically grueling position in baseball. That said, it is less grueling in modern times than it was in the past. Nowadays, most games are played at night when the temperatures are cooler; the equipment is improved; double-headers have been virtually eliminated; nutrition and training is better; etc. Defeating the rigors of catching was just as difficult as defeating the opponent—and Campanella was one of the best ever at both tasks. He'd proven his ability to defeat the opponent day in and day out for a decade, but there was still a durability record he badly wanted. "With nothing at stake, I ordinarily would not have had to catch any of those last three games [of the 1957 season]," recalled Campanella. "But I needed one more [game] to give me a league record of catching a hundred games nine years in a row. Ballplayers don't usually watch such things too closely. But I was proud of it. The reporters of the club reminded me of it. They told Alston, too." So, on September 27, Alston sent Campanella out to start the game against the Phillies at Connie Mack Stadium. He played just three innings before giving way to John Roseboro.

Campanella never caught another game after that. He pinch hit in the last game of the season on September 29, but he never again took his place behind the plate. "I had no idea it would be my last game ever [catching]." he said of the game on September 27, 1957. When the season ended and the Dodgers made official their intentions to move to Los Angeles, Campanella reassessed his original reluctance to make the move. He soon embraced the scenario and admitted that he was looking

1957

Brooklyn

DODGERS

ROY CAMPANELLA
CATCHER

				ROY CAMPANELLA									Catcher	
31	HEIGHT: 5'9"		WEIGHT: 190			BATS: RIGHT			THROWS: RIGHT					
	BORN: NOVEMBER 19, 1921							PHILADELPHIA, PENNSYLVANIA						

			MAJOR	LEAGUE	BATTING	RECORD							
	Games	At Bats	Hits	2B	3B	HR	HR%	R	RBI	BB	SO	SB	BA	SA
YEAR: 1957	103	330	80	9	0	13	3.9	31	62	34	50	1	.242	.388
CAREER: 10 YRS	1215	4205	1161	178	18	242	5.8	627	856	533	501	25	.276	.500

8-17-57: One of the true Brooklyn Dodger greats, 3-time M.V.P. winner **ROY CAMPANELLA** slammed his last homer in a 7-3 loss to the Bucs at Ebbets Field. The shot came in the 2nd inning when Roy drilled Ron Kline's first pitch into the left-centerfield seats. With wear and tear taking their toll on the 35-year-old, Roy saw his offensive production dip sharply in 1957. Nagging injuries often sidelined him, and his round-tripper on this day was his first in over a month. Still, none of the 6,830 fans in attendance could have imagined that they were seeing Roy's last long ball, but his career was tragically cut short when he was was paralyzed in a winter car crash.

WHO SAYS I'M SLOWIN' DOWN?!

ROY CLUBBED TWO CIRCUIT BLASTS IN A WIN OVER THE GIANTS ON 5-24-57!

forward to taking aim at the short right field fence at the Los Angeles Coliseum. But the car accident changed everything. It was his uplifting personality and his durability on the ballfield that made it so shocking for baseball fans to comprehend the idea that this fate—paralysis—could befall Campanella. How could this happen to such a wonderful person? How could this happen to such a strong man? As it turned out, though, the spirit and resolve he displayed in dealing with his misfortune earned him more fame and adulation than he ever enjoyed during his playing career. Other great catchers—Bill Dickey, Gabby Hartnett, Mickey Cochrane, etc.—had slipped out of the public consciousness once their playing careers ended. *New York Times* writer Robert McGill Thomas, Jr., summed it up best when he wrote, "The accident transformed Campanella from a sports hero into a universal symbol of courage."

*   *   *

There were 14,416 spectators on hand to watch the Dodgers and Pirates split a Sunday double-header at Ebbets Field on August 18. Brooklyn took the opener, 2–1, behind a fine, complete game effort by Sal Maglie; then dropped the nightcap, 8–6, in a long, sloppy affair. Stadium organist Gladys Goodding played "Happy Birthday" during the first game in honor of Roberto Clemente's 23rd and Bob Kennedy's 37th birthdays. "It was also, for the benefit of the ancients, in honor of Burleigh Grimes' birthday," wrote the *New York Times'* Roscoe McGowen. "The Lord of Burleigh is a bit older than the other two." The old right-handed spitballer turned 64 that day, and it was nearly 37 years since a young Grimes had lost two games in the 1920 World Series as Brooklyn was defeated by the Cleveland Indians. Thoughts of a return trip to the Series were fading fast from the minds of 1957 Dodgers fans, however, as Brooklyn had slipped 8½ games behind the league leading Braves by the time this day's twin-bill got under way. When all was said and done, it seemed more like it was Duke Snider's birthday rather than the others as he celebrated by clouting two home runs into the Ebbets Field seats. Snider hit his 30th of the season in the first game, a long drive into the centerfield stands off Bob Friend. Number 31 came in the second game and was hit to almost the exact same spot as number 30, but this time it was Elroy Face who served up the gopher ball.

After a day off on Monday, the Dodgers were back in action with another Ebbets Field double-header on Tuesday, August 20. This time they earned a sweep, routing the Reds, 11–5, in the opener; then edging them in the 12-inning nightcap, 6–5. Snider seemed still to be celebrating the birthdays of Clemente, Kennedy, and Grimes as the Duke slammed two more circuit blasts. He launched number 32 in the first game, a two-run shot off right-hander Tom Acker in the third inning. Snider's 33rd came at 1:07 a.m. off Johnny Klippstein, the solo shot ending the marathon nightcap. A nice sized crowd of 16,132 turned out for the double-feature despite an increased likelihood that the Dodgers would move to Los Angeles after the season. The fear that the Dodgers would vacate Brooklyn had been heightened on the Monday off-day after the Giants officially announced that they were leaving for San Francisco at the conclusion of the 1957 season. Facing anxious reporters, Walter O'Malley said, "Nothing has happened to the Dodgers. There's no announcement to make."

It didn't matter what O'Malley said—Brooklyn fans knew they had every reason to believe their Dodgers would also flee to California, especially now that the Giants had made their move official. Plus, O'Malley and Brooklyn city officials were still in a very public standoff. O'Malley wanted his stadium to be built at the corner of Atlantic and Flatbush avenues in Brooklyn. That was not an option for city official Robert Moses who instead offered a site at Flushing Meadows in Queens. "Flushing Meadows is a great site for a new stadium," said O'Malley. "Not for the Dodgers, though. Fans in Brooklyn couldn't get there." O'Malley's statement rang a bit hollow to Brooklyn fans, however. While the commute would be difficult, Flushing Meadows was just a little over ten miles from Brooklyn. Chavez Ravine, on the other hand, was nearly 3,000 miles away.

The Dodgers and Reds concluded their series at Ebbets Field on August 21 in front of a small crowd of 8,125. Perhaps the previous day's six-hour-and-38-minute double-header marathon kept the attendance down. Perhaps it was due to the reality of the Giants' move announcement sinking in. Whatever the case, the few that went to Ebbets that day saw big Don Newcombe pitch a beauty—a five-hit, 8–0 shutout. As if aware of the endurance contest the day before had been, Newk worked fast, putting the Reds away in just two hours and 15 minutes. It was Newcombe's fourth whitewashing of the season, but it was his first win in over a month and it ended a personal four-game losing streak. Elbow trouble had plagued him all season, but this outing gave hope that Newcombe might help Brooklyn make a desperate run at the Braves down the stretch.

The year 1957 was a star-crossed season for Newcombe, and this day was a microcosm of that. Feeling fine after his great day on the mound, Don slid behind the wheel of his car to drive to his parents' home in Linden, New Jersey, for dinner. Accompanying him was his father, wife, and two children. They had nearly reached their destination when a four-year-old boy darted into the street from behind a parked car and was struck by Newk's automobile. The boy suffered serious injuries and was taken to the hospital in critical condition, but fortunately he survived. Newcombe was not charged in the incident, but it sapped the joy out of his tenth win of the season—and joy was sometimes hard to come by for Newk in 1957.

*   *   *

If a desperate stretch run was to be made by the Dodgers at the pace-setting Braves, August 22 provided the perfect opportunity to get it started as Milwaukee pulled into Brooklyn for a three-game set. Crafty Braves right-hander Lew Burdette had other plans, however, and shut down the Brooklyn attack, winning 6–1 and picking up his 12th victory of the season. Newcombe, perhaps still troubled by the events of the previous day, took out his frustration by steadily hurling insults at home plate umpire Frank Secory. By the fourth inning Secory had heard enough, so he thumbed Newk from the game.

The loss made the Brooklyn situation more dire as they took the field for game two of the series on August 23. This time it was Gene Conley who silenced the Dodger offense, and he held a 2–0 lead as he took the mound for the bottom of the ninth. Brooklyn staged a desperate rally, however, and drove Conley from the game. Right-hander Don McMahon relieved Conley with the score 2–1, but McMahon failed to stave off the Brooklyn comeback, and when Gino Cimoli singled home Carl Furillo, the Dodgers were 3–2 winners. There was no carryover effect for Brooklyn the next day, August 24, as they dropped the series finale, 13–7. Nippy Jones, Hank Aaron, Andy Pafko, and Felix Mantilla powered the Braves to victory as they each battered Dodgers pitching for home runs. The loss put the Dodgers on the brink of elimination as they fell to third place, 7½ games behind the first-place Braves. It wasn't hopeless yet, but it was bleak for Brooklyn as they found themselves nine games back in the loss column with just 30 games left to play.

August 25: The Barber Trims the Cards

10,883 Ebbets Field fans were on the edge of their seats as Sal "The Barber" Maglie entered the August 25 game in the ninth inning with two out, the bases loaded, and the Dodgers leading the Cardinals, 6–5. St. Louis had already pushed across two runs and were threatening to tie the game—or take a lead—as the dangerous Ken Boyer stepped in to hit. Used almost exclusively as a starter for Brooklyn that season, Maglie coolly took the hill as if he'd closed do-or-die ballgames every day. He fired his first pitch across for a called strike, then made Boyer look foolish as he whiffed on the next two offerings. Three pitches and The Barber got the save—the only one he'd record with the 1957 Dodgers.

Maglie was at the core of much of the heated animosity that boiled between the Dodgers and Giants from 1950 through 1955. Dodgers players believed that The Barber doled out too many "close shaves" when pitching against them, so they held him in high contempt. And Brooklyn fans truly hated him. First, to Dodger fans, Maglie looked the part of a villain. He was dark with hooded, sleepy eyes, and when he took the mound he wore a heavy five o'clock shadow, bolstering his sinister appearance. He seemed to glower at Dodger batters from the mound, and the Brooklyn fans reviled him. He looked like a castoff from a mobster movie, and Dodger fans often called him "Public Enemy No. 1," a moniker that seemed appropriate. A villainous appearance would not be enough to engender the type of hate the Dodger fans had for Maglie. Their hate was magnified by the fact that he had their team's number.

From 1950 through 1954, Maglie was 22-and-6 with five shutouts against the Dodgers. And he was especially good against them in their own park where he was 11-and-3. Maglie attributed his success at Ebbets Field to the heightened focus he had at doing battle with the best, and the Dodgers were by far the best team in the National League from the late-40s until they departed for Los Angeles. But he also later attributed his success at Ebbets Field to the pitcher's mound. It was only after he joined the Dodgers that he revealed that the Ebbets Field pitcher's mound was his favorite in the league due to the fact that it sloped less severely than any other mound in the league.

The Dodgers seemed to turn the tables on Maglie in their championship season of 1955, but The Barber still owned a lifetime record of 23-and-11 against Brooklyn when they brought him on board to help them in mid–May of 1956. It was believed that Maglie was finished when the Dodgers acquired him. Age (he was 38) and a bad back had slowed him with the Giants in 1955. They gave up on him and waived him on July 31, 1955, then the Indians picked him up. Cleveland's motives for signing Maglie were clear—to stop the Yankees from getting him. But Maglie saw little action with the Indians through the remainder of the

'55 season and early '56, so he was happy to join the Dodgers when he learned that they had purchased him from Cleveland. The question was would the Dodger fans and players be happy to have him join them?

Many fans found it difficult to accept the fact that the hated Maglie would now wear the sacred Brooklyn jersey—but the players accepted him right away. Brooklyn players understood the fact that during his time in New York Maglie was simply doing what any pitcher worth his salt would do to help his team win. In The Barber's case, that meant pitching inside and, as believed by the Dodgers, doctoring the ball with scuffs, saliva, or whatever was available—an accusation Maglie always denied. They'd seen firsthand what he could do on the mound, so they were happy to have him join in their effort to return to the World Series in 1956. The past was the past and this was business—a brutal fact that baseball fans are often reluctant to accept. Plus, the players knew that Maglie only hit a batter intentionally when ordered to do so by his manager with the Giants, Leo Durocher, so the bulk of their vitriol was aimed at The Lip instead of The Barber.

Carl Furillo was one of Maglie's most thrown-at targets. Furillo ended up in the hospital in 1949 after being beaned by Giants pitcher Sheldon Jones. Jones later apologized and said, "I just did what Durocher told me to do." Maglie came too far inside to Furillo in 1950 and Carl hollered at him. Maglie came even further in on the next pitch and Furillo whistled the bat at the mound, causing Maglie to "skip rope." So, there was some history between the two when reporters asked Furillo how he felt about Maglie joining the Dodgers. "All that's happened in the past is forgotten," said Carl. "I'll tell you this—he's now wearing the same uniform I'm wearing. If trouble starts, I'll be out there with him."

Jackie Robinson was often the target of Maglie's brushback pitches. Robinson would retaliate in the only way a batter could—by bunting down the first base line and roll-blocking Maglie when he came over to field the ball. Still, it was all in the game and Robinson held no grudges when Maglie joined the Dodgers. "I'm only sorry he didn't come here sooner," said Robinson, "say about five or six years ago." By the time the 1956 season had ended, Robinson was a bona fide Maglie fan. "Playing ball with Sal last year, I learned he doesn't have a vicious bone in his body. He pushes the batter back and sets him up for the curve on the outside corner. That's his bread-and-butter pitch. Fortunately, he has great control."

Pee Wee Reese was all for Maglie coming to Brooklyn, but he acknowledged it would be odd to see him wearing a Dodgers uniform.

"It'll seem strange to see him come walking through that door," Reese told reporters while motioning to the entrance to the Dodgers clubhouse at Ebbets Field. "I've always admired him. It's not bad to have him going *for* you instead of *against* you." Carl Erskine agreed. The Dodgers were watching the clubhouse TV when they got their first look at Maglie wearing a Brooklyn cap and jersey. The scene took place at the Dodgers offices where the announcement was made that Brooklyn had signed Maglie. Erskine took in the surreal image of Maglie wearing the Dodgers cap and jersey and said, "What show is this, *Masquerade Party*?" Still, Erskine was the first one to greet Maglie and shake his hand when Maglie finally entered the Dodgers clubhouse.

The players never regretted their acceptance of Maglie. The Dodgers were playing listless ball and sputtering along in third place when Maglie joined them in May of '56. Walter Alston broke him in slowly at first, using him out of the bullpen while he pitched himself into shape. Eventually, Maglie joined the rotation and the results were magical. He won and won, and the Dodgers climbed and climbed in the standings, ultimately overtaking the Braves to claim yet another pennant. Maglie was seemingly on the mound for every must-win game down the stretch, and he almost always won. First, he beat the Braves on September 11, a game that saw Brooklyn finally overtake Milwaukee for first place. Then, with the Dodgers desperately needing a victory against the Phillies on September 25, Maglie responded by hurling a no-hitter. Finally, Sal beat the Pirates in the first game of a double-header on September 29, and the triumph clinched at least a tie for the pennant.

Brooklyn went on to win the N.L. flag but lost to the Yankees in the World Series. Maglie had appeared in the World Series with the Giants in 1951 and '54. He felt the sting of team defeat as the Giants lost in '51, but he enjoyed team victory in '54 when New York defeated the Indians. Still, he had yet to get a World Series win for himself as he took a loss in game four of the '51 Series and a no-decision in game one of the '54 Series. But Maglie finally got a Series win for himself in 1956 when he started game one and bested the Yankees' Whitey Ford. Often forgotten, however, is the fact that Maglie was the tough-luck loser when Don Larsen pitched his perfecto in game five. The Dodgers were losers to the Yankees in the 1956 Series, but Maglie was a winner in the hearts of his Brooklyn teammates and *most* of the Dodger fans. Some fans would simply never fully accept him into their fold.

Maglie's comeback story made him a popular speaker on the Knife & Fork circuit prior to the 1957 season. One banquet was at the B'nai

1957

Brooklyn

DODGERS

SAL MAGLIE
RIGHT-HAND PITCHER

32 **SAL MAGLIE** Right-Hand Pitcher
HEIGHT: 6'2"   WEIGHT: 180
BORN: APRIL 26, 1917   BATS: RIGHT   THROWS: RIGHT
                                           NIAGARA FALLS, NEW YORK

MAJOR LEAGUE PITCHING RECORD

	Games	IP	Won	Lost	Pct.	Hits	Runs	ER	SO	Walks	ERA
YEAR: 1957*	19	101.1	6	6	.500	94	42	33	50	26	2.93
CAREER: 10 YRS	303	1723	119	62	.657	1591	684	603	862	562	3.15

8-25-57: With the 3rd-place Dodgers struggling to stay in striking distance of the 1st-place Braves, Brooklyn eeked out a 6-5 win over St. Louis at Ebbets Field. Clingling to a 1-run lead with two outs and the bases loaded in the bottom of the 9th, skipper Walt Alston summoned the unflappable **SAL MAGLIE** to the mound. All Sal did was whiff the dangerous Ken Boyer on three pitches to end the game. Once a mortal enemy of the Dodgers while with the Giants, 40-year-old Sal pitched well for the Brooks in '57 when not sidelined with injuries.

I'M OFF TO GET MY WORLD SERIES SHARE!

BROOKLYN SAID SO LONG TO SAL WHEN THEY "WAIVED" HIM TO THE YANKEES ON 9-1-57!

* Only statistics from the 1957 Brooklyn Dodgers are displayed. Sal played in an additional 6 games with the 1957 New York Yankees.

B'rith Sports Lodge where Maglie received an award for "high principle and achievement in sports." He collected another honor from *The Barber's Journal* when he was named as one of the nation's ten best groomed men. He capped the off-season by signing his 1957 Dodgers contract— for a $4,000 raise. Maglie claimed it wasn't a raise—just a return to the $30,000 he was making in 1955 before the Indians slashed him to $26,000 in '56. The great comeback; the banquet money; the raise in salary—it all had Maglie in good spirits as the Dodgers opened spring training of '57. A late arrival to camp was Sandy Amoros who'd been holding out for his own raise. When he finally showed up and stepped into the batting cage for his first hacks, it was Maglie who was on the mound to welcome him. "Do you have your helmet on?" shouted The Barber.

"Si," said Sandy with his bright white smile. Then Maglie fired a pitch that struck Amoros in the rear end. They all laughed and then got down to business. That was where the honeymoon ended for Sal. He struggled to get in rhythm during spring training, and then after just two starts in the regular season he went down with a neck injury. Then he fractured a thumb during a collision while shagging flies in practice. Then it was a bum shoulder. Then a bad back. At 39 years of age, Maglie's body was rebelling. He was finally feeling pretty well by July and, for the most part, remained in the rotation for the duration of the season. Although they don't tell the full story, his season-ending numbers with Brooklyn look pretty good—6-and-6 in 17 starts with a 2.93 ERA. Those numbers, and the recollection of what Maglie did down the stretch in 1956, inspired a few teams to inquire in August of '57 as to whether Sal was available for sale or trade. In the end, Sal was dealt to the Yankees for $37,500 and two Triple-A players to be named later. It meant that Maglie would join the ranks of the few who had worn the jerseys of all three New York clubs—Giants, Dodgers and Yankees. His impact on the Yankees was minimal as he pitched in just six games for them as they cruised to a pennant, winning it by eight games over the White Sox. Maglie was unavailable for the Bombers in the World Series against the Braves since he'd been acquired after the post-season roster deadline. The Yanks could have used him, too, as they lost to Milwaukee in seven games.

The Dodgers players liked Maglie-the-man *and* Maglie-the-player. Many players were upset at the front office for letting Sal go, and they saw it as conceding the 1957 pennant to the Braves even though there was still a month left in the season. They'd seen what Maglie could do in a stretch run just a year earlier, and they were still hopeful that he could bottle lightning again and help them repeat as N.L. champs. If overtaking the Braves was an impossibility, they still wanted Maglie battling for them to help secure second place in the National League, which meant more money in their pockets—but his trade ended that thinking. As it was, the Dodgers ended up in third place and voted their pal Sal a full $1,057.18 share. Commissioner Ford Frick cancelled their gesture, however, approving instead the larger $1,745.85 share the Yankees voted for Maglie.

It was amazing—in just a little over a year with the Brooklyn Dodgers, Sal "The Barber" Maglie completely undermined the menacing, glowering, head-hunting legacy he'd seared into the minds of Dodger players and fans. Sal was a swell guy! He may well have been, but the legend of The Barber as villain lives on. Sal's wife, Kathleen, summed it up best years ago. "He isn't tough at all," she said. "He lets his beard grow before a game so he'll look fierce. I used to wonder what people were talking about when they said he scowled ferociously at the batters. Then I stayed home one day and watched him on TV. I hardly knew him."

* * *

Ernie Banks added to Don Newcombe's 1957 miseries when the Cubs' young superstar shortstop sent Newk to his 11th loss of the season on Tuesday, August 27, at Ebbets Field. Chicago had already nicked Newk for a run when Banks stepped up to the plate with two on and two out in the top of the first. Moments later a Newcombe fastball was flying into the lower leftfield stands to extend the Cubbie lead to 4–0. Newcombe escaped the first with no further damage, but when he struggled again in the second, Walter Alston quickly went to the mound to pull him. Unwritten baseball etiquette states that the pitcher being replaced should stay on the mound with the manager until the reliever arrives, but Newcombe was such a bundle of emotion and anger in 1957 that he, on occasion, violated this baseball axiom. Big Don's most recent transgression of this unwritten rule occurred during Brooklyn's August 7 loss to the Giants at Jersey City. Newk held a 5–3 lead on the Giants through eight innings that day, but the roof caved in on him in the ninth when New York's Hank Sauer clouted a go-ahead, three-run home run. Alston came out to yank Newcomb, so Don handed Walt the ball and stormed off the field—*before* reliever Clem Labine arrived at the mound. The fans immediately recognized Newcombe's encroachment and proceeded to boo him unmercifully. Newk was apparently unfazed by the fans' reaction back on August 7 because he now again handed Alston the ball and stalked off the field before reliever Danny McDevitt arrived. The fans again booed vociferously.

August 28: Furillo Stays Hot

The fans cheered vociferously the next day, August 28, as Carl Furillo Night was held at Ebbets Field. Furillo, 35 years old, was in his 12th big league season, all spent with the Dodgers. He was an institution in Brooklyn, and the fans were eager to show him their appreciation that evening. Dodgers broadcaster Vin Scully, 29 years old, was master of the 40-minute ceremony in which Furillo, his wife Fern, and their sons Carl Jr. and Jon were showered with over 100 gifts from friends and admirers. Among the $10,000 in presents was a brand new Cadillac for Carl and a Shetland pony for the Furillo boys. Furillo also received an inscribed silver tray from his teammates and congratulatory telegrams from President Eisenhower; New York Governor Averell Harriman; and George M. Leader, governor of Carl's native state of Pennsylvania. After the ceremonies and shortly before the game began, umpire Jocko Conlan demonstrated the respect the umps had for Carl by pulling him aside and saying, "We wanted to get you something, but we're not allowed." Furillo later exhibited his class and thoughtfulness by donating to an orphanage the 150 pounds of candy and the huge 10-layer cake given to him that night.

As if the added attraction of Carl Furillo Night was not enough to make the price of the game ticket more than a bargain that evening, upon conclusion of the festivities the fans were treated to extra baseball in a 4-hour-and-14-minute, 14-inning marathon that ended at 1:00 a.m. sharp when Elmer Valo lined a pinch-hit single to drive in the winning run. Furillo delivered a run-scoring triple and a single in the 4–3 victory, but particularly notable in the game was Ed Roebuck's nine innings of scoreless relief to earn the win.

The Brooklyn Dodgers were an aging team in 1957, and no one on the ballclub felt the negative effects of age and wear-and-tear more than Carl Furillo. His body was breaking down, the natural result of three hardscrabble minor league seasons, three grueling years in the Army during World War II, and over 1,500 rough-and-tumble games in a Dodger uniform. Two of the worse maladies Furillo suffered from in 1957 had their genesis in 1956—a bad throwing elbow and myste-rious abdominal pain. "The Arm's" elbow was injured late in the '56 season when Furillo crashed into the right field wall, and it had never been "right" since. The abdominal pains that plagued him in '56 were attributed to a "festering appendix," so Furillo had surgery to remove the appendix after the season—but this failed to solve the problem and he continued to be troubled by this mystery pain.

The veteran-loaded 1957 Dodgers mostly bore the stamp of Branch Rickey despite the fact that he'd been gone since 1950. Furillo, however, along with 38-year-old teammate Pee Wee Reese, went back even fur-ther and were the last of the MacPhail men. MacPhail, on a quest to build up the Dodger farm chain, purchased the Class-B Reading Chicks fran-chise and its players for $5,000 prior to 1941. "They got about 15 players, a set of old uniforms, and a broken-down bus," Furillo later recalled. "I was the only one out of the whole crowd that ever made it to the majors." The bus, a hard-to-get commodity in the months before Pearl Harbor, might have been the thing MacPhail coveted most when he purchased the Reading team, but he also knew he might have a diamond in the rough in Furillo, a tough kid from Stony Creek Mills, Pennsylvania, who looked like a big-league hitter and had an arm like a bazooka. It was the combined efforts of a recreational league coach and a local sportswriter that made it possible for Furillo to land with Reading. First, they gar-nered 18-year-old Furillo a spot on the roster of the Class-D Pocomoke City Chicks of the Eastern Shore League in 1940. Then, when Furillo put together a fine year at Pokomoke, they saw to it that he was sent up to Reading at the end of the season.

Furillo continued to develop with a full year at Reading in 1941 and a solid year with the Montreal Royals in 1942, but he shelved his base-ball career for three years in the Army, 1943 to 1945. Already tough as nails, Furillo grew even tougher in the Army where he served on the front lines in the Pacific. While there he was wounded and subsequently awarded a Purple Heart—which he rejected because he felt he had not been valiant enough to earn it. Upon his return to the States he earned a spot on the Dodgers roster in 1946 and never looked back. Furillo was the foundation of Branch Rickey's youth movement and a vital cog in the success the Dodgers enjoyed throughout his career. He was steady and productive, and seemed to get better each year—but his contribution was often overshadowed by more personable Dodgers stars like Duke Snider, Jackie Robinson, Pee Wee Reese, Gil Hodges, Roy Campanella, and Carl Erskine. But Furillo's role in the Dodgers' ascent to greatness was equal to anyone who wore the uniform during his era, and by 1957 he had played in six World Series with Brooklyn.

The Dodgers were the youngest club in the National League in 1947, and by 1957 they were the oldest. Despite his physical troubles of 1956, Furillo rejected the notion that he was over the hill when the 1957 season began, and he resented the trade rumors involving him. "What's all this talk about trading me because I'm getting old," he told Dick Young of the *Daily News*. "That's all I keep hearing. I'm so old that I would have won the batting title if I didn't get sick in August. I was hitting .320—and was climbing—when I got the virus, and then the appendicitis pains." He played through it all, however, and finished the '56 season at .289 and 21 home runs. Still, Dodger V.P. Buzzie Bavasi told Furillo he'd had a bad year when it came time to negotiate his 1957 salary. Enraged, Furillo gave Bavasi an earful, and Buzzie eventually backed down and conceded that Carl deserved the same salary he'd earned in '56.

Furillo got off to a good start in 1957. His four runs driven in on April 21 put him at 903 for his career, making him just the fourth Dodger to pass the 900 RBI mark, the others being Zach Wheat, Gil Hodges, and Duke Snider. By May 20 Furillo had driven in 29 runs in 27 games, far surpassing his pace of 1956. But a few weeks later Carl was suffering from pains in his side, something Dodgers physician Dr. Richard Kubiak speculated was just harmless (but painful) adhesions that may have formed after his appendix surgery. "He said the dozen x-rays they took of my abdomen didn't show a darn thing wrong with me," said a frustrated Furillo. Carl continued to fret about it, though, and his batting average began to plummet. He covertly went to the Long Island College Hospital for further examinations, but they sent him away with a vague diagnosis of "debilitation" and "anemia." Finally, in mid–July, he was benched.

The '57 All-Star break offered Furillo a chance to escape his worries, and he did so by chartering a fishing boat. His only concern was that he'd have to cancel his reservation if he was elected to the midsummer classic. Amazingly, Furillo—who seemed to hit 15 to 20 homers each year, bat around .300, drive in 80 to 90 runs, and play brilliant right field—was never an All-Star. Not even in 1953 when he led the league with a .344 average. He was an alternate that year, as he was the previous season, but he had never been an out-and-out All-Star, and that seems to bolster the now-accepted narrative of many that Furillo was always underrated due to the more accessible personalities of many of his superstar teammates. As it turned out, Furillo's worry that he might have to cancel his fishing trip was for naught as he again failed to make the All-Star team.

With his batting average at an un–Furillo-like .257 on July 21, Carl started the nightcap of a twin-bill against the Cubs that day and rapped out two hits. It seemed to be the spark he needed, and by August he was back as a starter in right field and his average steadily rose until the end of the season when he finished strong at .306. It wasn't unusual for Furillo to heat up in the dog days of August just when many players were slowing down from the heat and the grind of another long season. It was his pattern for many of his 12 years with the Dodgers. As Dick Young put it, "Furillo is quite a physical specimen, and has a well-developed pride to match," and these strengths helped Carl excel with regularity down the stretch.

Furillo blistered the ball at a .447 clip for the first nine games of August, but his bum elbow flared up again and forced him to sit out the next six games. "That's the way it goes," a defeated Walter Alston told reporters. "A hitter gets hot and then something happens to him." During his hot streak Furillo took the opportunity to be a guest on the *NBC Game of the Week's* pregame show starring Leo Durocher. It was quite an eye-opening event since Furillo and Durocher had been involved in a long, well-publicized feud. The bad blood began right away when a young Furillo joined the Dodgers in 1946. Fresh out of the service and flat broke, Furillo was forced to sign what he felt was an unfairly low-ball contract. "Take it or leave it," Dodger manager Durocher flatly told Furillo—and Furillo hated him from that day on. There had already been trouble between the two when Durocher, through some misinformation, believed Furillo to be a heavy drinker. Furillo was a "soda pop" guy, and he told Durocher so, but Leo had made up his mind for the time being. Furillo would have to prove his integrity, which he did—but the animosity between the two continued to fester. The Durocher–Furillo feud increased when Leo left the Dodgers to manage the Giants in the middle of the 1948 season—and began ordering his pitchers to throw at Carl. The situation came to a head in 1953 when Ruben Gomez drilled Furillo with a pitch in a game on September 6. Carl had had enough. Instead of going after Gomez, however, Furillo took off after Durocher and nearly killed Leo when he clamped down on The Lip's skull with an unrelenting, vise-like, death hold.

Furillo would always retain his disdain for Durocher, but Carl knew it was in his best interest to play nice, so he agreed to appear on Leo's pregame show on August 3, 1957. Durocher charmingly asked Furillo why he'd charged him and set off the now-famous rhubarb back in 1953? Sparing the viewers the long backstory, Furillo simply said, "I had been hit by the pitch and I saw fire." Shifting away from his very-personal incident with Durocher, Furillo added, "There will be numerous other player scraps *this* season due to the hot pennant race and the way the pitchers are pitching the hitters tight." Carl's Dodgers, however, would not be in the thick of it when the season ended, but on this day they were still within reach at just 2½ games back when Furillo sat down with Durocher on NBC.

Continuing to be a hot topic at that time was the matter of whether the Dodgers would move to Los Angeles in 1958. The question troubled Furillo all season because it was an unknown entity in Carl's everyday quest to earn money, provide for his family, and save every cent he could for the future. Simplifying a very complex struggle between Walter O'Malley and Brooklyn city planner Robert Moses, Furillo asked, "Why don't these politicians let the fans vote on whether the Dodgers stay here—why?" But no vote was needed to determine whether the Brooklyn fans wanted the Dodgers to stay—they most certainly did. The sad reality for the fans was the realization that they had absolutely no say in the final decision. Still, they let their voice be heard. One prominent voice in August of '57 was that of Brooklyn-born actor-singer-performer Phil Foster, who would later go on to star as the father of Laverne DeFazio (actress Penny Marshall) on the 1970s TV comedy *Laverne & Shirley*. Foster released a clever single on Coral Records called "Let's Keep the Dodgers in Brooklyn." Sung in a heavy Brooklyn accent, the song's lyrics aimed to drive home the theme that the Dodgers and Brooklyn were meant to go together. The two were inseparable. In the case of Skoonj, the lyrics paired the names Erskine and Furillo, saying to remove these players from Brooklyn would be "like a bed without a pillow."

Schmaltzy, yes, but the sentiment was heartfelt—and ineffective. In spite of the efforts of Phil Foster, the Dodgers would leave for Los Angeles, and as hard as it was for Brooklynites to imagine Carl Furillo in L.A., he did, in fact, move there with the team. Even Carl had a tough time getting used to it, though. "It's funny to say 'Los Angeles' Dodgers," Furillo told Dick Young early in '58. "I find myself saying 'Brooklyn' Dodgers most of the time, and people correct me. You now who it's gonna be hardest on—the kids. The kids in Brooklyn. Just before I left home, I was talking about it with my wife. We wondered about the kids who used to come to the games, and what they're going to do now. What's going to become of the Knothole Gangs?"

	Games	At Bats	Hits	2B	3B	HR	HR%	R	RBI	BB	SO	SB	BA	SA
YEAR: 1957	119	395	121	17	4	12	3.0	61	66	29	33	0	.306	.461
CAREER: 15 YRS	1806	6378	1910	324	56	192	3.0	895	1058	514	436	48	.299	.458

8-28-57: A festive night at Ebbets field finally ended at 1:00 AM when Elmer Valo hit a 14th-inning game-winning pinch single to lift the Dodgers to a 4-3 win over the Cubs. The festivities were on account of it being "CARL FURILLO Night" whereupon the great Brooklyn rightfielder was bestowed with nearly 100 presents in a pre-game ceremony. Gifts included a new car for Carl and his wife Fern, and a Shetland pony for the Furillo boys. Carl presented the fans with a run-scoring triple and an 11th-inning single. Carl was red hot with the bat in August and September, collecting 55 hits in his last 137 at-bats to lift his season-ending average to .306.

* * *

August 30 saw Carl Furillo continue his "salary drive," as some sportswriters came to dub Skoonj's annual end-of-season hot streaks, by walloping his 10th home run of the season in a 10–0 rout over the lame-duck Giants in the opener of a three-game series at Ebbets Field. Furillo chipped in two more hits, boosting his August average in 15 games to .440 and his overall season mark up to .284. The Dodgers closed out the month of August the next day with their third win in a row, a 7–5 triumph over the Giants in front of a noisy Ebbets Field crowd of 22,267. Gil Hodges slammed his 24th home run of the season in the win, a two-run clout off right-hander Al Worthington. The long-ball was Hodges' seventh in the last 12 Dodger games, and it left him just five homers short of 300 for his career. Dodger fans knew Hodges would easily reach the 300-homer milestone, but they could not be sure whether he'd do so in 1957 since there was only a month remaining in the campaign. And with the unsolved question of where the Dodgers would be playing in 1958, it left some to ponder whether or not Gil would reach the milestone as a Brooklyn Dodger.

SEVEN

September

The month of August ended with the Brooklyn Dodgers in second place in the National League, seven games behind the Milwaukee Braves and a half-game ahead of the third-place St. Louis Cardinals. Brooklyn had been in this position before—as recently as 1956. The Bums were in second place as September began in 1956, but they were just 2½ games in back of the Braves. Overcoming that deficit had seemed like a miracle, so the seven-game deficit of '57 seemed nearly impossible to erase. Distracted by their negotiations to move the ballclub or not, the Dodgers' front office seemed detached from the on-field developments. They failed to make any significant moves to help the team's chances to make a run as they did in 1956 when mid-season acquisition Sal Maglie carried the club to a pennant. Many players and fans felt the front office had given up on 1957 and was looking forward to 1958—in Los Angeles— and their suspicions were bolstered when Maglie was sold to the Yankees on September 2. The players would keep playing, and the Flatbush fans would keep rooting, but the only real question that seemed to be remaining was: Would September 1957 be the last month that Brooklyn would be home to the Dodgers?

* * *

Going for a sweep of the Giants on Sunday, September 1 at Ebbets Field, the fans watched it slip away as Roy Campanella watched a called third strike go by to end the game, giving New York a 7–5 verdict. Campanella ducked away from the Marv Grissom bender, but it broke back over the plate according to home plate umpire Lee Ballanfant. Campy argued loudly, but the 17,936 fans on hand seemed split on whether or not it was a strike. The punch-out ended what would turn out to be the last game ever played between the New York Giants and the Brooklyn Dodgers at Ebbets Field.

With Maglie ferried off to the Yankees following the Bums' loss

178

to the Giants, an ominous dark cloud seemed to settle over the Dodgers and Brooklyn. The cloud cast a shadow on everything, including a September 2 twin-bill against the visiting Phillies. When the day was over, Brooklyn had dropped both ends of the double-header to the fourth-place Phils. Dodger pitchers Danny McDevitt, Clem Labine, and Don Bessent were hammered for 17 hits and 10 runs in the opener, while Roger Craig and Ed Roebuck took it on the chin in the nightcap by surrendering 14 more hits and seven more runs. The 18,895 cash customers had little to cheer for, but they were treated to Duke Snider's 35th and 36th round-trippers, as well as additional Dodger home runs by John Roseboro and Carl Furillo.

Brooklyn closed out their long homestand with a 3–2 loss to the Phillies in 12 innings at Jersey City on September 3. The game was the last in the Roosevelt Stadium experiment, something in which the Dodger brass had obviously lost interest as their attention had turned to California. Most of the 10,190 in attendance seemed to care only about booing Duke Snider, but, if they were paying attention, they were witness to a fine pitchers' duel. Don Drysdale gallantly pitched all 12 innings for the Dodgers but was undone by a game-tying two-run homer by Phils rookie outfielder Harry Anderson in the ninth. The go-ahead run was scored in the top of the 12th when former Dodger Chico Fernandez crossed on a sacrifice fly by Puddin' Head Jones. Brooklyn's last chance died when pinch-hitter Elmer Valo was rung up looking at strike three to end the contest.

The game pushed Brooklyn's 1957 attendance to 1,000,927 with nearly an entire month still left to play. It was the 13th consecutive time the Dodgers had topped the one million mark, something no other major league club could claim. It was a clear statement that attendance was not the central reason for the talk of a Dodger move. It was all about what kind of deal the city, be it Brooklyn or Los Angeles, was willing to give Walter O'Malley.

* * *

With the end of the 1957 season fast approaching, Brooklyn left town for a 2½-week road trip beginning with a pair of games against the Phillies at Connie Mack Stadium. By the time the Dodgers returned to Brooklyn, there would be just four games left in the campaign. After dropping four in a row to wind up their homestand, the Dodgers began the road trip by taking both games from Philadelphia—12–3 on September 4 and 3–1 on September 5. Don Newcombe was the beneficiary of the offensive onslaught in the series opener and he gained his 11th victory. Five Dodgers had multi-hits, including Don Zimmer who banged out a single and a three-bagger in the seventh. Carl Erskine, making just his fifth start of the season in the series finale, saw less firepower behind him than Newk enjoyed, but Oisk looked like the Oisk of old, allowing just one run in 7⅔ innings to earn the win.

Next, Brooklyn traveled up to Harlem for three games against the Giants at the Polo Grounds. By now it was old news that the Giants were leaving after the season, so everyone knew this was the last chance to witness the storied Brooklyn–New York rivalry as this was the final time the two clubs would meet in 1957. Fully understanding the scope of the situation, a lively crowd of 21,373 turned out on September 6 for game one of the historic three-game series, but Johnny Podres ensured that they had no outlet for their enthusiasm. In one of his best games of the season, Podres crafted a three-hit shutout for a 3–0 victory. The whitewashing was his league-leading sixth of the campaign, a statistic that was even more impressive when considering that the win was only the 11th of the year for Podres. Johnny often said that he pitched his best ball in 1957 despite the fact that he didn't have the wins to show for it, and his victory on September 6 was a perfect illustration of his point.

Back in the lineup after a couple of days off to rest his troublesome knee, Duke Snider delivered a three-run homer to help lift Brooklyn to a 5–4 win over New York on September 7. Trailing 3–1 in the top of the sixth, Snider unloaded on Ruben Gomez, sending the ball screaming into the leftfield lower tier. It was Duke's 37th home run of the season. Danny McDevitt started the game but wasn't sharp, so he was relieved by Roger Craig with two out and the bases filled in the fourth. Craig fanned Ray Jablonski to end the threat, and then, in one of his best performances of 1957, pitched the rest of the game to wrap up the triumph for Brooklyn.

*   *   *

Veteran *New York Times* sportswriter Louis Effrat covered the last game the Brooklyn Dodgers played against the New York Giants—September 8, 1957. With an all-business approach, Effrat wrote,

> The break was a clean one—no tears, no dawdling—as the Giants and the Dodgers met for the last time yesterday at the Polo Grounds. In 1 hour 53 minutes and before 22,376 fans, many of whom had made the long trip from Brooklyn, the Giants beat the Dodgers, 3–2. The next time the clubs engage each other, one will be the San Francisco Giants. The other will be the

Dodgers, Brooklyn or Los Angeles, but certain it is that never again will the teams perform in the lee of Coogan's Bluff.

Starting pitchers Don Drysdale and Curt Barclay pitched well, and both defenses were stellar, but it was the big bat of Hank Sauer that would be the difference maker. Trailing 2–0 in the fourth, the 38-year-old Giants slugger uncorked a three-run bomb off Drysdale that would prove to be the only scoring the Giants would need. "The turnout was excellent," wrote Effrat, "and as the spectators filed out of the ballpark, one was heard to say, 'If the Giants had played this well more often in the past, they wouldn't be heading for California. There would be no worrying about attendance here.'"

September 10: Fred Kipp—Brooklyn Dodger for Life

From New York, the Dodgers traveled to Chicago for their final series of the season against the Cubs. Cubs fans were well aware that this might be their last chance to see the *Brooklyn* Dodgers but it didn't inspire them to turn out to Wrigley Field for the series opener on September 10. Maybe it was fatigue over the Dodgers story, or perhaps it was simple disinterest in their own club which was sitting in last place, but only 3,489 paying customers attended. The small but loyal Cubbie crowd was rewarded, however, with a 9–2 victory, fueled mostly by a pair of homers by Ernie Banks.

The Dodgers were already trailing the Cubs, 4–0, when 25-year-old rookie left-hander Fred Kipp was sent in to relieve Don Bessent with none out and a man on first in the third. It was Kipp's first big-league appearance—and it would be his only appearance of 1957. It didn't go well. Kipp got a quick out by forcing Jim Bolger at second on an attempted sac bunt by Dale Long, but the next batter, Bobby Morgan, belted a home run into the left field stands. Kipp held the Cubs in check for the rest of the third, fourth, and fifth innings, but then surrendered a big three-run blast to Banks in the sixth. Kipp got out of the inning when Bolger grounded out to third base but Fred's initiation into the major leagues had been a bittersweet affair.

Kipp was the top lefty in the Dodger farm system at the close of the 1956 season. It was believed that he'd be the first of the franchise's prized young southpaws to be called up to the big club in 1957, but when that time came in June the call went instead to Danny McDevitt. Meanwhile, Kipp remained in Montreal where he suffered through a tough season that saw him lose a league leading 17 games for the Royals. He still had the same high-quality stuff—a good fastball, curve, change and knuckler—that helped him win 20 games for Montreal in 1956. The difference, however, was that the Dodgers, with an eye on their possible move to Los Angeles, had moved many of their best farmhands westward to their St. Paul affiliate, leaving the '57 Royals somewhat depleted. The Dodgers knew better than to be too concerned by Kipp's 1957 record with the Royals, though. He'd been a solid performer in their farm system since 1953, so he still figured in their plans for the future.

Lean and lanky at 6-foot-4 and 200 pounds, Kipp, who hailed from Piqua, Kansas, distinguished himself in basketball and baseball in high school and subsequently at Kansas State University and Emporia Teachers' College. Following graduation, Kipp hopped on a train to Vero Beach for Dodgers spring training of 1953 and was soon signed by longtime Dodgers scout Bert Wells, himself a Kansan from Larned. Kipp made Wells look brilliant by immediately paying dividends, winning 15 games for Class-B Asheville while also nabbing the Tri-State League's Earned Run Average title with a 2.23 ERA. While in Asheville that season Kipp demonstrated his ability to swing the bat quite well by batting .343 with two home runs. Despite his humble assessment of his hitting skills—"I was a good hitter *for a pitcher*, but I was not a good *hitter*"— his .281 career minor league average and his .243 career major league average say that Kipp was more than capable at the plate. Kipp's capacity to swing the bat was just a bonus for the Dodgers, though. It was his left-handed slants that they were most excited about, and they were looking forward to seeing what the kid would do in 1954 following his fine '53 campaign at Asheville—but Uncle Sam intervened and Kipp spent 1954 and most of '55 at various U.S. Army outposts.

He was discharged from the Army in time to help the Mobile Bears win the Southern Association's league playoffs, followed by winning the Dixie Series over the Shreveport Sports of the Texas league. Then came his 20-win season at Montreal in 1956 where he won the International League's Rookie of the Year Award. The Dodgers rewarded Kipp by allowing him to pitch batting practice during the 1956 World Series against the Yankees. While there he experienced something he'd never forget—watching Don Larsen pitch his perfect game.

Kipp was on the Los Angeles Dodgers roster for all of 1958 where he appeared in 40 games—nine of them as a starter. He requested a trade prior to the 1959 season when he continued to find himself stuck behind Danny McDevitt on the depth chart. Instead of trading him, however,

		Games	IP	Won	Lost	Pct	Hits	Runs	ER	SO	Walks	ERA
YEAR: 1957		1	4	0	0	.000	6	4	4	3	0	9.00
CAREER: 4 YRS		47	113.1	6	7	.462	119	67	64	64	48	5.08

9-10-57: Dodger hopes of returning to the World Series continued to dim as the Brooks were drubbed 9-2 by the Cubs at Wrigley Field. Lots of new names were appearing on Brooklyn line-up cards with the expanded September rosters, and one of those names was **FRED KIPP**. A left-handed reliever from Piqua, Kansas, Fred made his major league debut when he entered this game in the 3rd inning. Cubs slugger Ernie Banks stole a little of the joy from the occasion, however, by singling off Fred in the 4th and then tagging him for a 3-run homer in the 6th. Fred, a former college basketball star, was a 20-game winner with Montreal of the International League in 1956.

H.M.M. WHAT ARE THEY TRYIN' TO TELL ME?!

AFTER FAILING TO CRACK THE LINE-UP, FRED WAS OPTIONED TO MONTREAL ON 4-26-57!

the Dodgers sent him down to St. Paul where he posted an excellent season. A late season call-up allowed him to pitch in the playoffs against Milwaukee, but he was not eligible to be on the World Series roster against the White Sox. The trade Kipp wanted finally came through in the winter before the 1960 season as he was dealt to the Yankees. The Dodgers thought highly of the gentlemanly Kansan, though, and told him he'd always have a job with the organization after his playing days if he chose to go that route. Kipp thanked Walter O'Malley for treating him well, then headed off to join the Yanks. But things were no different there, and Kipp spent most of 1960 with Triple-A Richmond, appearing in just four games for New York. After two more years on the Yankee farm in Richmond, Kipp saw the writing on the wall and called it quits. Instead of returning to the Dodgers for the job they held for him, Kipp ultimately founded his own construction firm back home in Kansas.

Kipp has no bitterness over the fact that his major league career may not have reached the heights he'd dreamed of. Instead, he's proud to have made it to the show at a time when only a select few gained admission. He's proud that he played for two Hall of Fame managers—Walter Alston and Casey Stengel. He's proud to have played with Hall of Fame teammates Jackie Robinson, Pee Wee Reese, Duke Snider, Roy Campanella, Sandy Koufax—and George "Sparky" Anderson. He's proud to have played on pennant-winning teams in the majors and minors. He's proud to have been inducted into the Kansas Baseball Hall of Fame. All of those things are great in Kipp's mind, but what Fred is most proud of is that he, thanks to a single four-inning appearance on September 10, 1957, will always be a member of the *Brooklyn* Dodgers. He holds that distinction in higher regard than being a *Los Angeles* Dodger or a New York Yankee. Those ballclubs, while storied, still exist and add new members to their roster every year. The door has been closed on the Brooklyn Dodgers for over 50 years, and Fred Kipp is happy to have slipped in before it was locked forever.

Kipp, now officially a *Brooklyn* Dodger in the record book, was safely back on the bench in the bullpen the next day, September 11, when he watched his teammate, Johnny Podres, pitch a gem against the same Cubs that had battered him and the rest of the Dodgers pitchers the day before. The Wrigley crowd was again sparse—just 3,461—but this time they had no offensive fireworks to enjoy as their Cubbies were completely dominated by Podres, who went the distance while defeating Chicago, 9–1. The only thing that kept Podres from pitching his seventh shutout was Ernie Banks who continued to swing a hot bat, slugging his

37th home run in the second inning. After witnessing Banks take himself and Don Bessent deep the day before, Kipp was not surprised to see Ernie continue to pound Dodger pitching. The triumph was Podres' 12th of the season, a new single-season career high for him, and he seemed to be gaining strength as the season wound down having surrendered just one run in his last 18 innings. Carl Furillo led the Dodger attack while continuing his standard end-of-season surge as he collected four hits and raised his average to .308.

* * *

Brooklyn opened up a season-deciding three-game series against Milwaukee on September 12. The first-place Braves held a seven-game lead over the third-place Dodgers. Even if the Dodgers were to fortunate enough to sweep the series, they'd still be trailing the Braves by four games with just eleven to play—and no head-to-head match-ups between the two teams remaining. The idea of a Dodger sweep was a moot point when Milwaukee captured the series opener, 2–1, but the way in which they won the game went a long way to snuffing out any fighting spirit the Dodgers may have still had. Leading 1–0 in the fourth, the Dodgers looked to add to their lead when Jim Gilliam stepped in to hit with the bases loaded and just one out. Gilliam hit a sinking liner that Andy Pafko seemed to catch in right field. Roy Campanella held at second and Danny McDevitt stayed on first, but Charlie Neal tagged at third and scored what appeared to be the Dodgers' second run of the game. But Pafko fired the ball in to second baseman Red Schoendienst who tagged Campy and then stepped on second to force McDevitt. The ruling was that Pafko had not made the catch and Eddie Sudol, the umpire in right, had signaled as such, setting up the unorthodox double-play. The Dodgers argued vehemently, but to no avail—the double-play stood and the run didn't count.

If it looked to Brooklyn like some good old-fashioned home cookin'—Milwaukee style—it only got worse in the bottom of the ninth. With the game tied, 1–1, Danny McDevitt, hurling a brilliant two-hitter, pitched to Wes Covington with Johnny Logan on first and none out. Covington quickly bounced into a threat-killing double-play—or so the Bums thought. It turned out that the plate umpire, Dusty Boggess, had called time out. McDevitt didn't hear time called, so he threw the pitch. Covington, who had asked for time, for some reason still swung at the pitch. The twin-killing was nullified, and the Dodgers again engaged in a spirited debate. Given a new life at the plate, Covington singled and

Johnny Logan moved to third, then scored the winning run on a long single over the head of a drawn-in Carl Furillo. "The victory, no matter how tainted," wrote Roscoe McGowen of the *New York Times*, "was greeted with rousing cheers by a majority of the 32,353 fans." It was as if the Braves fans knew that this victory signified that it was, after many years of playing second fiddle to the Brooklyn Dodgers, *their* year.

Despite their bitter loss in game one of the series, Brooklyn rallied to take the next two from Milwaukee. Don Drysdale went the route for the Dodgers on September 13 to nab a 5–1 victory. The win was his 15th of the campaign. Carl Erskine got the triumph in the series finale on September 14 by limiting the Braves to just four hits as he cruised to a 7–1 complete-game win. His arm trouble had reduced Erskine to just four previous starts in 1957, but he put it all together on this day to raise his record to 5-and-2. The game ended when Del Crandall grounded to Pee Wee Reese at third, who threw to Gil Hodges at first. Without hesitation, the entire Dodger team rushed to Erskine to congratulate him for a great performance. They all knew the pain he was enduring to pitch. And they all respected him as one of the finest men in the game—so their joy for his success was heartfelt. Even the Milwaukee fans couldn't help but root for Erskine in spite of the fact that their confidence was shaken a bit by watching their Braves lose two of three to the Bums. "Midway through the game," wrote McGowen, "many of the 40,775 fans in County Stadium gave a round of applause to the little Hoosier right-hander as he went to bat. That sort of thing is on the unusual side in this hotbed of partisan fandom."

September 17: The Little Pitcher with the Big Heart

The Brooklyn express rolled south to Cincy after the Milwaukee series, then ground to a halt as the Dodgers lost back-to-back games to the fourth-place Reds. Hal Jeffcoat, Bob Thurman, Ed Bailey and Frank Robinson exploded for home runs while leading the Reds to an 11–6 romp on September 15. Then on September 16, despite a fine effort from Johnny Podres, the Reds again came out on top, 3–2, when Ed Roebuck walked in the winning run in the 10th inning. The Dodgers were in a different city, St. Louis, the next day, September 17—but the result was the same as they again lost. The 12–5 whipping handed them by the Cardinals was Brooklyn's third straight loss and moved the Dodgers increasingly closer to elimination from the pennant race. Leading 5–3 as the game headed into the bottom of the seventh, the Cards battered Brooklyn hurlers for six runs by the time Walter Alston signaled little Jackie Collum to the mound. The scrappy five-foot-seven-inch left-hander, acquired from the Cubs back on May 23, was making just his third appearance for Brooklyn, but he, too, took his licks from the Cardinals that day, surrendering two earned runs on four hits in 1⅔ innings pitched.

While he was part of the Dodgers defeat that day, just being in the big leagues was a victory for the little pitcher with the big heart. The odds were stacked against him from conception when his DNA determined that he would grow to just five-and-a-half feet tall. Clubs wanted big pitchers by the 1950s, so one look at Collum was enough to make most teams skeptical of his ability to help them. As if his diminutive size wasn't enough of a disadvantage, Collum suffered a near fatal accident as a child that left his pitching hand permanently disfigured. Born into a farm family in Iowa, four-year-old Jackie was helping his mother and father load hay into the loft when his left hand got caught in a pulley—the force pinning him to a pole. A large spike in the pole ripped into his neck and jaw, narrowly missing his jugular vein, while the pulley severed the tips of Collum's index and middle fingers. Miraculously, he recovered with the only lasting effects being that the two injured fingers would forever be a half inch shorter than the corresponding fingers on his right hand. While not nearly as disfiguring as the farm injury that mangled the pitching hand of Mordecai "Three-Finger" Brown, Collum's injury would have the same effect for him—it improved his pitching repertoire. While he admitted that it was more difficult for him to grip the ball securely, Collum added, "Those short fingers enable me to put more twist on my screwball." And it was his sinking screwball that became his signature pitch.

After a standout high school career where he developed his pitching and hitting skills by playing with older kids in population-deprived Grinnell, Iowa, Collum enlisted in the Air Force and eventually found himself pitching in the 1945 Pacific Theater Championship Series. It was there that he defeated a team that featured several major leaguers including Pee Wee Reese, Stan Musial and Joe Garagiola. Collum's Air Force batterymate was Bernie Gerl, a tall, lanky catcher who'd spent 1944 with Lynchburg (Virginia), the St. Louis Cardinal's Class-B Piedmont League affiliate. Gerl knew Collum had the stuff it took to make it in pro ball, so Bernie made a call to the Cards who followed through by sending scout Walter Shannon to Iowa in the middle of a blizzard in the winter of 1946. Shannon signed Collum without ever seeing him pitch. Actually, Mr. Collum signed the contract since his son was just 19 years old. And there would be no signing bonus—just the promise of a chance to make the roster of one of the Cards' many farm teams. And make it he did, thanks in part to advice from Cardinals lefty Harry Brecheen who'd ridden his own screwball to 55 wins and World Series glory from 1943 to '46. Like Gerl, Brecheen saw potential in Collum, but Harry knew Jackie needed another pitch—so he taught him how to throw the screwgie.

Armed with his new pitch, Collum distinguished himself starting and relieving at various Cardinals outposts until he was finally given a big-league call-up with St. Louis in September of 1951. He made his debut on September 21 and responded by tossing a shutout against the Chicago Cubs. He finished the 1951 season at 2-and-1 with a 1.59 ERA in three appearances, but the Cards were still not convinced, so they sent him down to Rochester after just two early-season appearances in 1952. Dealt to the Reds in May of 1953, Collum logged respectable seasons for Cincinnati through 1955. Peppered within those years were some noteworthy occurrences. There was an interesting fact about Collum unknown to most fans and players—Jackie could throw with either hand. It became common knowledge one day when Collum stepped off the mound with runners on first and second. The little lefty slipped the glove off his right hand and then transferred the ball to his right hand. Seeing that the baseball was now in Collum's non-throwing right hand (or so he mistakenly thought), the baserunner at second relaxed— then Collum whipped a right-handed throw to shortstop Roy McMillan who tagged the runner out. Umpire Al Barlick called time and ruled it a non-play, sending the runner back to second and saying that Collum had deceived the runner. "Tell me when a runner who is picked off isn't deceived," said Collum. The Reds argued that pick-off rules were irrelevant since Collum was off the rubber when he threw to second, but Barlick would not be moved and his call stood.

After posting an excellent first half for the Reds in 1954, Collum received a telegram asking him to join the N.L. All-Star team as a batting practice pitcher. It was that experience that introduced him to another Jackie—Jackie Robinson, someone Collum would always cite from then on as a person he truly liked and respected. "I don't know how he took all that abuse," Collum said of Robinson. "He was not only a great player, but a great person. He was very intelligent and determined to play ball in spite of everything happening around him." Before the 1954 season was over, Collum added another item to his resume—he hit a home run.

Folks in the minor leagues knew the little southpaw was a good-hitting pitcher as he compiled a lifetime .260 batting average down in the bushes. He was even occasionally seen playing outfield or pinch-hitting during his 12 seasons in the minors. But as of September 11, 1954, he had yet to display any power in the majors. But that day he unloaded a big three-run tater off the Giants' Ruben Gomez at the Polo Grounds. That turned out to be Collum's only big-league round-tripper (he hit nine in his minor league career), but he went on to post a fine .246 lifetime major league average in 118 at-bats compiled over nine seasons.

Collum was traded back to the Cardinals in 1956 and was then dealt to the Cubs prior to the '57 campaign. He'd had a fine spring training for Chicago that season and was voted "Best N.L. Relief Pitcher" by *Sporting News* beat writers as the season opened, but he got off to a rough start with the Cubbies. Frustration boiled over on April 24 when Collum was ejected by plate umpire Stan Landes and subsequently fined $35 by N.L. president Warren Giles. Collum wasn't one who usually popped off, but Landes issued a record nine walks to Reds batters that inning, three by Jackie—so Collum let Landes know he felt Cubs pitchers were being squeezed. "The pint-sized Cub was the first National League player to be chased and fined this season," wrote the Associated Press.

Despite his slow start with the Cubs that April, the Dodgers liked what they'd seen in Collum over the years, so they jumped on the chance to acquire him when he became available in late May. He was dispatched to Montreal where he pitched very well and, as always, was a favorite of fans. Collum drew double-takes at Miami Stadium prior to a July 24 game against the Marlins when he pitched batting practice right-handed. "I once pitched a double-header in high school from both sides," he explained to amazed reporters. "Right now, I can throw just as hard with my right arm—I just don't know where the ball is going!" Despite his effectiveness at Montreal, including a great outing against Brooklyn in an exhibition game on August 19, the Dodgers were loaded with southpaws and didn't call Collum up until September. Jackie would appear just three games for the Brooks before the '57 season came to a close. He'd have a fine spring with the '58 Los Angeles Dodgers, but would appear in just two games for them in May before returning to Montreal.

Being with the 1957 Brooklyn Dodgers gave Collum the opportunity to play with the man he felt was the toughest hitter he ever had to pitch against—Carl Furillo. "He didn't try to overpower the ball," said Collum. "He would hit it wherever you threw it." Being with Brooklyn

	Games	IP	Won	Lost	Pct	Hits	Runs	ER	SO	Walks	ERA
YEAR: 1957*	3	4.1	0	0	.000	7	4	4	3	1	8.31
CAREER: 9 YRS	171	464.1	32	28	.533	480	247	214	171	173	4.15

9-17-57: The Cards punished Dodger pitching on this day, whipping Brooklyn 12-5 at Sportsman's Park. One of the unfortunate Dodger pitchers was little JACKIE COLLUM, a 5-foot-7-inch southpaw from Victor, Iowa. The game was well out of hand by the time Jackie entered in the 7th, but the diminutive lefty didn't have it on this day and was touched for four hits and two runs in 1-2/3 innings pitched. Jackie was acquired by Brooklyn from the Cubs on May 23, whereupon he was sent to Montreal where he pitched well until his September call-up.

*Only statistics from the 1957 Brooklyn Dodgers are displayed. Jackie played in an additional 9 games with the 1957 Chicago Cubs.

also gave Collum the chance to work with Roy Campanella, a man Jackie came to appreciate as the best catcher he would ever pitch to. "He knew the strengths and weaknesses of the hitters," Collum said of Campy, "and I could put the ball where he wanted it." Collum loved the game and worked hard to maximize his talent and overcome physical shortcomings that might have stopped less determined players from achieving their dream of making it to the majors. A lifetime record of 32-and-28 is a testament to that. But he humbly summed his career up this way: "I was a mediocre player, no doubt, but I was lucky enough to have had a chance to play with the best of them—18–19 Hall of Famers." But who's counting, anyway.

* * *

Big Don Drysdale put the Dodgers on his back on September 18 and snapped Brooklyn's three-game losing streak by pitching a 6–1 victory over the Cardinals at Busch Stadium. A two-run homer by Charlie Neal in the third inning helped Drysdale get the win. The Redbird loss dampened the hopes of St. Louis fans who, unlike Brooklyn fans, were still harboring hopes of capturing the pennant. The triumph was Drysdale's 16th of the season. Ed Roebuck helped button up the win by taking over in the ninth after Drysdale walked the first two Cardinal batters. But Big D's one run allowed over eight innings lowered his ERA to a league-leading 2.67—just .02 percentage points better than teammate Johnny Podres' 2.69 ERA. The Dodgers hustled aboard their plane after the game for a long flight to LaGuardia Field. Once back in Brooklyn they would begin their final homestand of 1957, a homestand many back in Brooklyn feared might be the last ever.

Understanding the significance of the fast-approaching end of the season, forces on both coasts were increasing their activities aimed at wooing the Dodgers. Los Angeles city officials adopted a resolution to open official negotiations with the Brooklyn baseball club for construction of a stadium in the Chavez Ravine area. "We are at the crossroads," Los Angeles Mayor Norris Paulson told his colleagues. "Are we going to be a bush league town or are we going to be major league in everything?" With that, Los Angeles put together a proposal so beneficial to the Dodgers that it left officials in Brooklyn wondering what they'd have to do to counter. Three hundred acres of free land at Chavez Ravine, ownership of half of the potential mineral and oil rights of the tract, city-funded access road construction—and more.

Back in Brooklyn, millionaire businessman-politician Nelson A.

Rockefeller had gotten into the act of trying to keep the Dodgers in Brooklyn with a last-ditch plan. Rockefeller's scheme involved he himself purchasing the site at Flatbush and Atlantic avenues in Brooklyn for $2,000,000; the city funding the razing of existing structures, clearing the land and relocating tenants and public utilities; and the Dodgers funding the building of the new ballpark. Rockefeller would give the Dodgers 20 years of free rent on the site with an option to buy the site at any time for the original price paid by Rockefeller. There were other details, but when it was all said and done, Walter O'Malley said no. "Any proposal involving $2,000,000 for the land prices the Dodgers out," said O'Malley. Who could blame him for his position when officials in Los Angeles were giving O'Malley an offer too great to refuse?

* * *

The Brooklyn Dodgers began their final homestand of 1957 on Friday, September 20—an evening affair against the Phillies. By the time Flatbush warrior Carl Erskine strolled up the old familiar Ebbets Field mound to start the game, his Dodgers had been eliminated from the pennant race by an afternoon game that saw the Braves defeat the Cubs. News of the Bums' elimination resulted in the smallest Ebbets Field night crowd of the season, just 6,749 paying customers, but Oisk still gave them their money's worth. Carl pitched the Dodgers to a 2–1 lead after eight innings but faltered in the ninth. By the time he was lifted with two outs, the Phils had taken a 3–2 lead—and that's how it ended. Many of those in attendance took out their frustration by booing their heroes, Duke Snider and Don Zimmer to name a couple, but even the most disappointed fans couldn't help but cheer Erskine's effort, as well as that of Gil Hodges who blasted his 27th home run of the season.

For those who missed out on Friday's Dodgers collapse, an exact repeat performance was offered up the next day, Saturday, September 21. Behind the excellent hurling of Johnny Podres, the Dodgers again led the Phillies, 2–1, going into the ninth inning. Podres got a quick out to open the last frame, but then issued back-to-back doubles. Walter Alston, who waited too long to rescue Erskine the night before, went to the pen quickly on this night and brought in the normally reliable Ed Roebuck. But Roebuck eventually walked in what would be the winning run as Brooklyn finally went down by a score of 3–2.

* * *

September 22: A Diamond in the Rough

After two consecutive gut-wrenching defeats to the Phillies, the Dodgers and their fans were in desperate need of a win in the series finale on Sunday, September 22. Don Drysdale proved to be up to the task as he pitched the Dodgers to a 7–3 triumph. The win was his 17th of the season—good enough to lead the Brooklyn staff. Drysdale's quest for victory was helped by an offensive output that included two homers from Duke Snider, numbers 39 and 40, and a round-tripper off the bat of six-foot-three-inch rookie first baseman Jim Gentile. A late season call-up was Gentile, and the homer was the first hit of his career. And it was a beauty—a towering fourth-inning bomb off Robin Roberts that crashed off the facade of the centerfield stands. It was the first of 179 long-balls Gentile would belt in his nine-year big league career, a career highlighted by a 1961 season with the Baltimore Orioles that saw Gentile smash 46 homers and 141 RBIs.

Glory for Gentile in Baltimore, however, was still years away in 1957, and for young Jim it probably seemed completely unattainable at that time. Not because he wasn't delivering the goods in the minors— he was. It just seemed that no matter what he did he couldn't crack the Brooklyn Dodgers' star-studded roster. So deep was the Dodgers' talent pool of the 1950s that Gentile had already spent five years in the Brooklyn farm system without so much as a sniff of the big leagues by the time the 1956 season ended. Despite racking up 136 home runs from 1953 through 1956, there just wasn't a spot for him on the big club with Gil Hodges still going strong at first base. So, the Dodgers chose to keep Gentile buried in the bushes rather than deal him to another team and risk having him come back to hurt the Dodgers down the road.

A star athlete at Sacred Heart Cathedral Preparatory in San Francisco, Gentile passed up basketball scholarship offers from USC and Stanford to sign with the Dodgers in the spring of 1952. It looked like he was ticketed for the Yankees like his idol Lou Gehrig, but when the moment came the Dodgers simply made an offer too good to refuse when they offered Gentile a signing bonus of $50,000. "I wanted to go with the Yankees," he later confessed to Yanks scout Paddy Cottrell, "but it was strictly a question of dough." The bonus was so rich that Gentile was even willing to sign as a left-handed pitcher when his real desire was to play first base and swing for the fences. Gentile was 12-and-1 with a 0.72 ERA and 135 strikeouts as a senior at Sacred Heart, but it was his performance in the 1952 East-West All-Star game that really put him on the radar of the Dodgers. Gentile struck out 17 batters that day and was named the game's MVP. For his effort he was rewarded with a trip to New York to see the 1952 World Series where he would watch the Yankees and Dodgers square off. While the New York and Brooklyn players battled on the ballfield, their respective team executives battled to sign Gentile. The Dodgers lost the Series but won Gentile.

They gave up on their experiment to groom Gentile as a pitcher after his rookie season in pro ball at Class-C Santa Barbara in 1952. It wasn't that he was completely awful—he was 2-and-6 with a 3.65 ERA— it was simply that his upside as a power hitter far outweighed his upside as a pitcher. Gentile explained it best in spring training of 1953 when he told sportswriters,

> Until my senior year in high school I played first base. But they needed a pitcher in my last year and I was elected because I could throw harder than any of the other boys. After I was signed to a Dodger contract by Bill Brenzel I figured I'd be able to go back to first base, which I prefer. But in Santa Barbara I ran into the same trouble as in high school—they needed a pitcher. I've got a fastball and nothing else. I was terrible. But in the last couple of weeks of the season I was used on first and I hit two homers.

The Dodgers moved him to first base permanently in 1953 and Gentile responded by leading the Class-A Western League with 34 home runs at Pueblo. He split 1954 between Pueblo and Double-A Mobile and again clouted 34 homers. Gentile produced 28 homers after a full season with Mobile in 1955, then erupted for 40 dingers with Double-A Ft. Worth in 1956.

If there were any doubters left, Gentile went a long way to convincing them after the '56 season. Jim would later say,

> I traveled to Japan with the Dodgers that off-season and I led the team in everything, every category—and home runs. Everything. They had always told me that it would take three to four years to make it to the big leagues. I was thinking now I was going to get a shot. They were talking about moving Gil Hodges to third base to bring me up in 1957. Well, it never came around.

While his big tour of Japan didn't net him a spot on Brooklyn's 1957 opening day roster, Gentile made believers out of a lot of his future Dodgers teammates. Duke Snider marveled at a couple balls that Gentile "rapped a country mile." Seeing Gentile continually powdering the ball in Japan led Roy Campanella to conclude that the kid was a true diamond in the rough. Soon, everyone was calling him "Diamond" Jim Gentile, a nickname that stuck permanently.

194

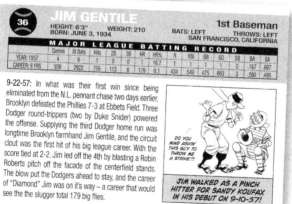

				MAJOR LEAGUE BATTING RECORD											
	Games	At Bats	Hits	2B	3B	HR	HR%	R	RBI	BB	SO	SB	BA	SA
YEAR: 1957	4	6	1	0	0	1	16.7	1	1	1	1	0	.167	.667
CAREER: 9 YRS	936	2922	759	113	6	179	6.1	434	549	475	663	3	.260	.486

9-22-57: In what was their first win since being eliminated from the N.L. pennant chase two days earlier, Brooklyn defeated the Phillies 7-3 at Ebbets Field. Three Dodger round-trippers (two by Duke Snider) powered the offense. Supplying the third Dodger home run was longtime Brooklyn farmhand Jim Gentile, and the circuit clout was the first hit of his big league career. With the score tied at 2-2, Jim led off the 4th by blasting a Robin Roberts pitch off the facade of the centerfield stands. The blow put the Dodgers ahead to stay, and the career of "Diamond" Jim was on it's way – a career that would see the the slugger total 179 big flies.

JIM WALKED AS A PINCH HITTER FOR SANDY KOUFAX IN HIS DEBUT ON 9-10-57!

Gentile was dispatched to Triple-A Montreal at the end of 1957 spring training. He hit 28 round-trippers while there and joined Brooklyn when the International League season ended. He made his Dodgers debut on September 10 against the Cubs, pinch-hitting for Sandy Koufax in the bottom of the second inning. He walked and was replaced in the top of the third when Don Bessent was sent in to pitch. Gentile's next appearance came a week later when he grounded into a fielder's choice in the ninth inning against the Cardinals on September 17. Next came his aforementioned home run of September 22—the first of his big-league career. Gentile played first that day and went 1-for-3. It turned out that the Dodgers had finally followed through on their talk of moving Hodges to third base to make room for Gentile. Hodges did fine at third, and the experiment continued once more on September 24, but that was the last time Gentile would play in a big-league game for the Dodgers. Hodges went back to first base for the Dodgers in 1958 and Gentile went back to the minor leagues. Diamond Jim spent '58 with the Dodgers' Triple-A affiliate in Spokane, then spent '59 with Triple-A St. Paul. "I was blocked from playing with the Dodgers by Gil Hodges for seven years." said Gentile. "Two in Single-A, two in Double-A, and three in Triple-A. They had so many players I never got a chance. They kept us around for a long time, going up and down, up and down, but they never gave me much of a shot."

The Dodgers mercifully freed Gentile by trading him to the Baltimore Orioles after the 1959 season. Finally given the opportunity to play regularly in the big leagues, Gentile bludgeoned the ball for the Orioles from 1960 to 1963, averaging 31 homers while making the All-Star team three times. Maybe the Brooklyn Dodgers would have won another pennant in 1957 had they followed their plan and moved Hodges to third base and added Gentile's big bat to their lineup that season. With the Dodgers gone in 1958 and 1959 and Gentile buried in the minors, most Brooklyn fans never gave it a thought. But when the name of Diamond Jim Gentile started making the sports pages in 1960, it couldn't help but remind Brooklyn fans of their last failed run at a championship in 1957, and the slugger that never got a shot in Flatbush.

September 24: McDevitt Stands Tall at Ebbets' Last Stand

The Brooklyn Dodgers played their last home game of the 1957 season on September 24. While the future of the Dodgers in Brooklyn was still uncertain that day, most locals had by then resigned themselves to the likelihood that the Dodgers would be leaving. The mood was somber amongst the Dodger players, employees, and fans that evening. Wrote Roscoe McGowen in the *New York Times*:

Danny McDevitt pitched his second shutout of the season as a farewell to Ebbets Field last night and the Dodgers beat the Pirates, 2–0, Everybody, including the 6,702 cash customers, assumed that the Dodgers were playing their final game in the old ball yard that was opened 45 years ago. Between innings Gladys Goodding, who started playing the pipe organ at Ebbets Field after Larry MacPhail became the head man there 19 years ago, played numerous tunes with the farewell motif. ...

After the Brooks had scored their first run in the opening inning, [the organist] played, "Am I Blue?" and "After You're Gone." "Don't Ask Me Why I'm Leaving" accompanied the scoring of the second run in the third inning. As the game neared the end, Miss Goodding grew more and more nostalgic. "Que Sera Sera" was an inevitable choice of the organist. There were others, such as "Thanks for the Memories," "How Can You Say We're Through?" "When I Grow Too Old to Dream," and Bing Crosby's old theme song "When the Blue of the Night Meets the Old of the Day." Miss Gooding, at the end of the game, started playing, "May the Good Lord Bless You and Keep You," but somebody turned on the record always played after Brooklyn games, "Follow the Dodgers." This was eventually silenced, and the organist was able to close out her program by playing "Auld Lang Syne."

Vin Scully recalled the night prior to a Los Angeles Dodgers game on September 24, 2014.

On this day back in 1957 the Dodgers played their last game ever at Ebbets Field—and it was a very sad night. The Dodgers won the game, two to nothing. A little left-hander, Danny McDevitt, beat the Pittsburgh Pirates. But the story that night I'd never forget was the organist, Gladys Goodding. Gladys was known to have a drink or three once in a while, and she showed up that night with a little brown bag. She went into the room where the organ was. She locked the door—you couldn't get in there. The first song she played was "My Buddy," which is one of the saddest songs you'll ever want to hear, and she went DOWN from there! I think she was taking a nip here and there while she played the organ. By the time the game was over, it was the most depressive night you'd ever experienced.

When McDevitt took the mound that night, he wasn't thinking about the fact that he might be starting the last game ever played at hallowed Ebbets Field. He was just hoping to recapture the form he'd had earlier in June when he arrived from St. Paul and pitched to great success. McDevitt had come back down to earth since then, so he was hoping to pitch well that day to give notice that he planned to be back on the club in 1958—whether they were in Brooklyn or Los Angeles. The five-hit shutout he tossed ensured that he would be in the Dodger plans for 1958, but it also cemented him forever into baseball history when fate later determined that it was, in fact, the last game the Dodgers would ever play in Brooklyn.

McDevitt seemed destined to pitch in New York—but with the Yankees, more likely, not the Brooklyn Dodgers. "There are numerous interesting facts in the McDevitt life story, which began in the Medical Center in New York on November 18, 1932," wrote Dan Daniel in the *Sporting News* soon after the young southpaw burst on the scene. "McDevitt was born not far from the mound of the first Yankee ballpark, which was at Broadway and West 165th Street, [current] site of the vast Presbyterian Hospital and Medical Center." The McDevitt's moved south just beyond the New York state line to Hallstead, Pennsylvania, when Danny was two years old, and it was there that he grew up. Despite the move, Danny was a die-hard Yankees fan as a kid.

His father, Leo, an excellent semi-pro pitcher, did his best to help his son become a ballplayer that might be good enough to play for the Yanks one day. Danny blossomed into a great athlete at Hallstead High, playing on back-to-back championship basketball teams, running the hundred and broad jumping on the track team, and starring on the baseball team. McDevitt entered St. Bonaventure in the fall of 1951, but eventually dropped out to achieve his dream and sign a contract with the Yankees. He recounted,

> Bill McCorry and George Selkirk made the deal with me, I had a bonus offer of $6,000 from Brooklyn, but I wanted to be a Yankee. So, I accepted a much cheaper and more involved offer from McCorry. The mistake cost me exactly $4,500. McCorry said the Yankees would pay me $1,500 down, and another $1,500 if I stuck.

What followed his signing was a long series of failures, interruptions and reassignments that left him on the brink of quitting by the spring of 1957. The Yankee leash was short, and after a miserable 1951 campaign spent mostly at Class-D LaGrange, the Yanks cut McDevitt loose. "Then Brooklyn came back." said McDevitt. "Not with $6,000 again, but an offer of $1,500. I was in no mood to argue. I took the dough and went to work with Greenwood [Dodgers of the Class-C Cotton States League]."

Things took a turn for the better at Greenwood in 1952 and McDevitt won 12 games, but his progression was halted as he spent 1953–54 in the Army. The years of 1955–56 were spent shuttling between Elmira, Ft. Worth, Cedar Rapids and Macon, but he struggled to rediscover the gains he had made before entering the service in 1952. "I began to have some doubts about myself," McDevitt admitted. "My record with the Dodger chain was a 'glorious' 23-and-40. I said, 'Give it another year.' It took a lot of talking to myself to keep me from quitting." His stick-to-itiveness was rewarded in 1957. It started with a good season in winter ball in Venezuela where McDevitt and his catcher, Al Ronning, stumbled on a formula that helped Danny set a league record with 114 strikeouts. His Venezuelan advancements continued with the 1957 St. Paul Saints. McDevitt threw a hard fastball, but it was his secondary pitches—the sinker, curve, and change—that formed the repertoire that would lead him to the Dodgers in June of '57. "I was on my way," said McDevitt.

After winning four of his first five starts for the '57 Dodgers in impressive fashion, most folks agreed that McDevitt *was* on his way. Not everyone was convinced, though. Cincinnati skipper Birdie Tebbetts took a shot at McDevitt after his Reds lost to the lefty in Danny's big-league debut on June 17. "The kid had little," chirped an unimpressed Birdie. Cardinals manager Freddy Hutchinson was a believer, however, after McDevitt beat his club in Danny's second start on June 21. "What I liked about McDevitt was his poise, his ability to keep the ball low, and his control." There were still nonbelievers out there, though—like the security guard at the players' entrance to the Polo Grounds. As McDevitt tried to enter prior to the Dodgers' game against the Giants on July 2, he was stopped because the guard didn't believe Danny was a player— he simply didn't look old enough. At five-foot-ten-inches and a slight 165 pounds, McDevitt definitely had more of the appearance of a teenage fan rather than a player. McDevitt hollered for Clem Labine who had entered before Danny. Labine came back and vouched for McDevitt. "Sorry, I didn't know you," the guard apologized. "We're even, then," cracked McDevitt, "I don't know you either!"

McDevitt started 17 games for the 1957 Dodgers, winning seven and losing four while pitching to a 3.25 ERA. His arrival helped Brooklyn stay relevant in the '57 pennant race much longer than they would have been without him. He struggled with the '58 Dodgers but rebounded to win ten games with the World Champion 1959 Dodgers. His last appearance with the Dodgers came in 1960 before he wound down his career with stints with the Yankees, Twins and Athletics through 1962. With a career record of 21-and-27, McDevitt will never be confused for Hall of

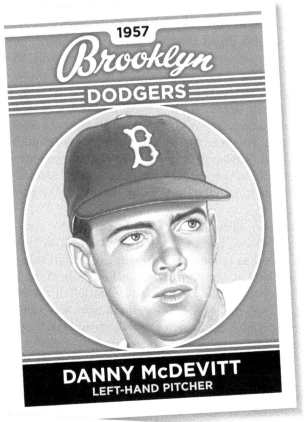

1957
Brooklyn
DODGERS

DANNY McDEVITT
LEFT-HAND PITCHER

37

DANNY McDEVITT

HEIGHT: 5'10" WEIGHT: 175
BORN: NOVEMBER 18, 1932

Left-Hand Pitcher

BATS: LEFT THROWS: LEFT
NEW YORK, NEW YORK

MAJOR LEAGUE PITCHING RECORD

	Games	IP	Won	Lost	Pct	Hits	Runs	ER	SO	Walks	ERA
YEAR: 1957	22	119	7	4	.636	105	55	43	90	72	3.25
CAREER: 6 YRS	155	456	21	27	.438	461	266	223	303	264	4.40

9-24-57: In a brilliant 5-hitter pitched by rookie **DANNY McDEVITT**, the Dodgers beat the Pirates, 2-0, in Brooklyn. Although it wasn't "official," most fans at the game knew that this was to be the last game ever played at Ebbets Field – and it was. Resigned to the reality that their Dodgers were leaving, only 6,702 paid to see the lame duck ballclub's final home game. It was unfortunate, too, because McDevitt returned to the electrifying form he displayed early on when he burst on the scene with dominating wins in three of his first four starts. Longtime Ebbets Field pipe organist Gladys Gooding closed out the game by playing "Auld Lang Syne" after the final out.

I TOLD YOU IT WASN'T SO TOUGH UP HERE, KID!

DANNY PITCHED A COMPLETE GAME WIN IN HIS BIG LEAGUE DEBUT ON 6-17-57!

Fame Dodgers pitchers like Koufax or Drysdale, but history has decided that Danny's name holds a lofty place in Brooklyn Dodgers lore—the last man to pitch at Ebbets Field for Dem Bums. And he did it in style, too, with his 2–0 complete game gem. "I didn't think of it as the event it has turned out to be," said McDevitt back in 2007 when he returned to Brooklyn with his batterymate, Joe Pignatano, to recreate the classic moment prior to a Brooklyn Cyclones minor league game. It had been 50 years, but people in Flatbush still remembered McDevitt. "It was my turn to pitch, and that was just a lucky turn for me. It's my one claim to fame. I never thought it would become as big as it has, but the fans in Brooklyn have kept that alive."

September 27: Harris est Très Bon

The Dodgers did not play for two days following Danny McDevitt's September 24 triumph at Ebbets Field. Their season, and their history as it would turn out, would come down to a final three-game series at Philadelphia to wind down the 1957 campaign. The World Series was already set. It would be the Milwaukee Braves versus the New York Yankees. There was a particularly empty feeling for the Dodgers and their Brooklyn fans as their series with the Phillies got under way on September 27. The Dodgers had been in the World Series in 1955 and 1956, so their exclusion was daunting, and the uncertain future magnified the feeling.

The Phils were 18½ games back and long eliminated, but 11,595 fans braved chilly conditions at Connie Mack Stadium, refusing to accept that the baseball season would soon be over. Their Phillies came through with a win, 3–2, as rookie Jack Sanford won his 19th game while sending Dodgers rookie right-hander Bill Harris to defeat in his big-league debut. Sanford took a 3–0 lead into the ninth inning but had his shutout bid ruined by a Sandy Amoros two-run homer. Harris represented himself well on the mound for seven innings, but a sixth-inning solo shot by Willie Jones turned out to be the margin of victory for Philadelphia. Harris also represented himself well at the plate, collecting what would be his only major league hit—a sixth-inning line drive single.

Bill Harris spent 15 seasons pitching in pro ball—well over 400 games, with all but two of them coming in the minor leagues. He toiled in the Dodgers farm system for 12 of those seasons, but the Dodgers were rich in pitching, so Harris found it tough to get a chance with the big club year after year. Harris was seven full years and 106 minor league victories into his career in the Dodgers organization before he finally got his long-awaited taste of the big leagues on September 27, 1957.

Born in Duguayville, New Brunswick, Canada, on December 3, 1931, Harris, like Danny McDevitt and Jackie Collum, would find his small stature a stumbling block to being taken seriously by major league scouts and executives. Harris was stockily built but stood just five-foot-seven-inches. Harris' size didn't deter Brooklyn scout Bill O'Connor from inking the 19 year old to a contract while Harris was playing in a hockey tournament in Buchans, Newfoundland, in 1951. Harris was an excellent hockey player and may have had the opportunity to play professionally, but after signing with the Dodgers he put his focus on making it to the big leagues. "I signed that contract with the Dodgers because Montreal was the farm club, and that's where I wanted to play," Harris said in 2008. "Being a Canadian, Montreal was THE place to play."

Harris soon found, however, that he'd have to overcome size prejudice to make it. He was headed south to the Dodgers' Vero Beach spring training facility in the spring of '51 when the train stopped in New York and a "big, husky, athletic looking guy" boarded. He sat close to Harris and the two began talking when they eventually discovered that they were both destined for Vero Beach. "He looked at me and said, 'You're not going to make it,'" Harris recalled. "I said, 'Why?' And he said, 'You're way too small.' Well, it just so happened that we got on the same team in spring training, and after four months he got released and I was there for 16 years."

The little righty began tearing through the Dodger farm system by winning 18 games at Class-D Valdosta in 1951 and 25 games at Class-B Miami in 1952. Harris' 0.83 ERA at Miami remains the lowest ever recorded in organized baseball for a pitcher who tossed at least 200 innings in a season. Eleven victories and a perfect game came in Double-A Mobile the next season, followed by 12 more wins with Mobile in 1954. That earned him a call-up to Triple-A Montreal at the end of the '54 campaign. Harris won 40 games for Montreal from 1955 to 1957, production that finally earned him a call-up and a start with Brooklyn in 1957. But it was back down on the farm in 1958, after which Harris made just one more major league appearance—a perfect 1⅔ innings of relief pitching against the Cubs on September 26, 1959.

The bulk of Harris' pitching came with Montreal—right where he wanted to play when he signed with the Dodgers. But the tail end of

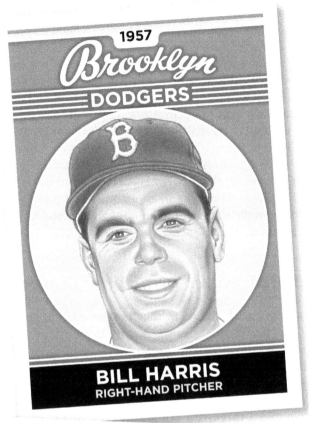

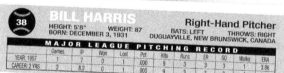

	Games	IP	Won	Lost	Pct	Hits	Runs	ER	SO	Walks	ERA
YEAR: 1957		7	0	1	.000	9	3	3	3	1	3.86
CAREER: 2 YRS	2	8.2	0	1	.000	9	3	3	3	4	3.12

9-27-57: Making his major league debut, Canadian-born **BILL HARRIS** pitched well for Brooklyn, but lost a 3-2 decision to the Phillies at Connie Mack Stadium. Bill had been called up earlier in the month after piling up 16 victories with the Montreal Royals. In addition to a respectable showing on the mound, Bill did well at the plate, too, lining a single off Philly's rookie sensation Jack Sanford. Despite winning 174 games during a 15-year minor league career, Bill would get just one more taste of the bigs — a 1-1/3-inning appearance with the Los Angeles Dodgers on September 26, 1959. Bill hurled a no-hitter with the Mobile Bears on June 14, 1953.

HARRIS REPORTING FOR DUTY, SIR!

BILL HURLED MONTREAL TO VICTORY AND WAS IN BROOKLYN THE NEXT DAY ON 9-8-57!

his career was spent in the state of Washington pitching for Spokane and Tri-City from 1960 to 1965. Harris and his family liked the area so much they settled there. Harris eventually opened a sports bar called Billy's Bull Pen where he enjoyed talking about his baseball career—including his game with the Brooklyn Dodgers. "We were teammates, and I must say with all sincerity that he was one of the finest competitors to ever take the mound," said Dodgers legend Tommy Lasorda at Harris' induction into the Canadian Baseball Hall of Fame in 2008. Sparky Anderson, another of Harris' good friends, was also at the ceremony and added, "Billy came along at a tough time. If he'd have been with another organization, or if he took the mound today, he would be a regular and big winner." No doubt that Sparky is correct about Billy. But, had Harris come up with another organization, or had he come along in a later generation, he would not have been one of an elite and finite group—the Brooklyn Dodgers.

September 28: Da Youngest Bum of Dem All

Thanks to Ladies Day and the Knothole Club, game two of the Philadelphia–Brooklyn series drew even better than game one. This time a crowd of 19,789 filled Connie Mack Stadium on September 28 to watch two teams with nothing left to play for but pride. For proof that the players still cared, one need look no further than Phillies rookie right-hander Don Cardwell flipping Don Zimmer directly after Randy Jackson clouted a three-run homer into the upper leftfield stands in the top of the third. Following protests from the Dodgers, plate umpire Bill Baker went to the mound and warned Cardwell, then directed another warning to Phillies manager Mayo Smith in the home dugout. Things calmed down—although Cardwell later plunked Gil Hodges for good measure—but the Phillies were unable to dig out from Jackson's long-ball and lost the game, 8–4. The win would go in the books as the last victory recorded by the Brooklyn Dodgers.

Buried in the box score of that game was the fact that the last out of the Dodgers' half of the ninth inning was recorded when rookie Rod Miller struck out while pinch hitting for Randy Jackson. That at-bat would be Miller's only big-league experience, but it was Rod's golden ticket into the soon-to-be-closed fraternity of Brooklyn Dodgers. Miller was just a few months shy of his 18th birthday when he debuted with Brooklyn. An outfielder at Lynwood High School in California, Miller was signed by scout Lefty Phillips for a $4,000 bonus following graduation and then dispatched to Class-B Cedar Rapids. The young and inexperienced Miller should have been in a much lower league, but because of his high signing bonus the Dodgers were forced by the rules to keep him on their roster and were prevented from sending him any lower than Class-B ball. Miller struggled at Cedar Rapids and hit just .183, but he still found himself called up to the big club in September. "The biggest thrill of my career was going into the Dodger clubhouse, seeing all these legends, and putting the major league uniform on," Miller said in 1998.

Miller was perfectly content to sit on the bench and observe, so he was surprised when Walter Alston called for him to grab a bat and hit in the September 28 game versus the Phillies. Recounting the story, Miller said, "It was the next-to-the-last day of the season in Philadelphia. The Dodgers were up, 8–3, in the ninth inning when Alston told me to pinch hit for Randy Jackson. I didn't believe him at first. I thought he was kidding. I had to be coaxed by Pee Wee Reese and Duke Snider that he wasn't kidding me. The pitcher for the Phils was Jack Meyer and the catcher, Joe Lonnett, was telling me the pitches—but I struck out swinging." Miller returned to his spot on the bench following his at-bat as Reese replaced him in the field for the bottom of the ninth.

Alston earned Miller's eternal respect the moment he sent him in to pinch hit. Miller had learned all about Alston's one big league at-bat—a strikeout after being called up to the Cardinals back in September of 1936. Miller had no idea that he would suffer the same fate as Alston, but he was aware of the possible parallel. Miller pondered this as he stood in the on-deck circle. "I thought about the compassion Walter Alston had for me, letting me get to bat," said Miller. "He was the classiest human being I've ever known."

Classy was not a word used to describe many of the cynical writers that covered the Dodgers. They descended upon Miller the next day and pressed him for a story. Dick Young summed up the scene this way:

The kid told how he came from Lynwood High in California, which is Duke Snider's native land, and how everybody idolizes Duke out there. "He used to show up at our affairs," said Rod, "and he'd talk to us and answer questions. I got to know him," the kid said with a self-conscious grin, "because I guess I asked him more questions than anybody." "Did you ask him," said a newsman smugly, "how come he can't hit lefty pitching?" The kid bristled. "Oh, he hits them pretty good." At that moment, Rod Miller wasn't a member of a big-league ball club. He was a Duke Snider fan, defending his idol with the feeling of any Brook rooter.

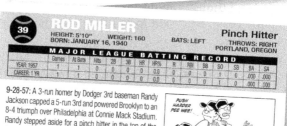

		Games	At Bats	Hits	2B	3B	HR	HR%	R	RBI	BB	SO	SB	BA	SA
	YEAR: 1957	1	1	0	0	0	0	0.0	0	0	0	1	0	.000	.000
	CAREER: 1 YR	1	1	0	0	0	0	0.0	0	0	0	1	0	.000	.000

9-28-57: A 3-run homer by Dodger 3rd baseman Randy Jackson capped a 5-run 3rd and powered Brooklyn to an 8-4 triumph over Philadelphia at Connie Mack Stadium. Randy stepped aside for a pinch hitter in the top of the 9th as skipper Walt Alston sent a very nervous 17-year-old ROD MILLER in to make his big league debut. In spite of the fact that Phils catcher Joe Lonnett was tipping pitches to Rod, Miller still struck out in what would be his only major league at-bat. If there was one man who could sympathize, it was Alston himself, who also fanned in his only majors at-bat. Rod always expressed gratitude to Alston for giving him his one shot in the show.

Miller spent the next three years at Dodgers outposts in Thomasville, Columbus, Reno, Kokomo, and Great Falls, but a subsequent four-year stint in the Marines ended his continued pursuit of returning to the big leagues. Forty-five years later, Miller was still trading on his brief major league experience in his work with an athletic training equipment manufacturer. "You can't imagine the residual benefits I've had in my life from that one time at bat," Miller said. "It's opened more doors than I ever could have imagined."

September 29: Kennedy Makes History

As if in a hurry to lay the season to rest, the Philadelphia Phillies defeated the Brooklyn Dodgers in one hour and 58 minutes to put an end to the 1957 campaign for both ballclubs. Making no reference to the Dodgers' uncertain future, Roscoe McGowen stuck to the game details in his *New York Times* game recap:

> The Dodgers always contribute to the unusual, whether they win or lose. Today they lost, 2–1, to the Phils at Connie Mack Stadium in the season's finale. And they lost to a left-handed pitcher for the first time since Luis Arroyo of the Pirates beat them in a relief job on September 22, 1956. Seth Morehead, a 23-year-old rookie southpaw making his first major league start, held the Brooks to four hits and one unearned run in nine innings.

The game started with a bit of a different look for the Dodgers. Instead of team captain Pee Wee Reese handing the Brooklyn lineup to the umpires at home plate, it was a "new captain" who presented the card to the umps. Rube Walker was the new captain, a step up from his usual rank as "captain of the humpties" as he was affectionately known by his teammates. Walker was Reese's roommate, and Pee Wee's last day hand-over of the captainship to Rube was a gesture of the friendship the two shared.

The Dodgers scored first when Gil Hodges pushed Gino Cimoli across with a sacrifice line drive to centerfield in the top of the first inning—but that was the only run the Flatbush bats would generate in the game. Roger Craig started and pitched well for Brooklyn, but he surrendered a two-run homer to Ed Bouchee in the sixth, and that was all the support Morehead would need on this day. The game and the 1957 season came to an official end when Dodger leftfielder Bob Kennedy made the final out on a fly ball to Phillies centerfielder Don Landrum. If asked prior to the season to speculate on who would make the final out in Brooklyn Dodger franchise history—*IF*, of course, the club were to leave after the 1957 season—36-year-old Bob Kennedy would have been an unlikely choice for anyone to make. He wasn't even on the team at the start of the season. After joining the ballclub via the waiver wire on May 20, Kennedy saw action in just 19 games, mostly as a left-handed pinch-hitter. He received just 31 at-bats and delivered only four hits— one of them a round tripper off Ruben Gomez on August 8 at Ebbets Field. Never a power hitter, the circuit blast was the 63rd and last homer of Kennedy's 16-year playing career.

Kennedy had already announced that he would retire as a player after the 1957 season, and the Dodgers' loss at Connie Mack Stadium neatly bookended his career. He'd played his first big league game at that same ballpark (then called Shibe Park) as an 18-year-old White Sox rookie way back on September 14, 1939. He grounded out while pinch hitting against Philadelphia Athletics right-hander Nelson Potter. Kennedy got his first big league start the next day as he played third base and secured his first major league hit in the sixth inning when he singled off A's righty Lynn Nelson. Kennedy would hit safely another 1,175 times over his long career.

As Kennedy was born on the South Side of Chicago, it made sense that he would play for the White Sox. But he was born on August 18, 1920—just a couple months before the Black Sox scandal became official when eight White Sox players were indicted by a grand jury. The fallout would affect Kennedy's youth experience in baseball, as well as his later pro days in Chi-town. Noted baseball writer Phil Cola:

> As he grew up into a strong, hard-throwing teenager playing amateur ball in and around Chicago, there were times he was held out of games because one of the banned Black Sox, Buck Weaver, was playing that day. According to Bob's son, Terry, himself a major league player and minor league manager, Bob was held out of those games by his coaches because anyone who played in a game with Weaver could be banned from the major leagues, and Bob was thought to have a future in the big leagues.

When Kennedy joined the White Sox in 1939 they had still not recovered from the Black Sox Scandal, spending most of the previous 20 years mired deep in the second division. Minus the years he lost to service in World War II, Kennedy would toil with middling-to-bad Sox teams through June of 1948 when he was dealt to Cleveland where he batted .301 as a part-time player and rode the Indians' surge to a World Series title.

Cleveland provided Kennedy with the best years of his career, although he was traded to the Orioles just days after the opening of

1957

Brooklyn

DODGERS

BOB KENNEDY
OUTFIELDER/3rd BASEMAN

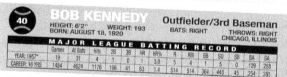

BOB KENNEDY — Outfielder/3rd Baseman

	Games	At Bats	Hits	2B	3B	HR	HR%	R	RBI	BB	SO	SB	BA	SA
YEAR: 1957*	19	31	4	1	0	1	3.0	3	4	1	5	0	129	258
CAREER: 16 YRS	1484	4624	1176	196	41	63	1.4	514	514	364	443	45	254	355

40 HEIGHT: 6'2" WEIGHT: 193 BORN: AUGUST 18, 1920 BATS: RIGHT THROWS: RIGHT CHICAGO, ILLINOIS

MAJOR LEAGUE BATTING RECORD

9-29-57: The record book of the Brooklyn Dodgers was closed for good when **BOB KENNEDY**, the Brooks' 37-year-old leftfielder, flied out to end the final game in franchise history. It was also the final game in Bob's history, as the 16-year veteran retired after the game. For the record, the Phillies defeated the Dodgers 2-1 at Connie Mack Stadium. Bob was winding down his fine career with the White Sox when the Dodgers acquired him on May 21 to strengthen their bench. Bob clubbed his only homer in a Dodger uniform on August 8, 1957.

* Only statistics from the 1957 Brooklyn Dodgers are displayed. Bob played in an additional 4 games with the 1957 Chicago White Sox.

"HAPPY BIRTHDAY" WAS PLAYED ON THE EBBETS FIELD ORGAN FOR BOB ON 8-18-57!

the 1954 season and thereby missed out on a second pennant with the Indians as they rolled to a 111-wins campaign that year. Kennedy was a true nomad after he left Cleveland, roaming from the Orioles back to the White Sox, then to Detroit, and back to the Sox before finally landing in Flatbush in May of '57. He'd batted just .221 in 78 games divided between the White Sox and Tigers in 1956, so he knew he was going to have to make some changes if he wanted to stay in the league in 1957. Kennedy started with an off-season workout regimen that put him in the best shape he'd been in for years when he reported to spring training for Detroit in March of '57. "He is at his lightest in six years and is hitting harder and running better," said Tigers manager Jack Tighe, indicating that Kennedy may have saved his job by getting in A-1 physical condition. At 36 years of age, Kennedy was also experimenting with glasses for the first time in his career, opting to wear them during night games. "I got to thinking about my play last season," he explained. "I wasn't able to see as well at night as during the day. I had trouble following the ball, so I thought I'd give glasses a try."

Despite his off-season improvement efforts, the Tigers released Kennedy on April 8, just a week before the season opened. It wasn't the best etiquette to cut a veteran with so little time to catch on with another club before opening day, but Kennedy was a class act and took full responsibility for his release while also wishing his former club well. He wasn't jobless for long as his old club, the White Sox, signed him shortly thereafter. "With Jim Rivera shifted to first base, we needed an extra hand in the outfield in case of emergency," said Sox manager Al Lopez. "Bob is a pretty handy guy to have around, because he'll bolster our pinch-hitting strength." That was the same philosophy the Dodgers had for signing him themselves when the White Sox later waived him in May.

Kennedy was true to his word and retired as a player after the 1957 season, so his last at-bat, major or minor league, was in a Brooklyn Dodgers uniform. He went on to a long career as a scout, coach, manager, and successful front office executive for many teams, including a one-year return to the Dodgers organization as manager of the Double-A Albuquerque Dodgers in 1966. Bob's son Terry followed his father's footsteps into the major leagues and became an all-star for the San Diego Padres and several other clubs. While with the Padres, Terry joined the World Series RBI club in 1984 when he drove across two runs in his first Series at-bat against the Tigers. With that, Bob and Terry became the first father-son-duo to drive in World Series runs. Bob's World Series RBI came way back in 1948 while he was with the Indians, and it was one of the highlights of his career. Despite all he did in his long career, that RBI is often one of the first things listed in biographies about Kennedy. Often, however, even before mentioning that World Series RBI, Kennedy's making the last out in Brooklyn Dodgers history is cited first. He certainly had no idea of its importance as he trotted off the field after his fly ball out to end the game. He would have much rather reached base safely, leaving on-deck hitter Randy Jackson to deal with the possibility of making the last out of the season. But it was Kennedy who made the iconic out, and while not completely fair, it'll most likely stand as his most remembered contribution to baseball history.

* * *

With their season-ending loss to the Phillies in the book, all that was left was for the players to file back into the visitors' clubhouse, dress, and catch the plane back to New York. Once there, they would collect their things from their Ebbets Field lockers, say good-byes, then scatter their separate ways for the off-season. The players had a lot to ponder as they prepared to walk out of the old ballpark, many of them for the last time. Some of the worries that faced them were concerns about the team's shortcomings that led to failure in 1957; some worried about their personal futures.

They needed more punch at the plate. Their team home run total of '57 was the lowest it had been since 1948. Defensively, their infield strength up the middle was not up to par in 1957. Too often they missed on double-plays when Jim Gilliam was playing second base. Charlie Neal had proved to be a good shortstop, but he, too, had under-performed with the glove at second base when he'd played there in 1956. The '57 campaign also showed that the Dodgers needed to bolster their catching corps for 1958. Age and injuries had slowed Roy Campanella, so the Dodgers would need to intensify their search to find his long-term replacement. John Roseboro looked like a legitimate candidate, but he was still unproven. While the outfield was aging and injury-prone with Duke Snider and Carl Furillo, when healthy they were as good an outfield as there was in the league with the addition of young Gino Cimoli. Third base was a question mark. Pee Wee Reese, 38 years old, could not be the full-time answer, so the Dodgers were possibly going to look to Dick Gray at their St. Paul affiliate. Much to the dismay of Jim Gentile, the team seemed set at first base with Gil Hodges showing no sign of slowing down. And their pitching, despite Don Newcombe and Sal Maglie posting sub-par campaigns, had been very good in 1957 and seemed to have the potential to be even better in 1958 with Don Drysdale and Johnny Podres getting stronger and stronger.

Based on trade rumors in the air, some players feared being dealt away in the off-season. Don Zimmer, Rube Walker—and even Carl Erskine—had been the subject of trade talks. Most guys, however, simply turned their focus to their usual off-season activities. In an era of low salaries, many guys would return to jobs back home—and lots of golf playing. Snider would get to work on his avocados and lemon trees after a brief stay with Carl Erskine in Indiana and a visit with Preacher Roe in Missouri. Erskine planned to do some hunting and fishing in Wisconsin before returning home to attend to his restaurant and gift shop and real estate activities. Podres was going on a fishing trip in Canada before returning to Brooklyn to sell cars. Cimoli was scheduled to appear on the *Red Skelton Show* in Los Angeles, then he was heading home to San Francisco with no solid plans. Newcombe would look after his Newark liquor store. Neal intended to hunt near his home in Longview, Texas, but had no other plans as of yet. Joe Becker would be at home in Arkansas training mules. At this news, Roscoe McGowen couldn't help but say, "After handling pitchers, training a Missouri Mule ought to be a sinecure."

Gilliam: golf at Rahway, New Jersey. Jake Pitler would play golf near his Binghamton, New York, home—and rest. Don Bessent would sell cars in Jacksonville, Florida, while Ed Roebuck would sell cars in Los Angeles—NOT Brooklyn, noted McGowen. Roger Craig would work in his Durham, North Carolina, clothing store. Elmer Valo had a public relations job for a brewery near his home in Allentown, Pennsylvania. Hodges would relax at home in Brooklyn and play golf. Campanella planned to do some fishing and yachting as well as overseeing things at his Harlem liquor store. Drysdale and Koufax were set to fulfill their military obligations. Reese would be hunting, golfing, and bowling while also running his storm window business. Zimmer planned to play golf, fish, work in the construction business—and lose ten pounds. Alston planned to shoot skeet, play pool, fish, hunt, and entertain his grandson Robbie. Billy Herman: hunting, golfing, and fishing at his new home in Vero Beach. There were a bunch of guys who would play winter ball—Sandy Amoros, Rene Valdes, Danny McDevitt, Joe Pignatano, Fred Kipp, Johnny Roseboro, and Bill Harris to name a few. So, it was business as usual for the players, but, as McGowen wondered, "But when spring does come, then what?"

*   *   *

Epilogue

Roscoe McGowen would not have to wait for spring for his question to be answered. On October 8, 1957, the Dodgers announced that they'd played their last game in Brooklyn. "Dodgers Accept Los Angeles Bid to Move to Coast," blared a headline in McGowen's *New York Times*. "Team Will Play in California in '58 After Representing Brooklyn Since 1890," the headline continued. The $30,000,000 price to condemn a downtown Brooklyn slum area and build a new stadium was too steep, and the Los Angeles offer was too good to refuse. It was incompetence, poor attendance, and financial loss that spurred the Giants into their move to San Francisco. The Dodgers, however, had excellent attendance and were one of the most financially successful teams in the National League. They'd amassed a $1,800,000 profit from 1953 to 1957—a healthy sum in that era. It was this fact that made the Brooklyn fans particularly bitter about losing their ballclub. "That's the one ugly and inescapable fact that sets this deal apart from all other franchise transfers," wrote Arthur Daley. "The only word that fits the Dodgers is greed."

Los Angeles gave Walter O'Malley the keys to the kingdom, and the deal he scored was a great personal triumph. "But is it a triumph?" asked Daley. "The feeling here is that it is not. The feeling here is also one of galling resentment. Perhaps Messrs. O'Malley and Stoneham should be wished good luck and Godspeed in true sporting fashion. But these are not true sporting deals. They go without even a goodbye."

* * *

For those who still found it hard to believe that the deal to rip the Bums out of Brooklyn would not somehow be reversed, reality set in when the Los Angeles Dodgers opened the 1958 season in California—while Ebbets Field stood silent. Vin Scully was at the microphone for the last game at Ebbets Field and he was also at the mic for the first game in California. And Scully continued to broadcast Dodger games

213

until his retirement at 88 years of age following the 2016 season. It was prior to a Dodgers game against the Pirates on April 5, 2013, that Scully perfectly captured a blend of history, warm nostalgia and cold reality when he commemorated the 100th anniversary of the opening of Ebbets Field. Scully began his pre-game essay that day as history teacher, telling the story of how Charles Ebbets fulfilled his dream by purchasing some cheap land in Pigtown and building a ballpark there. Ebbets Field opened in 1913, Scully added, a game that saw Casey Stengel hit an inside-the-park home run for Brooklyn. Then Scully then shifted to nostalgic old timer, warmly recalling the 1973 Frank Sinatra song "There Used to Be a Ballpark," which Scully noted was written in memory of Ebbets Field. Still basking in warm nostalgia, he then began telling of his boyhood in Washington Heights, New York. Oddly out of place nearby was a castle made of Carrara marble, owned by a wealthy doctor. This castle embodied permanence to a young Scully.

But at this point of the essay Scully transformed into a teller of harsh reality. In a turn of events as cold as the Carrara marble itself, Scully informed viewers that when the doctor later died, the castle fell into the hands of his sister. The castle was sold, taken down, and in its place was built a towering apartment complex called Castle Village. "I bring that up because Ebbets Field is no longer, and there are apartment houses where Ebbets Field stood," said Scully matter-of-factly, adding, "Nothing is forever."

Bibliographic Essay

While great care and effort at content accuracy was made during the writing of this book, I would not be so bold as to classify it as a "scholarly" work with a bibliography and extensive notes section. My apologies go out to readers who like to trace the origin of every bit of information contained within a book's pages, but that type of publication was not my aim. Productions of that ilk are created by educated academics, brilliant writers, and hard-working journalists—not humble artists like me! What I've written in this book is simply text, rather informal in nature, that I thought would add flavor to the artwork I created for my 1957 Dodgers card set.

This book is not intended to be an all-encompassing history of the Brooklyn Dodgers. Countless great books have already been written that serve that purpose far better than I could ever hope to do. The pre–1957 history contained within these pages is a compressed version of the Brooklyn Dodgers' epic saga, boiled down to set the stage for the telling of the story of 1957, their final season. Many important Brooklyn Dodgers events and characters have been left out of this book in an effort to keep the page count under a thousand! But, if you haven't done so already, I'd recommend reading all the classic Dodgers histories you can lay your hands on should the condensed history in this book whet your appetite for the full, unabridged story of Dem Bums.

I have attempted to specifically credit sources within the text in any place I have used material directly quoted. The rest of the text is a rewritten mash-up culled from the works of many great sources. With apologies to the author of any source I may have inadvertently left out, here's a list of materials from which I gathered the bulk of information contained in these pages.

Books: *A Moment in Time* by Ralph Branca and David Ritz; *It's Good to Be Alive* by Roy Campanella; *Nice Guys Finish Last* by Leo Durocher; *Carl Erskine's Tales from the Dodger Dugout* by Carl Erskine;

Bibliographic Essay

What I Learned from Jackie Robinson by Carl Erskine; *When Baseball Was Still King* by Gene Fehler; *More Tales from the Golden Age* by Gene Fehler; *Bums* by Peter Golenboch; *When the Cheering Stops* by Lee Heiman, Dave Weiner, and Bill Gutman; *The Boys of Summer* by Roger Kahn; *The Negro Leagues Revisited* by Brent Kelley; *The Pastime in Turbulence* by Brent Kelley; *Sandy Koufax* by Jane Leavy; *Take Me Out to the Ballpark* by Josh Leventhal; *Green Cathedrals* by Philip J. Lowry; *Baseball Players of the 1950s* by Rich Marazzi and Len Fiorito; *The Greatest Ballpark Ever* by Bob McGee; *Brooklyn's Dodgers* by Carl E. Prince; *Carl Furillo* by Ted Reed; *Brooklyn Dodgers* by Mark Rucker; *The Duke of Flatbush* by Duke Snider and Bill Gilbert; *Few and Chosen Dodgers* by Duke Snider and Phil Pepe; *Twilight Teams* by Jeffrey Saint John Stuart; *The Ballplayers* by Mike Shatzkin, Stephen Holtje, James Charlton; *Once Around the Bases* by Richard Tellis.

Newspapermen: Milton Bracker, *New York Times*; Dan Daniel, *New York Times*; Arthur Daley, *New York Times*; John Drebinger, *New York Times*; Frank Gibbons, *Cleveland Press*; Herb Heft, *Sporting News*; David Hinckley, *New York Daily News*; Zander Hollander, *Sporting News*; Stan Isaacs, *Newsday*; Jack McDonald, *San Francisco Call-Bulletin*; Roscoe McGowen, *New York Times*; Jack Mann, *Newsday*; Tom Meany, *Sporting News*; Thomas Rogers, *New York Times*; Joseph M. Sheehan, *New York Times*; Gay Talese, *New York Times*; Gordon S. White, Jr., *New York Times*; Dick Young, *Sporting News*.

Online: *Sandy Koufax* by Mark Z. Aaron; *Jim Gentile* by Ed Attanasio; *Jake Pitler* by Stan Bard; *Dolph Camilli* by Ralph Berger; *Larry MacPhail* by Ralph Berger; *Casey Stengel* by Bill Bishop; *Reflections on Ebbets Field* by Daniel Campo; *Happy Chandler* by Terry Bohn; *Gino Cimoli* by Alan Cohen; *Bob Kennedy* by Phil Cola; *Preacher Roe* by Warren Corbett; *Sandy Amoros* by Rory Costello; *Twilight at Ebbets Field* by Rory Costello; *Fred Kipp* by Pat Doyle; *Babe Herman* by Greg Erion; *Eddie Basinski* by David Eskenazi and Steve Rudman; *Burleigh Grimes* by Charles F. Faber; *Clarence Mitchell* by Charles F. Faber; *Billy Harris* by Kevin Glew; *Ralph Branca* by Paul Hirsch; *Joe Pignatano* by Paul Hirsch; *Ed Roebuck* by Paul Hirsch; *Walter O'Malley was Right* by Paul Hirsch; *Carl Erskine* by Bob Hurte; *Walter Alston* by Bill Johnson; *Elmer Valo* by Mel Marmer; *Branch Rickey* by Andy McCue; *Greg Mulleavy* by Bill Nowlin; *What the Dodgers Meant to Brooklyn* by Yuval Rosenberg; *Carl Furillo* by John Saccoman; *Gil Hodges* by John Saccoman; *Koufax's Roundball Once Trumped His Fastball* by Richard Sandomir; *Wilbert Robinson* by Alex Semchuck; *Jackie Collum* by William L. Sherman;

216

Bibliographic Essay

Roger Craig by Rich Shook; *Dixie Walker* by Lyle Spatz; *Pete Reiser* by Mark Stewart; *Jackie Robinson* by Rick Swaine; *Roy Campanella* by Rick Swaine; *Sal Maglie* by Judith Testa; *Roy Campanella* by Robert McGill Thomas, Jr.; *Clem Labine* by Alfonso L Tusa C; *Randy Jackson* by Gaylon H. White; *Jim Gentile* by Doug Wilson; *Tommy Holmes* by Saul Wisnia; retrosheet.org; baseball-reference.com; sabr.org.

Index

Numbers in **bold italics** represent pages with illustrations

219

Index

Bolger, Jim 181
Bonanza 96
Bonnie, Al 121
bonus 137–38; signing 70, 101, 129, 143, 148, 188, 193, 198, 205
Bonus Rule 70, 144
Bordagary, Frenchy 13
Boston Braves 7, 19, 67, 113, 147
Boston Braves Historical Society 3
Boston Red Sox 7, 10, 22, 67
Bouchee, Ed 207
Boudreau, Lou 94
Boyer, Ken 96, 165
Bozman, Bill 3
Brady Bunch 77
Branca, Ralph 20–21, 28, 88
Breadon, Sam 17
Brecheen, Harry 20, 188
Brenzel, Bill 194
Brinkman, Ed 2
Brooklyn, New York 72, 212
Brooklyn Atlantics 9
Brooklyn Cyclones 88, 201
Brooklyn Daily Times see Meany, Tom
Brooklyn Dodgers: against Athletics 7, 48–49; against Braves 44, 46, 61, 67–68, 90–92, 96, 103, 106, 117–18, 124, 143, 146, 164, 167, 185–86; against Cardinals 16, 19–20, 61–62, 70–71, 92, 94, 96, 101–3, 106, 120–21, 131–32, 164–65, 186–87, 191, 196, 199; against Cubs 22, 58, 61, 70, 82, 84, 86–87, 104, 106, 108–9, 121–24, 126, 128, 136–37, 142, 146, 170, 174, 181, 184, 196; against Giants 20, 28, 46, 55–56, 65, 74, 76, 108, 110–11, 138, 146–47, 149, 151–52, 152–53, 156, 170, 177, 178–79, 180–81; against Indians 10–11, 162; against Phillies 16, 27–28, 49–50, 53, 55, 77, 79, 81–82, 111–12, 148, 160, 167, 179–80, 192–93, 201–4, 207; against Pirates 8, 10, 46, 52–53, 56, 77, 84, 86, 129, 152, 156, 162, 167, 197, 214; against Red Sox 10; against Reds 22, 63, 71, 73, 87, 90, 99, 101, 114–17, 132–33, 136, 138, 162–63, 186, 199; against Yankees 15–16, 19, 27, 28, 32, 33, 34, 49, 73–74, 131, 138, 151, 167; announce move to Los Angeles 126, 213; attendance (excellent 213; over one million 179; poor 13, 52–53); clownish reputation of 12–13; community of fans 21–23, 111, 131; debt of 13; eliminated from 1957 pennant 192; exhibition games 32, 44, 45, 48–49, 73–74; fog delays game of 86–87; last home game 196–97, 206–7; last home run 134, 136; last out 144, 207–8, 211; last pitch 144; legacy of 6–7, 15, 21; nickname 9–10; off-season player plans 212; organist *see*

Goodding, Gladys; play at Roosevelt Stadium 40, 53, 55, 61, 86–87, 90, 117, 151, 156, 170, 179; players (non-committal about move 114; opposed to integration 25–26; ranked 41); purchase (plane 37; Reading Chicks 172); Rookie-of-the-Year 52; sell Ebbets Field 37; set record for most strikeouts in a double header 109; song about 175; Sym-phony band 22–23, 32, 134; tour Japan 42–43, 194; World War II effect on 16, 19
Brooklyn Eagle see Murphy, Jimmy; Parrott, Harold
Brooklyn Eckfords 9
Brooklyn Excelsiors 9
Brooklyn Eye and Ear Hospital 16
Brooklyn Grays 9
Brooklyn Hartfords 9
Brooklyn Mutuals 9
Brooklyn Parade Grounds 48
Brooklyn Robins 11
Brooklyn Superbas 9, 32
Brooklyn Technical High School 19
Brooklyn Wonders 9
Brosnan, Jim 84
Brown, Joe L. 79
Brown, Mordecai 187
Brownsville (Pennsylvania) High School 137
brush back pitches 43, 49, 91, 114–15, 132, 165–66, 174–75, 204
Bruton, Bill 91
Buchans, Newfoundland, Canada 202
Buffalo Symphony Orchestra 18
Buhl, Bob 106
Bum (cartoon) 40
Bums (Golenbock) 31, 88, 101
Burdette, Lew 68, 103, 164
Burns, Matt 8–9, 42
Bush, Donie 94

Cairns, Bob: *Pen Men* 149
Camilli, Dolph 14, 15, 101
Campanella, Roy 6, 33, 34, *161*, 212; against Braves 61, 90, 185; against Cardinals 102; against Cubs 58, 82, 84, 106, 124; against Giants 156, 178; against Phillies 111; against Pirates 56, 156–57; against Reds 87, 99, 115–16; assessed by Cobb 160; assessed by Collum 191; assessed by Erskine 159; auto accident of 17, 124, 156, 160, 162; catches 100 games nine years consecutively 160; criticism of 108; at demolition of Ebbets Field 6, 17; differences with Robinson 157–58; gives Gentile nickname 194; helps Roseboro 41; injuries 46, 87–88, 157, 158, 211; mentioned 9, 27, 28, 33,

220

Index

223

Index

Index

Index

Index

CPSIA information can be obtained
at www.ICGtesting.com
Printed in the USA
LVHW020557221122
733703LV00013B/118